# RELIGION AND SOCIETY IN TRANSITION:
## The Church and Social Change in England, 1560-1850

BY
ERNEST E. BEST

Texts and Studies in Religion
Volume 15

The Edwin Mellen Press
New York and Toronto

Library of Congress Cataloging in Publication Data

Best, Ernest E. (Ernest Edwin), 1919-
   Religion and society in transition.

   (Texts and studies in religion ; v. 15)
   Bibliography: p.
   Includes index.

   1. Sociology, Christian--England--History.
2. England--Church history.  I. Title.  II. Series.
BR744.B43  1982     306'.6'0942     82-21699
ISBN 0-88946-804-4

Texts and Studies in Religion, ISBN 0-88946-976-8

Copyright © 1982, Ernest E. Best

All rights reserved.  For more information write:

        The Edwin Mellen Press
            P.O. Box 450
      Lewiston, New York 14092

Printed in the United States of America

TO

George Kelsey,
Frederick Shippey,
and the late
Carl Michalson,

Sound Scholars, Good Teachers, Loyal Friends.

# Foreword

This book has emerged through a lengthy evolution. Throughout my adult life my central interest has been in the dynamic relationship between mature religious faith and commitment, on the one hand, and human culture, on the other. It was natural, therefore, that after a number of years spent in Nagasaki, Japan, in the aftermath of the atomic bomb, one should have asked how human beings developed relationships which eventuated in such tragedy. Thus an earlier book entitled *Christian Faith and Cultural Crisis: the Japanese Case*, a shortened version of my doctoral thesis, appeared. It sought to uncover the values which influenced both western and Japanese leadership as the latter struggled to modernize the nation during the Meiji period. At that time, two of my former professors at Columbia University, Charles Glock and the late Rudolf Heberle, encouraged me to do a similar study of the modernization of England, paying detailed attention to the religious dimension.

Though diverted by many another responsibility, the hope to complete the project never left me. It is not surprising, then, that earlier versions of parts of the manuscript appeared several years ago. One such was an article in *Religion in Life* (Winter 1955-56) entitled, "Involvement and Influence: An Illustration from Sixteenth-Century England." Another appeared in the theological journal *Encounter* (Winter 1973), at the centenary of the death of F. D. Maurice, entitled "F. D. Maurice in Perspective." Still further, much of the content relating to the eighteenth century, as well as the theoretical basis for the study, were discussed in graduate seminars given at

Tokyo University of Education and Tokyo University in 1974. The first at the invitation of Prof. Kiyomi Morioka and the second at that of Prof. Keiichi Yanagawa. I am indebted to the students of both those seminars, as well as to so many of my colleagues and students through the years who have added their criticisms, especially to my methodology.

I have indicated in my introduction that this is essentially a study in the sociology of knowledge. It is of necessity, therefore, eclectic and dependent upon so many of the primary and secondary studies of others. Obviously the errors of fact and judgment are my own.

Over the years a number of grants have made possible study and research in England and elsewhere: the Jones Foundation of Lafayette College and a research grant from The Methodist Theological School in Ohio. Finally, a grant from the Social Sciences and Humanities Research Council of Canada through Victoria University in The University of Toronto helped to make publication in its present form a reality.

I must make special mention of those who have been a great help in the final throes of publication. David Neelands, registrar of Trinity College, in The University of Toronto, and Peter Wickerson, professor of religious studies at Huron College, did the painstaking work of preparing the index. My daughter Bronwyn not only did the exacting work of typing the final manuscript but made many helpful suggestions for improvement in style. Finally, my wife, Helen, knows how much in my life would never have been accomplished were it not for her constant encouragement.

Ernest E. Best<br>
Victoria College<br>
University of Toronto

# TABLE OF CONTENTS

INTRODUCTION: . . . . . . . . . . . . . . . . . ix

## PART ONE

### PRELUDE: 1560-1688

CHAPTER I:     The Roots of Change . . . . . . . . .    3

CHAPTER II:    The Pivotal Period. . . . . . . . . .   39

## PART TWO

### THE GREAT TRANSFORMATION: THE EIGHTEENTH CENTURY

CHAPTER III:   The Context of Change: Politics,
               Economics and Society in the
               Eighteenth Century. . . . . . . . . .   83

CHAPTER IV:    In the World and of It: The
               Establishment in Distress . . . . . .  121

CHAPTER V:     The Extent of Dissent . . . . . . . .  145

CHAPTER VI:    Faith, Thought and Life: The
               Vital Issues at Stake . . . . . . . .  163

## PART THREE

### THE NEW ORDER UNDER JUDGMENT

CHAPTER VII:   The New Age: Its Strengths and
               Weaknesses. . . . . . . . . . . . . .  195

CHAPTER VIII:  A Fresh Vision: A Prophetic
               Alternative . . . . . . . . . . . . .  247

CHAPTER IX:    Conclusion. . . . . . . . . . . . . .  293

NOTES          . . . . . . . . . . . . . . . . . . .  305

BIBLIOGRAPHY   . . . . . . . . . . . . . . . . . . .  321

INDEX          . . . . . . . . . . . . . . . . . . .  331

# Introduction

When this manuscript was in an earlier and lengthier form, an historian was asked to give his critical assessment of it. He sensed so clearly my intention in undertaking this study that I know no better way to introduce it than through his words. "The author," said he, "rightfully strides through many fields of study *all too frequently kept strictly fenced apart*. Without this *Lebensraum* he could not do what he wants to do. What we have here I take it, is a huge case study in the interrelation of the history of Christianity with the history of man." This is, of course, an exaggeration. It *is* a case study in the interrelation between the history of a segment of Christendom and the social history of those who lived within it over a particular period of time.

This book is not meant to be an historical monograph, though, especially in Parts I and III, I make use of a number of original sources. Elsewhere I have drawn upon historical monographs which have dealt in detail with religious, economic, political and social factors. It *is* an attempt to analyse a period of history both upon the basis of empirical evidence and a sociological theory. It is an historical study in the sociology of religion. Its justification stands or falls on the actuality of the relationships traced and the accuracy of the generalizations made on the basis of them. It is my conviction that its underlying thesis, while not exceptional, is acknowledged far more in the breach than in the observance. The point that leaps from this account is that life is all of a piece; that it is as false a view of reality to fail to see *the relationship between things* as it is to see their uniqueness. My concern is to show the interrelationship between the individual and the society of which he is a part as well as to demonstrate the way in which events which take place within one structure of a society affect those occurring within the other structures. Moreover, just as man is always man-in-society in reaction to his physical and social environment, so his thought affects his action and the latter reacts upon the former in a continuous symbiotic fashion.

For two reasons I have chosen a particular period in English history to illustrate these arguments. This period, the axial point of which is the eighteenth century, enables us to see the relation between religion and social change in a time when change, though not as rapid as in our own day, was nevertheless of critical importance. We may, therefore, gain some insight from that experience in this time of very rapid social change. The second reason is that varied assessments have been made of religion as a factor in social change in eighteenth century England, and none of them to date has been personally satisfying to me. Studies such as J. W. Bready's *England Before and After Wesley* attributes too much to religious motivation alone, and those such as T. S. Ashton's *An Economic History of England, the 18th Century* and his *The Industrial Revolution*, dealing chiefly with economic factors, attribute too little.[1]

It is not that any of these represent necessarily the most recent, the best or the most exhaustive studies of the period, but for a long time they symbolized standard alternative interpretations. One's reaction to them, it was reasoned, depended upon whether one was "religious" or not.

While it is true that eighteenth century England takes centre stage in this study, it was necessary to trace its roots in changes that go as far back as the English Reformation. With equal logic the full impact of what occurred during the century cannot be grasped without an

Introduction                                                        xi

understanding of events which took place in the first half
of the nineteenth century in response to them. The most
important of those responses brought the individualistic
presuppositions of the earlier day into serious question.
Karl Marx is the name the vast majority of men would rightfully associate with that reaction. The name of Frederick
Denison Maurice is known to far fewer, but he represents a
creative response from within the strictly Christian community to the same shortcomings. He saw the basically social
nature of man and the distortion of reality which takes
place when it is ignored. It is this insight which brings
this study, which begins with the fragmentation of the
social order at the close of the medieval period, to its
logical conclusion with the fresh recognition of the need
for social wholeness by Marx and Maurice in the middle of
the nineteenth century. A sociological study such as this,
which is interested in defensible generalization, is more
concerned with identifying such "trends" which persist
through a considerable period of time than it is with particular events considered vertically. That is the justification for dealing with a period the furthest horizons of
which cover three centuries.

In Part I, I deal all too briefly with what amounts to
a radical redistribution of power. Between 1560 and the end
of the seventeenth century the authority of the Church of
England so declined that it could no longer represent the
interests of the whole people as it had claimed to do for
centuries previously. The monarchy, too, was so attenuated
by that time that it could not move save by leave of parliament, a body dominated by the "middling sort of men."
Until both of these movements had occurred, bringing to an
end the contextual, organic, if authoritarian, society of
the high middle ages, the individualistic age of *laissez-
faire* could not emerge.

In Part II, I trace the implications the new values had as they were implemented in the political, economic, familial, intellectual and spiritual areas of the nation's life. Each of the areas is treated both as a dependent variable and as an independent one. Each is relative to the others. Moreover, if thought affects practice, the opposite is also true. What becomes obvious is that the dominant world view of the eighteenth century which affected everyone and everything immersed in it was a very different one than that shared during the period sometimes known as medieval Christendom. A social change had taken place. As the weaknesses of the new order appeared it was inevitable that it should in turn be challenged.

In Part III, I deal, again briefly, with the criticism of some of those who, from the standpoint of the Christian faith which a great many men still claimed as the justification for their ways, were convinced that the new individualistic values simply could not stand the test. They called for a new organic view in which men freely acknowledged both dependence on, and responsibility for, their neighbours, as well as a common dependence upon God. Other men, such as Marx and Engels, equally convinced that the new order would not do, sought alternatives through visions that owed relatively little to the religious traditions of the past.

The methodology used in this book, while kept in the background, is an essential part of any contribution the book may make to further understanding. It is meant to be an adaptation of the social theory of Talcott Parsons which in turn built upon the pioneer work of Max Weber. It is an adaptation for at least two reasons. First, Parsons' theory tends to presuppose a natural consensus at the centre of things, an almost automatic "governor" which assumes that while change takes place it will be confined inevitably within tolerable limits. It tends to overlook the coercive

## Introduction

xiii

nature of the *status quo* at any given time and therefore does not take sufficient account of conflict as an element in human relationships. Such conflict may lead either to new developments within a continuing cultural configuration or to its breakdown. A more adequate account of both "consensus" and "conflict" is recognized in modern "field" theory.[2] Both factors, "consensus" and "conflict," feed back into the ongoing life of mankind, affecting the basic requirements for creative life both human and, as we recognize now, sub-human.

The second reason an adaptation has been effected in Parsons' theory is because in it as well as in most "scientific" theory insufficient attention is paid to the implicit presuppositions through which it views reality. For example, while any adequate analysis of English society during the period under discussion would disclose the remarkable way in which the religious interest found new and frequently creative ways to influence society, it is not possible to interpret them without making value judgments which must be termed theological, or, if you prefer, theoretical. Such judgments are inevitable in all such enterprises and must be disclosed in any theory which seeks to be consistent, whole and, above all, objective.

The model which informs this work is a "differentiated" organic one. It assumes that there are conditions under which human existence thrives. Such conditions hold when unity and diversity in their dynamic, ongoing relations serve each other. When they do not, conflict occurs which may or may not be overcome. Depending on the context and circumstances, the challenge may call for incremental or radical change. In this sense the approach is more dynamic, comprehensive and flexible than Marxian dialectic. The metaphor on which the model is based is as modern as that of *Mankind at the Turning Point*, the second report of the club of Rome, and as ancient, at least, as Paul's first letter to the Corinthians.[3]

Whether such judgments are convincing or not depends upon their ability to touch springs of recognition in the consciousness of others.  The thesis that human existence must be understood as a whole *even though this can never be achieved in anything save a relative sense*, that unity is as real as diversity, that generalization is as necessary and as vital as specialization, that we must see things in their interrelationships if we are to understand what is going on in any adequate sense, is a *normative* judgment throughout this work.  Whether or not the assessment strikes the note of reality awaits the response of the reader to the way in which the account which follows interprets events that continue to have significance far beyond the border of a tiny island in one corner of the globe.

# PART I

# PRELUDE: 1560-1688

Chapter One

THE ROOTS OF CHANGE

In order to see eighteenth century England in perspective it is essential to understand in broadest outline the forces which were at work in English society from the time of the English Reformation. At every stage the account demonstrates the interdependence of religion and society and discloses changes incipient at the time which were to become the dominant characteristics of the new age.[1]

I

During the reign of Elizabeth I two factions strove for supremacy within the Church of England. It is no exaggeration to say that the struggle between them went on for a century and a half and was not resolved until the Glorious Revolution of 1688 with fateful implications for the relationship between religion and society in England from that time forward. It is important, therefore, that we understand what was at stake between them.

One party stood for the Elizabethan settlement. That is, the Queen was recognized as "Supreme Governor" of the church and of the state. She was to be served by her Bishops who were regarded as Lords Spiritual though they served, along with Lords Temporal, in the government not only of the church but of the state. In opposition to them stood a party which was convinced that church and state should be institutionally separated after the Genevan pattern. According to them, the church should be governed by ordained presbyters and elders sufficiently educated to fulfill their responsibilities. Political authority was to be carried out by laymen who should also be elders in the church but should wield their political power in a state institutionally separate from the church. In this way the church would act as conscience of the state but not exercise direct political power within it.

At this time both parties were strongly under the influence of the Reformation. Calvinist views of double election were widely shared though highly controversial. The deepest difference between the parties was over the sources of religious authority. For the established church authority was to be found not only in the Bible but in nature reflected in human reason as well as in Creeds and Councils. Each was fitting in its proper place. For the presbyterian party the final authority for the whole of life was to be found in the Bible.[2] The former faction was epitomized in the lives and careers of John Whitgift (1530-1604), Richard Bancroft (1544-1610) and Richard Hooker (1554?-1603), and set forth in the latter's "Of the Laws of Ecclesiastical Polity." The presbyterian position was defended by such men as Walter Travers (1548-1635) and Thomas Cartwright (1535-1603), whose works are available only in fragmented form.

Whatever may be true in the twentieth century, traditional religious faith deeply motivated men in the sixteenth. Whether one wears a surplice or not appears to us to be a matter of petty concern. In a day when religious conformity was insisted upon as essential to an orderly society, such behaviour identified one's whole theological position. When Cartwright's sermons preached at Cambridge in 1565 led to services conducted without the surplice, the gauntlet had been thrown down. Open controversy was inevitable between the whole position of the established church, led by John Whitgift at this time Master of Trinity College and then Vice-Chancellor of Cambridge, and that of presbyterianism, led by Cartwright who was Lady Margaret lecturer in divinity there.

At the same time Whitgift had to defend a position distinct from the English catholic community related to Rome, the recusants, who it was feared were sympathetic to Spain. These distinctions were clearly set forth in the respective sermons of Hooker before the lawyers at the Temple in 1585 and the "lectures" of Travers in the afternoons in the same chapel. Hooker's "Of Ecclesiastical Polity" reveals a profound faith in natural human goodness and the integrity of human reason as well as in the authority of traditional practice. Quite apart from divine revelation man can distinguish good from evil and has a natural instinct towards the good. Man's sin does not make it impossible for him to create customs, laws and practices that tend toward their own perfection. Yet human goodness cannot produce true faith, hope and love. The gospel and the church do this. Their task is complementary to the state in the sense that they carry man to a higher spiritual perfection. In his belief in eternal, natural and divine law supplemented by revelation Hooker was influenced by Aquinas rather than Calvin.[3]

The ecclesiastical implications of these basic theological propositions are what is of greatest interest to us. Since natural law, human reason and tradition are supplemented for the elect with divine revelation disclosed in the Bible, a Christian state will employ all of these in its order and so will its Christian ruler. Nevertheless, as in Calvin, the true church is invisible. The visible church in a Christian state, such as England, may be ruled by a king whose only limitation is his duty to God. Such a king may be head over both church and state, since externally they are co-extensive even though the purposes of both institutions differ. The church is the vehicle of salvation for men. It provides the Word, the Sacraments and the Ministry to that end. The king may or may not be a member of the church invisible. Yet there is nothing to prevent him being head of the church visible in the areas under his temporal control, since all visible churches include both elect and non-elect. The purpose of the state is to use its God-given power to see that the positive law with its punishments and rewards reflects the natural and the divine law. This, according to Hooker, is essentially the task of the king. He does not seem to envisage any serious clash between the interests of church, state and king. It is no wonder that both James I and Charles I were great admirers of Hooker's work! It accounts for their blindness to what was taking place in the England of their day. It gave them religious justification for their actions and made them resistant to necessary change.

Just as the king is part of both worlds, that of the church and the state, so the bishops should have power in both realms. Hooker granted high authority to the ministry as mediator not only of the Word and Sacrament but also as moral disciplinarian. In tracing the orders of the ministry he does not claim that the bishop's authority is *de jure divino* as some continued to do, but he does consider it as going back to the special place and authority of the apostles. Though there are only two basic orders within the New Testament canon, the presbyter and the deacon, there is seniority among presbyters. The bishop is senior presbyter.

While Hooker was concerned for the proper administration of the sacraments, he believed, like Calvin, they were to be observed within the context of the preached word. They were not to be a substitute for it nor, because helpful to personal salvation, a weapon which priests might use for their own privilege. He shared with his presbyterian opponents a concern lest a "dumb" clergy continue to decimate the life of the church.

The problem of the source of authority was fundamental for Hooker as it was for Travers and Cartwright. In Hooker the authority of the king was basic both for the church and the state so far as the external, earthly order was concerned. The church as an institution was not above the king any more than the state was above him. He was sovereign over both realms. The church was as subject to the laws of the state as the state was bound to the Christian responsibilities of the church. The true king was required by the purpose of his office to follow the natural and the divine law. He would follow reason and conscience informed by his spiritual advisers whose task it was to know the things of God. The king is fallible, a fact that later on Laud and Charles I seemed to forget. Evil is a reality but it is essentially a mistake to be corrected rather than a tragedy to be overcome. In setting the two realms, the eternal and the temporal, in relation to each other, the temporal may be self-sufficient though it cannot effect the eternal salvation of men. Only the gospel is efficacious here, and thus the ministry of the church is necessary.

Set over against this view the position of Travers and Cartwright, borrowed from Geneva, was something else. The most striking difference is the overall view of the human situation. The Calvinist position of these English reformers viewed man's alienation from God, reflected in distortions in all man's works, as a basic datum. With Calvin they regarded the natural law as provided by God for the ordering of man's earthly affairs. Nevertheless, it is never efficacious enough to bring about very much more than a truce among men. They certainly do not regard it as being capable of producing of itself the best possible order within the limitations of human existence. The task of the church is to be the leaven in human society which does make this possible.[4] There is no doubt that the scriptures rightly interpreted were for them more authoritative than any other single authority in church or state. The jurisdictions of the latter were to be kept strictly separate. It was assumed that the church could discern "the mind of Christ" both for its own good and for that of the state but that the *implementation* of civil law and order was the task of the state not the church. The task of the church was essentially redemptive; that of the state corrective.

The fact that the English presbyterian party, along with Calvin, fell back ultimately upon the authority of scripture applied to the whole of life led to critical differences in their view of the government of the church and its doctrine as compared with Hooker. What was not explicitly stated in scripture should have no place in the life of the church. The order of bishops was not part of the practice of the primitive church as disclosed in the New Testament. It was an order derived from the practice of man and so has no place in the church. This was also their objection to the book of Common Prayer. Moreover, while the "powers that be" are ordained of God and should be obeyed, there was no precedent in the New Testament for the king as "Supreme Governor" of the church. As James I later so keenly sensed, "No bishop, no king!"

Hooker thought the presbyterian movement subversive because he regarded its leaders, especially its lay leaders in parliament, as men seeking power that did not belong to them and because it would have the church telling the state what to do. In actual fact the Bill and Book presented by the presbyterian party in parliament in 1587 supported a scheme of church government that would have left the bishops as senior presbyters advised by a council of presbyters. They sought little actual limitation of the monarchy though potentially the right of rebellion was recognized should men be forced to obey God rather than men.

The presbyterians were calling for a re-ordering of the life of the church and of the nation that would have been a far greater break with the past than was the case, for example, with the church in Geneva. They sought a far more radical reformation in the liturgy, the government, the ministry and the practice of the established church than had been carried out at the time of the English break with Rome. It is clear that there were serious theological and ecclesiastical differences between the conception of the Christian faith, more especially of the church and its meaning, as held by Hooker on the one hand and Travers and Cartwright on the other. The life of England, its cultural heritage, helped to make the interpretation of Hooker what it was as the life of Geneva, with its very different background, made Calvin's solution there a possibility. The English situation could never have been transferred to Geneva, and, at this time if at any, the Genevan pattern could not be transplanted into English life. The hope of the presbyterian party that it could, without a far greater break taking place within the church itself, a church from which they were not prepared to separate, proved unrealistic. Rather, both positions representing alternative views of the meaning of the Christian faith were taken seriously so that men were prepared to continue to live, to suffer, and to die for them.

I have outlined in some detail the theological and ecclesiastical positions of the episcopalian and presbyterian parties at the outset because, except for secondary differences in interpretation, they did not basically change until the failure of comprehension, when the Church of England and Dissent went their differing ways, at the end of the seventeenth century. Indeed, they represent alternative approaches within the Christian churches up until the present. They provide the background against which the relations between religion and society must be understood in England at least until the middle of the nineteenth century.

Both points of view have theological standing in their own right. They arise out of genuine differences in religious perspective. As such, they were internally convincing to those who stood for them. Yet their relative strength and influence cannot be understood if theological considerations alone are all that are taken into account. Hooker's views had the influence they did partially because they coincided with, indeed were actually sponsored by, the interest both of the church and the crown, interests that were both political and economic.[5] It is equally true that the position of Cartwright, Travers and the early presbyterian classes was given currency by the patrons whose interest it was to challenge the crown and who had the political and economic power to do so.[6] The interest of Elizabeth I in the church was always political. She was prepared to press religious debate only so far as conformity served to unify the state. Therefore, until after the threat of the Spanish disappeared in 1588 she did not permit too close discussion of the Thirty-Nine Articles nor did she call for anything beyond external conformity. Nevertheless, in the rivalry for power between the rising gentry and the crown the presbyterian preachers and lecturers stood for a form of ecclesiastical government that limited the crown as well as the prelates. How could such a party help but deserve the patronage of the gentry, which in fact it largely received?

At the time of the break with Rome, Henry VIII had confiscated great land holdings of the church. He distributed many of them to the nobility in exchange for their loyalty. Both church and crown were weakened in this way until the reign of James I.[7] Frequently the crown and the nobility had little interest in their newly acquired land and so were prepared to sell it to landholders who were interested in its development. *It was the latter group who made up the rising gentry.* With the land went the right to appoint clergymen to various "livings" which for centuries had been related to it. This accounts for the unusual power which the laity had in the life of the church--a fact which is highly significant for the purposes of this study.

Elizabeth continued the land policies of her father. Furthermore, she was as interested in securing the loyalty of her bishops as she was of her courtiers. Therefore she conferred benefices upon those who would support her, at least for a price. It was in this way that certain abuses against the church arose which the Church of England was unable to shake until the nineteenth century and which made it doubly difficult for her to face the challenge of change creatively. The crown improved the treasury and thus strengthened its own power through requiring a financial settlement in money or land when a bishop was appointed. The bishop paid a tax known as "firstfruits" for the privilege of a church office. This meant that the price paid by a bishop was passed on to the "livings" of many of the lower clergy. Disaffection between the higher and lower clergy resulted. The reduced wealth of the church made it difficult for the bishops to live in lordly style which their status as well as their Queen required them to do. They felt forced to reduce still further the revenues of the lower clergy. Therefore, many, though not all, of the more competent clergy served as tutors and chaplains for the gentry because the gentry could more adequately support them. This tended to leave the offices of the lower clergy in the established church for the less educated, the careless, the incompetent.

Another major abuse to which the above policies led was pluralism. The same clergyman would hold more than one appointment in order that he could make ends meed financially. As a result he was frequently absent from one or another of his appointments and thus the church suffered. Moreover, since the whole system was tied to an agricultural economy, this made it very difficult for the established church to respond to changes that were taking place in the organization of society from an agricultural one to a mercantile and finally an industrial one. Indeed, the church was relatively impoverished when compared to the economic resources which were open to rival powers. The presbyterian party cried out against the abuses of the church and the clergy, but Archbishop Bancroft complained that it was the greed of the laity and the interest of the crown as well as the laity not in religion but in political power which accounted for the church's difficulties.

The necessity for uniformity in religion was taken for granted by all parties at this time. It accounts for the fact that religious loyalties were as political as religious. It also accounts for the fact that the presbyterian faction did not call for separation from the establishment even in the Bill and Book but rather for a reform of the church. It also explains why Elizabeth waited until after the defeat of the Armada before she permitted vigorous implementation of Archbishop Whitgift's demand for Conformity which was originally promulgated five years before. The basic struggle was really over who should have the greatest share of power as between crown, church and parliament. What had been the church and crown's relative loss was parliament's relative gain.

A significant group which threw its weight largely behind parliament, the gentry, and the presbyterian faction was the rising legal profession. The great change in land

# The Roots of Change

distribution in the sixteenth century necessitated exactness and skill in the drawing of titles as well as in defence of interested parties. Also as trade greatly increased legal contracts became more and more involved. The legal profession grew by leaps and bounds. Whitgift knew well what he was doing when he was careful to see that Richard Hooker rather than Walter Travers was appointed to the Temple as chaplain in 1585. It is significant that it was there the champions of the two different parties battled it out in sermon and lecture.

From the standpoint of those in authority in the church then, the presbyterian movement represented a many-sided threat. Archbishop Whitgift, deeply sympathetic with the Reformation theologically, saw in the activities of Travers and Cartwright and in the presbyterian classes that were springing up in certain quarters of the country a use on the part of the gentry of the religious cause to serve their own political and economic ends. Parliament, meaning principally the gentry in Commons, wanted to strengthen itself at the expense of church and crown. What better way to achieve this than through an aggressive, insubordinate, articulate clergy? The fact was that the crown, the church, and the nobility were still stronger than the rising gentry and were to remain so until the fall of Laud fifty years later. The relative power of the gentry expressed through Commons was no match for crown and church because the latter two had power which was as yet beyond the touch of parliament. For the moment the presbyterian-puritan cause seemed doomed. Yet, because the interests of all parties were not only strictly religious but always involved with relative economic and political power, no one faction at this time could totally defeat the other.

II

The first half of the seventeenth century in English history was a period of great flux, with an old order in its death throes and a new order seeking to be born. This was especially true in church, in state, and in economic life. The feudal orders were disappearing, and in the wake of the revolution at mid-century the new "man of property" had sealed his ascendancy. Even in family life the old patriarchal system had begun its demise to be replaced by "contract marriage."[8] The sturdy yeoman had either improved himself as a result of his use of new methods of farming or, because of competition and enclosures, been forced to sell his land and to join the growing ranks of landless poor. The nobility in turn had either become successful farmers, made money out of state monopolies, and so secured a continuing place in society, or squandered their patrimony.

It was during this period that the church and crown made their bid for direct political power. By 1660 a parliament made up of landed gentry and city merchants in Commons had clearly shown that they had the upper hand in English society even though they could not do without the diminishing power of the established church on the one hand, and the cohesive, symbolic power of the throne and the nobility on the other. The church they needed to stabilize the extremes to which the revolution had threatened to go, and the crown they needed for the same reason. But the church which emerged was one stripped almost completely of its former power, and Charles II would have belittled divine authority indeed had he claimed "divine right" for the crown he wore. In the intermeshing of the religious with the political, economic and social aspects of life in this period we see again how life is all of a piece and how unsatisfactory it is to talk as though these could be understood when separated.

There was a direct line of continuity in the life of the established church between the "presbyterian-puritans" of the Elizabethan period and those of the civil war over a half-century later.[9] Christopher Hill says,

> Most decisive of all was Perkins' establishment of a school of disciples in Cambridge, among whom we need only mention Preston, Sibbes, Ames, Cotton, Gouge, Thomas Goodwin to show their significance-- using the patronage of Rich, ministers of Perkins' school spread as a refreshing flood over East Anglia and the Midlands, and occupied key lectureships in London.[10]

Richard Baxter comes at the end of this procession for he began his influence only during the civil war but was at an early age deeply influenced by many of the above leaders.[11]

It was not until 1662 that a break came from the establishment. Up until that time the most significant theological-ecclesiastical issue of the period, that between "the presbyterian" and "episcopal" parties in the establishment, had been kept within the church. There had been no thought on either side of a divided church. The question was rather in which direction the church was to move. Both parties had their advocates of a serious religious life. Even Laud ran into trouble because he called the nobility to moral account before the Star Chamber and opposed the *Calvinists* on the charge that *they* were antinomian and thus encouraged a life of moral complacency. Baxter's view of the church, which he set forth at the Savoy Conference in 1662, was in all essentials similar to that set forth in a Bill and Book presented to parliament back in 1586-7. His failure at that conference marked the real beginning of Dissent for, according to the Act of Uniformity, one had either to consent to episcopal rule or be deprived of one's "living" as a clergyman. In the past the minority "presbyterian" party had always had a strong following in Commons which made its complete defeat impossible, but the post-revolution compromise between the crown, the church and the city no longer provided that support. Separation from the establishment was then the only alternative left for those who refused to conform. This, however, was the outcome of the struggle we seek to outline here.

Strictly speaking, from a theological point of view, what is striking about the period from 1603 to 1640 is its homogeneity. For reasons of state and ecclesiastical polity even Laud, who supported a mild Arminianism, was more fundamentally latitudinarian in matters of strict doctrine. He was for a *via media* theologically if not ecclesiastically. Yet, the predilection for the Arminian cause was present in Andrewes, Cosin, Bancroft and Laud, all of the "episcopal" party as opposed to the strict double predestination doctrine of the Calvinist "presbyterian" party led by Preston and later by Baxter. The Arminians had claimed that salvation was conditional upon the response in faith as well as the moral seriousness of the believer and that Christ's atoning work was for all mankind. Montagu had claimed that Calvinist doctrines of double election led to the moral laxity of the time and offered "cheap grace" rather than a life of discipline, whereas a proper sense of man's part in his election would lead to moral improvement in the nation. Hooker's views anticipated those expressed by Montagu, if they did not openly express them.

While the "presbyterian-puritan" party was anti-legalistic on the basis of New Testament exegesis, it was certainly not antinomian in terms of moral responsibility. While Perkins insisted that a man could have a reasonable assurance of his election, what he did stress was that one could scarcely claim election if he did not display moral responsibility.[12] John Preston more than a generation later taught that one could have a much more certain assurance of election than Perkins would have allowed, but even here it was properly speaking an assurance of faith as distinguished from a piece of intellectual information.[13] Thus Montagu's charges did not wash.

The York House Conference of 1626 in which the Duke of Buckingham, as well as many other lay leaders in parliament, took part clearly demonstrates that these issues were of deep personal religious significance to leadership both in church and state.[14] It has been pointed out that John Donne resolved this issue by coming out for universal election and that since no one charged him with heresy, these issues were purely political rather than theological or he would have been so charged.[15] Yet it was for his eloquence that Donne was noted more than for his theology. This, together with the fact that his views on this issue were not shared in that day by any significant number, would account for the oversight.

The York House Conference was the last effort in this period at serious theological debate. Basically the issue was between the findings of the Synod of Dort and the "Arminianism" of the prelatical party. Neither side defeated the other. Preston led the "presbyterian" party. The views of Montagu were set forth as representing "Arminianism." One of the arguments advanced against Dort was that it spoke only for the Dutch church and so it could not speak for the Church of England which had its own traditions valid for it alone. Abbott, then Archbishop of Canterbury, was more Calvinist than Arminian and later on forced Montagu himself to recant his views when Montagu was made Bishop of Chichester. Had Laud been Archbishop then, of course the story would have been different, for with him Arminianism at least enjoyed ascendancy. It was this tendency than made Laud open to the charge of "papist" no matter how frequently and fervently he denied any such charge. After all, he was first and foremost for preserving the Church of England and as much of its moral, economic and political power as he possibly could. Joining Rome could scarcely have served that purpose.

Yet the views of Preston, religious or political, were scarcely in the interests of Charles I. Preston was for joining the power of Britain to the Protestant cause on the continent which was doing very badly at the time. Indeed it seemed to Preston that England was betraying the Reformation cause altogether since she was prepared to stand by while the Spanish and French forces had their way. But, as both James and Charles recognized, it was the Spanish and the French who were for a strong monarchy. They were not tarred with republican tendencies as were the Dutch. The "divine right" authoritarian, "Arminian" ideas of Charles I were antithetical to those of Preston, so that the latter's influence at court disappeared altogether even before the death of Buckingham in 1628, who had been his patron at court.

The locus of dispute then within the church continued to be, as it had been since the days of Henry VIII, primarily ecclesiastical and only secondarily theological. On the one side stood Whitgift, Bancroft, Laud and their intellectual champion Hooker representing the established "episcopal" side. On the other stood Travers and Cartwright, Perkins and Preston and, at the end, Richard Baxter, representing "the presbyterians." Was the church to continue to be characterized by its traditional practices and ruled by a hierarchy of bishops who were both Lords spiritual and temporal? Or was there to be a radical change that would

# The Roots of Change 19

reflect the patterns of Calvin's Geneva in which, peculiar to England, bishops would be "senior presbyters" advised by clergy and lay representatives and where there would be strict separation of church and state as institutions? Was the king to continue to be "supreme governor" of the Church or simply another member subject to the church's advice and discipline? It is not hard to see which of these alternatives would be favoured by the king on the one hand and the parliament, growing in strength, on the other. Was the sacrament of the Lord's Supper and the liturgy of the church as established to be the continued practice of all Christians or was the church to allow her authority to be challenged and limited by those who felt that such practice did not conform with their faith as understood through their interpretation of the Bible?

Even though Archbishop Bancroft would have had it differently under James I there was a reluctance to punish those who would not conform, for James I's early training had been in Scotland. By the time of the Hampton Court Conference in 1604, however, he had become frightened by the republican implications of Calvinism and so turned his back on it as an ecclesiastical system. Thus his well-known aphorism, "No bishop, no king," became his profound conviction.

Pressures for uniformity, then, from the standpoint of political expediency continued to keep theological controversy suppressed prior to the English Revolution. Nevertheless, the tendency was for those such as Bancroft and Laud to be identified with an Arminian position and the establishment while those, such as John Preston and later Richard Baxter, were Calvinists who supported the presbyterian faction and clung to the doctrine of double election. Even Laud, however, was not that anxious to engage in doctrinal debate. If pressed, he was latitudinarian. Richard

Montagu, the chief Arminian spokesman, as we have seen, did try to claim that Calvinist doctrines of double election led to antinomianism and thus to moral laxity while Arminianism, since in it man had a share in determining his eternal destiny, did not. He was not successful in pressing this claim, however, for the moral seriousness of the presbyterian party was not in question even if on other counts they were under suspicion.

Again at this time, therefore, it was the ecclesiastical implications of those doctrines that carried greatest import. In a very deep sense the doctrine of double election made all institutionalism of religion at best secondary, for then not even the church could do anything to determine a man's ultimate fate. Those who were predestined for heaven certainly did not need the help of a state-supported church. They belonged to an aristocracy of the faithful who in their relationship to one another were on an equal footing. Clergyman and layman stood together, both of them priests. They communed around a table. They were the chosen ones, a republican elite! They did not need an altar before which they were represented by a priest through whom salvation was mediated to them from above. Thus when Laud would have the altar placed against the east wall of the churches this was a direct challenge to theological conviction as well as to liturgical practice. Both had political implications. For the king, be he James I or Charles I, the "presbyterian party" was always dangerously republican if not democratic. As the bishops, most especially Laud,

> came more and more to demand expression of High Church ceremonial and to oppose the simplifying services of the Church's puritan wing, their opponents more and more dubbed them 'Arminian' meaning by the term sacramentalist, ceremonial, vestarian,

ritualist with little doctrinal significance implied. The theological and political ideas of Arminius and his followers were quite forgotten in the anti-prelatical and ritualist hurly-burly.[16]

It was James I and his Archbishop, Bancroft, after the Hampton Court Conference of 1604 who began to take action on the basis of what they presumed to be the political implications of the doctrine and polity held by the presbyterian faction. It was Bancroft, pressing Hooker's ideas to an illegitimate extreme, who was the first real advocate of "the divine right of kings" theory. With the cooperation of James I, who as a result of his experience in Scotland had become frightened of the republicanism of the Calvinists, Bancroft, under the authority of the Privy Council, proceeded to act against any who refused to conform to Whitgift's articles of 1583 and the Canons of 1604. This meant that one must acknowledge (1) the Royal Supremacy in ecclesiastical matters, (2) that the Book of Common Prayer contains nothing contrary to the Word of God, (3) that the Thirty-Nine Articles were agreeable to the Word of God.

From seventy-five to three hundred clergy were deprived of their livings at this time.[17] For many of those affected it meant exile in Holland or for others, later on, in the New World. This forceful action, together with other canons which were passed by convocation yet unratified by parliament, led to a deeper rift than ever between church and crown on the one hand and parliament on the other. The church's convocation had previously had no power to act apart from parliament, but Laud took it still further into opposition when it voted monies for Charles I without permission of parliament. Eventually this led to the deprivation of the powers of convocation to tax or to act on its own at all, even after the post-revolution settlement when there was some disposition on the part of parliament to be more conciliatory.

The efforts of Bancroft and Laud cemented relationships between their enemies, the presbyterian faction and parliament. Laud pressed the policies of Bancroft still further because he had come to see that the loss in the church's power economically had to be stayed by an alliance with the crown and an insistence on ecclesiastical authority and uniformity. He failed because his attempt was far too late to be praticable. All he did was to precipitate the events of the coming English Revolution by driving matters to the extreme. The rising influence of the common law, the growing power of parliament and the economic dominance of the city of London, plus all those propertied interests strengthened by developing capitalism, made both Laud's hopes and the claims of the crown impossible of fulfillment. The common man and the courtier disliked Laud's insistence on moral discipline; the "middling sort of men" disliked his radical interference in the economic order, for example, on the matter of enclosures; the parliament did not appreciate his readiness to grant monies raised by church taxation to a king who could not act because that parliament had already refused him such.

The major abuses of pluralism and ignorance among the clergy, mentioned earlier, only exacerbated the situation for Bancroft and Laud, who, while concerned about them, had too much on their hands to deal successfully with them. This added fuel to the fire as the presbyterian faction within parliament resisted aid to the church while such abuses continued. The "presbyterian-puritan" element, strongest in the growing cities and towns in which tithes were hard to collect, wanted such tithes directed to the support of an educated ministry rather than to the upkeep of an administrative hierarchy. The yeomen and the freeholders upon whom tithes fell heaviest were in no mood to support a priesthood at all. After all they had been told by some they had no need of priests to assure their eternal salvation. It was they who later filled up Cromwell's armies and whose hopes were expressed by the Levellers, the Anabaptists and the Quakers. At the same time they were a far cry from the presbyterian faction in parliament who were to them representatives of the propertied classes.

The problem of patronage both ecclesiastical and lay was of critical importance in this period and throughout the seventeenth century. The greater part of such patronage still lay in the hands of the church and a lesser part in the hands of the crown. As a result, Laud did have a decisive control over the nature of the ministry. He chose to use patronage in the main to strengthen the hierarchy and to increase its discipline over the practices and membership of the church rather than in a strong program to develop an educated ministry. The crown was fearful of an educated ministry which was likely to develop republican ideas already popular in such places as Cambridge.

On the other side, patrons among the gentry also held church patronage and wanted to hang on to this means of influence over the life of the church. It was one method of their fighting the power and the ideas of both church and crown. Yet, prior to 1640 only one quarter of the livings in London were under lay patronage, and although the numbers grew as the gentry and merchants acquired power and land at the expense of the church and state, it was a slow process. *Thus the "presbyterian" movement was never able to attain more than minority status and power prior to 1640.*

Actually, the fact that the patronage system continued to be in effect, no matter in whose hands it lay, worked against the reorganization and reformation of the parish system which was to be so necessary in seventeenth and eighteenth century England. Resting as it did on land, it meant that the church could not but help lose out as the basis of the economy moved from land to industry and from country to city. This also meant that the church was ill-equipped to meet the spiritual needs of the industrial towns.

The presbyterian faction on the other hand, gradually developed a system of voluntary support, at first confined to the gentry and merchant classes, and so had greater freedom to address itself to the new order.[18] Moreover, the fact that some patronage lay in the hands of the laity made it possible for the "presbyterian" movement to survive. *At the same time it also reinforced the growing conception of the absolute rights of property, for the lay patron held his ecclesiastical power owing to his property rights.* For Bancroft and Laud, the ministers who served under such patronage were simply the lackeys for the interest of those who supported them. When those who held these privileges had their interests threatened by such groups as the Levellers during the Revolution, many of them reacted swiftly and, together with the city merchants, were prepared to support the old ecclesiastical system in the post-revolution settlement even though that system was reduced greatly in both political and economic power. Thus "property" took precedence over "religion," and "freedom" was confined to the propertied classes.

The gentry was divided in its loyalty. Many were on the side of the king and of the establishment, especially if their economic wealth had been granted to them by either. Others for religious, political and economic reasons were for the growing power of the opposition. All of this forced a healthy re-thinking of the nature of the church and its relation to the state, of the congregation to the minister,

# The Roots of Change 25

and of the nature and role of the state itself. These tensions can be viewed as positive goods. For example, since contract was replacing tithes as an economic reality, some system in the church not so tied to a landed economy had to be worked out for its support. Thus the "contract" between minister and congregation, not something new but rather the old covenant idea found way back in Hebrew and Christian tradition, came to play a role which in an important sense was extremely fortunate for the future life of the church. It supported the concept of the congregation as a "gathered community." It made the voluntary religious community a viable option.

The political highlights of the period prior to and including the English Revolution are too well known to be repeated here. We are interested only in those facts which were fateful for church and state. Neither of the Stuart Kings, James I nor Charles I, was prepared to support any cause that did not in turn support a strengthened monarchy. Neither of them was of any significant help to the Protestant cause in Europe but were rather personally sympathetic to the royal houses of Spain and France because they were for a strong monarchy. English merchants, on the other hand, were sympathetic to the Protestant and the Dutch cause and so had one more reason to use the powers of parliament against their kings.

Prior to 1629 Charles I tried every expedient to prevail over parliament. His greatest problem was financial. One of the ways in which he raised revenue was to grant monopolies to particular companies for a price. Parliament put a stop to that with the Statute of Monopolies of 1624. When Charles I attempted to collect taxes not voted by parliament, he was frustrated by the Petition of Rights of 1628-29.

The most significant political fact for our interests,

however, is that William Laud, Archbishop of Canterbury, became chief adviser to Charles I in matters both of church and state. Through special Commissions church and state were interlocked. Laud sought a revived church authority through emphasis on tradition, sacrament, liturgy and a moral conformity imposed upon high and low alike through political power if necessary. At the same time he tried to re-establish and institute the old economic claims of the church that had been devastated by the crown ever since the days of Henry VIII. In return for the support of the crown, convocation gave monies to the king when he could not find them elsewhere. Laud, when impeached in 1640, was still trying to assert the divine right of kings, the divine origin of the episcopacy and the traditional power of the church expressed through Convocation High Commission, the Star Chamber and the ecclesiastical law. His was the final attempt of the Church of England to maintain the direction of English life through direct political power held in its own hands.

This was the beginning of the end not only for the unlimited authority of the crown but for the traditional power of the church. *For good or ill the institutional church was never again able to maintain in England a significant measure of secular power either political or economic.* Church and crown were able to share power until 1640 against the rising power of the gentry because they had a preponderance of power on their side. Neither could do without the other. After 1640 the balance of power shifted into the hands of the rising commercial and landed classes represented by parliament.

After the civil war there was a new alliance between the established church and parliament, but decisive power was on the side of the latter. Parliament took away convocation rights to impose ecclesiastical taxes and to pass any

# The Roots of Change

canon binding on laymen without the consent of parliament. The natural result of Laud's attempt at ecclesiastical absolutism was a strong anti-clericalism which persisted long after the revolution. It is no wonder that Convocation fell into limbo before long since it had no significant power. Parliament realized it needed the church in the late seventeenth and in the eighteenth centuries to maintain social order and also to provide votes for a government in power through the bishops, as Lords Spiritual, acting in the House of Lords. But the direct political power of the church was at an end. She was even at the mercy of the parliament so far as preferment, and emoluments which went with them, were concerned. No wonder that by the beginning of the eighteenth century the church was little more than an agency of English culture to promote the *status quo*. It was such a church that Wesley found to have lost its spiritual depth, its moral fiber and its social concern.

By the middle of the sixteenth century the age of mercantilism had begun to change the face of the old feudal economic order based purely on land. As the century progressed and we enter the seventeenth century the locus of this great new economic activity moved from Southern Europe, especially from Spain, to the north, to the Lowlands and to England. It was this economic revolution that was to be as fateful as the religious and political for the future of England. It is a revolution the implications of which continue to be felt throughout the world to this day.

The old feudal order was organic. In it every man had a function to fulfill based both on his relation to local land and his relation to local political power and authority. In the new day a new impersonal force, the market, based on impersonal laws of supply and demand stimulated by new methods of production and the availability of money for capital investment began to take over. This emerging impersonal market with its own impersonal laws marks the period 1600-1640 as a bridge between the old "organic" medieval society in which one's life was determined by social function to one in which it was to be largely determined by impersonal laws of supply and demand. At first this was only dimly understood even by those directly involved in it. It was even less understood by those whose interest was not primarily economic.

Within England itself economic power was shared by those involved in commerce and those whose interest was still primarily in land, the rising gentry.[19] There was no necessary separation between these two groups. They were often intermarried because land was still a status symbol and continued to be so in England through the nineteenth century. Thus the gentry's growing power rested on a mixture of interest in land and growing wealth in mercantilist and finally in capitalist enterprise. In this exchange it was the merchant who predominated, who bought into the gentry class and to whom the future belonged. It was he who knew, if anyone knew, the secrets of the marketplace and how to make them redound to his profit. As the seventeenth century wore on he did so ever more effectively, sweeping aside even the restraints of government which, after the revolution, he came to control increasingly.

Even this first economic revolution spelled a social revolution. If the poor were forgotten, as enclosures took place to make way for the new agriculture, the old nobility lost out altogether unless, like a few of their number, they were able to adjust to the new order and to become entrepreneurs. In so far as both church and crown were able to hang on to their lands and to join the effort to see that they were developed, they maintained some basis in the new economy. More frequently they were the losers because they were slow to adjust. To realize currency they sold many of their holdings.

Until 1624 the crown attempted to restrict the new mercantilist economy through monopolies granted by the crown in return for a price. One should properly say the crown attempted to use the new economy for its own purposes, but the parliament put a stop to this by Act in 1624. The future was to belong to "the men of property." This was why Laud's attempts on the part of the church which were tied to the old feudal order were so futile even though he utilized that order's last strength in the effort. This, too, is why the crown's power evaporated. From 1660 on, the future belonged to those who cooperated with the new "economic man."

In the early days of the century the merchants and the gentry exerted their new economic power to gain the ascendancy through parliament and through their rights as property owners, that is, through the common law. As yet they were not strong enough to challenge church and crown effectively, but the forces of the future were in their hands. It was natural that many of the gentry should align themselves with those religious forces which were also seeking change, especially if those forces tended to undercut the established authority and economic power of the church.

Yet it is a mistake to reduce the activity of the gentry and the merchant class, as well as the rising legal profession, to men who were not genuinely interested in religious faith. They did not *have to* support chaplains and especially lectureships such as the "Feoffees for Impropriations" which show the extent to which they were willing to go, at a considerable financial cost, to support their religious preferences. Yet it is true that those preferences corresponded to their political and economic interests. They resented Laud's efforts to prevent enclosures for which he hailed many of them before the courts. They also resented his insistence on the fulfilling of duties to the poor according to the Elizabethan Poor Laws, though many of them gave correspondingly more than others to the destitute in the first half of the sixteenth century. The merchants were opposed to the crown because of its interference with the development of a free market through the granting of monopolies. Even at that, many of the merchants who supported the "presbyterian-puritan" cause were also members of Companies granted monopolies in America. Indeed, the crown accused such men of using their meetings for business as covert associations for religious purposes. In any case, it could finally do little against a gentry whose wealth as early as 1600 was reputed to be three times that of the crown, nobility, church and rich yeoman alike.[20]

The question of usury, which is essentially the question of the new use of money in the emerging economy, is one of basic interest to us. Perkins, Ames, and Baxter, each of whom wrote extensively on the responsibilities of the "presbyterian-puritan" man, followed Calvin closely in the matter of usury.[21] They permitted usury when money created wealth as it did in the emerging order. They also hedged this permission with such restrictions to prevent extortion that little place was given for the explosive power of invested capital which occurred from the beginning of the sixteenth century on.[22] During this period through Ames to Baxter the classical leaders of "presbyterian-puritanism" continued to talk as though the personal relationships of village and town characteristic of the middle ages were still unchallenged by the new way of doing things.[23] Still their concern was not only for the poor but also for the wealthy, lest wealth corrupt. As Tawney points out, even though Baxter was at work in an emerging industrial town like Kidderminster, he showed little understanding of the labourer's concern over the rise and fall of his wages which, for the first time for any appreciable number of people, were the only source of income upon which they could rely. On the other hand, he admired Mr. Foley of the new entrepreneurial class because he had led an unostentatious life, a sober and responsible life, and in the process his wealth had, according to Baxter, deservingly increased. If the poor were poor, they should be thankful that they were not tempted by riches, and if they were themselves sober and deserving, there would be those whom they would find to help them.

If men such as Ames and Baxter had had greater economic insight, or, had they inspired others more competent in the area to see how the Christian faith might be applied to the great new impersonal forces of the market in such a way as to lift the standard of living for all, perhaps the great separation between religion and economics which was to increasingly take place might not have occurred. Whether the laity who were ready to support them in religious matters had such an interest may be doubtful. As Usher claims, while the "presbyterians" of parliament were ready to strip the church of its privileges, they seemed equally unready to suggest an alternative method for her support. His claim is that they were interested in securing the church's property for their own aggrandizement rather than for purposes of reform.[24] The only counter to this is evidence that the merchants of London more than any other group contributed large sums to charity in the early seventeenth century. They used also their patronage to support their own religious views within the church.

Nonetheless, after the revolution those with economic motives won out, and among them there were those little interested in religious reform, for they used the established church for their own purposes while they drove the dissenters out of public life altogether. Many of the latter also were restricted in their business opportunities for they had to work without the protection and privilege of government favour. From this time forward their giving to charitable institutions fell off while at the same time the poor were greatly increasing in numbers. In the Interregnum itself, even for men like Iverton and Cromwell, property rights were to be protected at all costs whether people were protected or not. *It was this spirit reflected in the new authority of contract that won out at the Restoration.*

After the Restoration it was the "economic man" whose leadership was dominant in parliament. It is from this point that Tawney traces the fateful separation between religious and economic concern. As religious ardor cooled in reaction to the extremes of the Revolution, a reaction which was more concerned on the part of the men of property with the threat to their economic interests of the Levellers than with religious matters, the purely "economic man" came more and more to the fore. His world view was dominated by a "new religion," that of political arithmetic, in which the impersonal laws of the marketplace based on property and ownership prevailed over personal rights. There was little then to control the acquisitive spirit in the larger marketplace while at the same time dissenting piety was by law confined to purely private relations.

We have frequently mentioned the condition of the poor in passing but we have not actually outlined their economic status. In the feudal order the poor were accounted for in vassalage and were widely used on the land. With the increase in enclosures which went on with ever increasing speed after the reign of Elizabeth a great pool of the dispossessed was created. Formerly freeholders and others were able to use the commons for grazing purposes. Enclosures made this impossible, with the result that many of them, and some of the smaller yeomen, were forced into the ranks of

# The Roots of Change 33

the poor. As the situation became more and more critical the Elizabethan Poor Laws were passed in 1598. By law each parish was required to look after its own poor. Workhouses were established in each parish to provide shelter. There were repeated attempts on the part of the church throughout the seventeenth century to see to it that the poor were cared for. Nevertheless, according to Gregory King, at the end of the century one-half of the population was dependent on the other productive half.

Laud failed, as the king failed, to impose either the authority of the church or of crown over the economic arena as well as the political. The early "presbyterian" movement hoped to maintain authority over society through the inwardly changed elect who would then exert control in the state as in Calvin's Geneva. Yet the Long Parliament had no interest in being ruled by presbyteries, for to the majority of the gentry and merchants "new presbyter" was simply "old priest writ large." Various attempts during the Commonwealth to assert such authority were always abortive and by the Restoration were out of the question. Indeed the initiative religiously was taken out of the hands of the moderate city "presbyterians" by 1646 and did not return in any measure until, through their compromise at the Restoration, the monarchy was restored and order rather than revolution became the passion of the day.

The reigns of the first two Stuarts then marked a period of growing tension in English history. It was an age of transition in which old feudal orders were disappearing and the new gentry, the new "man of property" whose wealth was most likely in land and commerce, was emerging to contend for power with church and crown. His economic power rested upon legal rights given to him as a result of new "contract" and "title" over which he was very jealous.

In this period the church, especially under Laud, made

its final bid for the right to use direct political power to strengthen its own predominance and authority over society as a whole. Laud attempted to use such power for at least three purposes. (1) He sought to preserve the faith. He struggled for uniformity through total conformity and so forced the issue between the "Arminian" and "Calvinist" positions. Like James I he appeared to be more concerned over the institutional implications of double election than he was over the theological though it would be wrong to claim that he was unconcerned for the latter. (2) He strove to recapture the earlier power and authority of the institutional church. He would have been wiser, had he been able to discern the future, to have thrown his weight with the economic interests of the gentry in Commons whose economic power was on the rise. Had he done so he might have brought about the limitations on the crown without the ravages of the revolution. He chose instead to use what power the church had left through convocation in alliance with the crown whose wings were also to be clipped. (3) He attempted to assert the authority of the church over the social values of the day. This was disclosed in his fruitless struggle against enclosures on behalf of the poor. He did not understand that the balance of power had begun to lie with those who, while they still used the power of land economically, were nevertheless gaining power through the rise of the new commerce.

    The crown also made a bid for direct political power and was prepared to use every resource, including religion, to reinforce it. The theory behind "the divine right of kings" was an effort on the part not only of the crown but also of churchmen like Bancroft and Laud to shore up traditional power by absolutizing the king's role as "Supreme Governor" in the church. The presbyterian cause, with its doctrine of double election, limited not only the role of the church but also of the crown because of its differing view of the church which was one of functional service rather than of mediation between the divine and the human. The doctrine of the priesthood of all believers is republican in implication if it is combined with that of double election, while it may be equalitarian if the doctrine of election is presumed. The presbyterian party wanted to use its power in land to support an educated ministry rather than to maintain the offices of the established church. However, since it transformed much of its new economic power gained through commerce into land and the political patronage that adhered to it, that party was as incapable of reforming the abuses of the church related to land as was the establishment itself.

The lectureships which they supported voluntarily, the "Feoffees for Impropriations," were nevertheless a witness to the profound seriousness of the religious interest of the presbyterian party and the Independents. Yet even the clerical leadership, especially later on under Richard Baxter, failed to see the ethical implications of the new "impersonal market" for basic human relationships; they did not understand the role to which labour was reduced in the mercantilist enterprise. At the same time the independent power accruing to the gentry, the merchants and the bankers, as a result of their economic role, made them more and more self-assertive and impatient of any control over them at the hands of the clergy. They were prepared to write their own rules both within the church and the marketplace, and since both seemed able to operate independently of one another, the fateful separation between religion and the other structures of human society began to emerge.

We may then come to the following broad conclusions as a result of our analysis of this period:
(1) The intimate relationship between the theological,

ecclesiastical, political and economic is evident throughout. Every interested party sought to use the influence and authority of one area in the other.

(2) Abuses in the church remained because she was still tied to a landed economy. Even the presbyterian party tried to use this relationship to further its cause.

(3) The evidence suggests that the gentry, especially those related to the new economic power, were increasingly anti-clerical after 1646 and appeared to be more interested in the "rights of property" rather than those of religion though there were many who went into unpopular Dissent after the Revolution.

(4) Property rights based on contract and title and reinforced by political power in Commons defeated both the authority of the church and the crown even though that defeat was not total and not permanent.

(5) The fateful separation of religion from the rest of life had begun to put in its appearance. The right of the church to speak for the poor was rescinded since the laity regarded it as a challenge to its authority in economic matters. Charity toward the poor was the result, rather than a place for them in society.

(6) The "organic" feudal order in which every man had his social function was being replaced as the impersonal mercantilist order emerged in combination with the landed order. The roles of the clergy, crown, nobility and gentry all changed as the power of the first three diminished and that of the last increased. The future for the yeoman as well as the poor was increasingly uncertain. In the value system the privileges now given to the practice of usury became more powerful than personal concern for human beings. Laymen dedicated themselves to economic enterprise for its own sake.

(7) Finally, after the failure of Laud in 1640 and of the

The Roots of Change 37

Westminster divines in 1646 to assert direct political authority, it was to become more and more apparent that the only authority left to the clergy was to be that of preaching, teaching, and that of personal moral example.

Chapter Two

THE PIVOTAL PERIOD

I

The Interregnum, the period from the calling of the Long Parliament in 1640 to the invitation to Charles II to return to England under certain conditions in 1660, was one of revolution and reaction.  It was a time of swift, sudden and often unpredictable change.  Above all it was a period of fundamental instability in which no one of the contending forces at work could gain a distinct and lasting advantage. Thus it ended as a "half-way revolution" in which many dreams were dashed for another two and a half centuries which some had thought would be realized in their own time. It changed England but only partially.  "Religion, property, and freedom prevailed," as Hill concludes, but it was the middle term which governed the other two.  Since the period is so complex and so much has been written of it in depth, we will confine ourselves only to those issues which seem to have had a lasting effect upon the relationship between religion and society in post-revolution England.

From a strictly theological point of view little new developed during the two decades though among the Independents such parties as the Levellers, the Seekers, the Diggers and the Fifth Monarchy men, as well as the Quakers all produced utopian and sometimes chiliastic interpretations of the faith familiar in the history of Christian radicalism.  Emphasis on the second coming of Christ, and the identification of some leaders with Christ himself, such as the Quaker James Naylor, are recurring patterns in the religious life of the lower classes in a time of great instability.

Again one's theological position was most deeply revealed in one's position on church government of which there were at least four. No one of them was able to prevail in its pure form with the result that deep concern for religious truth was brushed aside for alternatives that seemed more easily manageable.

The first ecclesiastical position was that of Laud which we have already outlined. In an effort to assert the authority of the church he finally tried to claim an authority *de jure divino* for bishops and, of course, embraced the divine right of kings theory in order to enhance the power of the king as head of both state and church. He was impeached in 1640 and executed in 1645 so that this alternative at the moment was swept aside.

The second position was that of the presbyterian party which through parliamentary action had set the Westminster Assembly of Divines to work in 1643 on a Reformed pattern of church government after abolishing episcopacy! Its famous Confession of Faith and Directory for Public Worship as well as its Catechism all reflect Calvinist views stemming from Geneva and practiced in Scotland. It advocated a uniformity in faith and morals governing the whole of life which was quite as thorough-going as Laud's had been. It replaced the authority of the episcopacy with the authority of presbytery, the latter a spiritual aristocracy of clergy and laity. It would have meant the exchange of Laud's High Commission and Star Chamber for that of clergy and ruling elder. Or so it appeared to many. For them, "new presbyter was simply old priest writ large." The position of the Assembly was never to prevail. Events overtook them as a more radical Independency represented by small tradesmen, yeomen and freeholders, swiftly rose to power.

The conservatives among the Independents were essentially congregationalists. They claimed that their position like that of presbyterians rested solely on Scripture and on the nature of the church as outlined in the New Testament which was the only standard to be followed. Each local church should be autonomous in the appointment of its officers and in the expression of its faith in so far as doctrine had to be expressed and documented at all. In the Agreement of the People of 1649 and the Humble Petition and Advice of 1657 certain broad principles generally shared by Christians were set down and latitude was granted among all Christians to differ so long as agreement was acknowledged on these principles. They excluded without question the practice of "prelacy" and "popery." Yet, in fact, the widest disagreement in matters of faith obtained among the Independents so that in the last analysis every man was his own authority. Later on, after the Restoration while under external persecution, the idea as well as the reality of "the gathered community" emerged and modified this extreme individualism. Nevertheless there was a shunning of overt external discipline. The pious simply separated themselves "quietly" from unbelievers. The broader Independent view meant that the ecclesiastical power of the church should be restricted to verbal influence and moral example. It believed that the laity should be responsible for the implications of the Christian social ethic through exerting its influence on citizens as political leaders or through accepting such leadership themselves. Tawney makes this important point very clearly:

> The transition from the idea of a moral code enforced by the Church, which had been characteristic of early Calvinism, to the economic individualism

of the later Puritan movement took place, in fact,
by way of the democratic agitation of the Independents. Abhoring the whole mechanism of ecclesiastical discipline and compulsory conformity, they
endeavoured to achieve the same social and ethical
ends by political action.[1]

The fourth position in terms of church polity was that
of the left-wing Independents represented by the Levellers,
the Diggers, the Seekers, the Fifth Monarchy men, and the
Quakers to name only the major groups. They were regarded
even by the more conservative Independents as anarchists
though they did not characterize themselves as such. They
believed that each man was his own priest; that each man was
in fact equal before God and man and therefore no other authority than that of the Holy Spirit reflected through the
conscience of the individual believer was required as an
authority in the church or finally, for that matter, in the
state. Their emphasis was on the internal and the spiritual
rather than the external and the institutional. As we have
said, they were utopian and chiliastic. They either wanted
to set up the Kingdom of God on earth now or they believed
it was about to break into history through an act of divine
fiat in the immediate future. Many of them wished to set up
a communist commonwealth here and now. It was ideas such as
these that frightened even the small tradesmen who made up
the majority among the Independents. They along with
Cromwell gave these radicals short shrift and in the last
analysis were prepared to cooperate with their former enemies to restore the monarchy in order to avoid what they
regarded as such extremes.

From the beginning of the Interregnum there was a growing anti-clericalism in reaction to the policies of Laud.
It meant that the clergy never again held significant political decision-making power in the life of the nation.

Through the Clerical Disabilities Act of 1642, reaffirmed again in the Humble Petition and Advice of 1657, no person in clerical orders could hold political office of any kind. In Independency where the clergy was elected by the laity the latter took even spiritual authority into its own hands. Even the right to preach was not the prerogative of the clergy among their left-wing brethren. At best the clergy were left with teaching and preaching, example and admonition alone.

This was a remarkable reversal in a very short time. It was another manifestation of the growing separation of the power of the secularized state from that of the church. *Though in the long run it helped to purge the institutional church and thus had its positive side, it also helped to bring about a fateful separation in the minds of men between the concerns of religion on the one hand and the collective power of the state and the machinery of economics on the other.* The clergyman was to be concerned with the things of the spirit and to leave the world to other men more practically fit for the task. After the Restoration, Richard Baxter realized that any power and influence the clergy had left lay purely in the realm of moral suasion.

The Interregnum was a critical juncture in the life of the nation. England desperately needed a unifying force. Religious faith failed to produce such a centre of loyalty capable of bringing a sufficient degree of stability to the nation for it to survive without either return to older and more tried ways or to the discovery of a new way. Since the latter was lacking, the former took place at the Restoration of 1660. After the death of Cromwell and during the reign of Cromwell's son, Richard Baxter, among others, was called upon to try to bring about agreement among the denominations on a common form of church government, essentially upon a common authority that the nation as a Christian nation could recognize. Agreement was not forthcoming and the attempt proved abortive. The Commonwealth collapsed. *With the consent of the presbyterian party the monarchy was restored and the hope for any common Christian unity recognizing a common authority, inward as well as outward, upon which the nation could unite in common cause was gone never to return. With its exit much of the direct influence of the Christian faith over British life, at least as expressed through a single institutional church was lost.* The authority of the government replaced the authority of the church and the crown. In this sense the Restoration introduced, albeit inadvertently, the first traces of a growing secularization. The interests of "property" were too strong, the insights of men of faith either too fanatical if they were on the left, or too bound to solutions already offered whether they be Anglican, Presbyterian or Independent on the right, for distinctly creative, Christian answers to have been found to the threatening anarchy of the day.

Men of peace and of common sense tended to turn away from a serious concern with religious faith which seemed to them to be divisive rather than helpful. The "religion" of the city after 1660, with certain notable exceptions, was the marketplace and its demands, even though its bankers and merchants might formally bow the knee to Canterbury. The Restoration compromise, when looked at from the perspective of the centuries, may well be the beginning of the new age of secularized man. Its latitudinarianism and its genuine fear of fanaticism were largely responsible for the lack of vitality and for the formalism in religion that marked much of the history of English religious life in the last days of the seventeenth century and the first half of the eighteenth. It was this very lack of ardor which eventually prepared the way for the work of Wesley and of the so-called evangelical revival a century later.

In all this it is important for us to understand the role which economics played in the final outcome of what at least began as a genuine political revolution. In 1640 it was to be expected that the landed gentry and those monopolists whose economic livelihood had depended upon the crown would support both king and Laud, as the king's chief adviser. The monopolists were no longer the most dynamic economic leaders in the city nor in the textile areas, for more independent businessmen had frequently become successful in spite of restrictions and opposition from the crown. The monopolists belonged to an order which, though it was scarcely apparent, was on the way out. It was also natural that the very poor, those most dependent upon the crown and the church, should also support Laud and the king. After all, Laud had fought hard against enclosures and for strict adherence to the Elizabethan Poor Laws. However, parliament consisted mainly, though by no means exclusively, of those merchants and newer gentry whose economic interests were continually frustrated by the profligate and inept crown and by its favourites to whom monopolies were now given indiscriminately, so the city was opposed to the king and refused him loans when he needed them most. Thus the City and the Commons brought him to heel.

The Independents were smaller tradesmen, still free, many of whom resented the new entrepreneurs who were making little more than lackeys out of them through a growing and complex "putting out" system. In turn, the army was full of small copyholders and yeomen who tried to get acts passed against enclosures just as Laud had done. They sensed the fate which awaited them. Though they were the "new" Sectarians they were no more successful than Laud had been. Because the army was composed of such men, the republican "presbyterian" faction in the city feared the army and turned away from it after 1646. Yet Cromwell and Ireton stopped short of the demands of the Sectarians because they challenged the fundamental rights of large property holders.[2] Cromwell felt that once the rights of property had been challenged nothing but anarchy would ensue.

Thus "the new freedom" meant freedom for those who held property, especially large properties. Formerly enclosures were *forbidden* on *moral* grounds as constituting a hardship for the poor. They were now *supported* on *moral* grounds as establishing the need for civil order as opposed to anarchy and of enforcing the rights of common law. By *The Instrument of Government* of December 16, 1653,

> instead of the old freehold franchise or of the rating franchise of *The Agreement of the People*, the franchise in the counties was to be given to the possessors of real or personal estate to the value of ₤200.

What had happened in the meantime that "property" should have come to enjoy such rights? Was it simply that enclosures were more efficient technically? Or was it that "men of property" had gained the unchallenged ascendancy in terms of effective power? It was this context which provided the womb out of which the theory of "possessive individualism," as C. B. MacPherson has called it, was born.

Those who were charged with maintaining order at the close of the Interregnum had come to equate anarchy with the inability to protect property rather than people. Therefore city merchants, joining hands with the gentry in Commons as well as with the established church and a restored monarchy in the person of Charles II, brought about the Restoration and through parliament were to take over the nation in the year 1660 as senior partner if not exclusive owner of the whole company.

## II

After the great instability of the Interregnum in which religious issues were both an actual cause of, and given as an excuse for, violent social dislocation, it was to be expected that there would be a fear of fanaticism and extremism, of further disruption and anarchy. That fear was an ever present factor in the life of the nation until after "the Glorious Revolution" of 1688. By then men were looking for those aspects of social life upon which they could agree. If religion was a cause for disagreement that was a good enough reason for it not to be taken too seriously. A degree of depth and truth was lost in the process as well as a sensitivity to humanity.

In his "Reliquiae Baxterianae" Richard Baxter gives an account of those who made up both the conforming and the non-conforming groups after the Act of Uniformity of 1662.[3]

On the conforming side there were the lower clergy who were asked to conform outwardly even if they could not agree inwardly. This the vast majority of them did. Baxter says they did so in order to stave off poverty for their families.

A second group thought that the conformity asked did not touch on matters of fundamental concern. Baxter calls them Latitudinarians, and he includes among them the Cambridge Platonists led, he says, by Henry More.

Those who stood firmly for episcopacy *de jure divino*, and who undoubtedly were supported by some for reasons of expediency, formed a third party.

Among the non-conformists Baxter identifies four sub-parties. One party stood for what they conceived to be the state of things in the reign of Edward VI when the winds of the early reformation blew strong theologically, and yet the Church of England also retained the beauty of her traditional worship liturgically while episcopacy was also regarded as traditional rather than essential. They wanted a truly Reformed religion *within* tha national church. A second party was made up of those, like Baxter himself, who wanted the church of primitive first and second century Christianity, a comprehensive church but led by a "local" episcopacy as represented, for example, at the end of the first century by Clement, then bishop of Rome. So Baxter, while unready to recognize the episcopacy *de jure divino*, was prepared to recognize an episcopacy of this kind, advisory and supervisory but not as holding any divine authority above local presbyters and elders. It was for this version of church government that Baxter was arguing at the Savoy Conference in 1661. But it was too far from traditional English practice, and the bishops who had been suffering for two decades were scarcely in a mood to accept this limitation on their powers. As it turned out, others in parliament saw to it that the episcopacy was rendered largely powerless at the hands of the state rather than at the hands of the church. A third group, among the nonconformists, was the Presbyterian in the full ecclesiastical sense of the word who wanted a Calvinist reformed church governed by presbyters and elders and without a bishopric altogether. A fourth group was, of course, the Independents who stood for local lay autonomy. Included among them were the more extreme sectarians and the Society of Friends.

The ecclesiastical struggles that had gone on within the established church between the Anglican faction and the presbyterian were finally brought to a head and resolved in the immediate post-restoration years. Officially the traditional views of Hooker prevailed, and "the presbyterian-puritan" party was driven into dissent. Since the "Presbyterian" party in parliament was largely instrumental in restoring the king to power, they, in the person of their

leader, Richard Baxter, had hoped to get wide concessions
for their position.  The Savoy Conference of April 1661
in which Baxter pled with the church authorities ended in
complete disagreement, and the Act of Uniformity of May
1662 marked the triumph of the traditional forces.  In
actual fact the powers of the bishops were greatly reduced,
for while they maintained seats in the House of Lords,
Convocation had no power to pass ecclesiastical legislation
that was not ratified by parliament.  They lost all power to
tax, and since there was a profound cleavage of interest
between the higher and lower houses of Convocation, that
body met rarely, and except for one occasion during the
reign of Anne and an abortive attempt to convene in the
1740's, fell into complete neglect for over a century.

    Cragg says that "the gathered church" after 1660 was
what was left of the Commonwealth.[4]  In an ecclesiastical
sense this was so.  In the teeth of the Clarendon Code the
dissenters had no alternative but to withdraw into small
groups which met together for worship.  Even these were
circumscribed by the Conventicle Acts.  Through preaching
and teaching, the first in household gatherings and the
second in academies since they had been excluded from the
Universities, or by flight to Europe or America, the movement persisted.  Even though many fell by the wayside the
old "presbyterian-puritan" man  now became Independent or
Presbyterian, or a member of the Society of Friends.  He
stood alone with God against church, king and parliament.
His straightened circumstances helped produce a narrow outlook as withdrawal from public life was forced upon him.
Dissent became more passive, but its virility was great
enough  that it persisted until it was granted limited
toleration in 1688.  *The sphere of private relationships
and the realm of business were areas where dissent was free
to express itself.*  It did so with vigor in both.  It

continued to recruit from the middle and the lower classes and thus tended to strengthen Independency and the radical egalitarian sects.⁵ There could be in these circumstances little social application of Christian principles and discipline. *Thus the individual and the social aspect of the faith became separate areas of concern with the latter falling into complete neglect.* The impersonal nature of the expanding money market and the as yet relatively imperceptible expansion of industry, producing greater wealth for some and growing economic insecurity for others, were the areas of activity for those who by virtue of their religious dissent could not have, in the nature of the case, political responsibility for the implications of their economic activity. *It was no wonder that in their minds economics and politics were separated, and that interference of the latter in the former was interpreted as just one more evidence of persecution and hostility.* This attitude provided the seedbed for the economic *laissez-faire* of the eighteenth and nineteenth centuries.

The Cambridge Platonists represented by Cudworth, Smith, Whichcote and especially Henry More, represent the most virile theological thought in the post-Commonwealth period. Henry More gave his time almost exclusively to an academic life at Cambridge. He attempted to combine the ontological idealism of Platonism with a moralistic volitionism rooted in the Biblical tradition. Reason and faith thus found their union in a living God who revealed Himself mystically to men as the Holy Spirit. The Cambridge Platonists were personally pious in the finest sense of the word and theologically, as well as intellectually, were closer to the tradition of Hooker than of Calvin. On the other hand, they cared little for "the externals of religion" creed, static dogmas, and the ecclesiastical institution. Perhaps this was their weakness. Had they moved out from the university and brought their influence to bear on the ecclesiastical and political leadership of the time, one of their students, who later became Archbishop of Canterbury, Tillotson, might have more readily recognized when he was sacrificing depth in faith for conventional morality. In the emphasis of a person like More on the individualistic inwardness of religious experience the Cambridge Platonists were closer to Baxter than they were to their pupil Tillotson. Lichtenstein claims that in the thinking of Henry More the tension between the intellect and the will to faith was finally given up in favour of the latter. This left the field theologically to the influence of men such as Locke who emphasized the intellectual and the moral at the expense of theological depth.[6] Thus Tillotson may have inadvertently sacrificed all three because he had not grasped how both comprehensiveness and depth might be maintained.

Richard Baxter continued to represent the old "presbyterian puritan" faction.[7] He was concerned primarily with personal piety, with consistency between inner faith and outward act. His emphasis was always practical; his theology centered in Biblical existentialism. He was persistently evangelical, and he rarely gave himself to theological speculation. As a result, he had little to bring to theology *per se*, though he contributed something in the area of personal ethics as applied to social problems of a political and economic kind. In this regard he was the heir of the earlier William Perkins. In him religious faith was too high and serious a matter to be associated with mere philosophical speculation. His call was to a radical confrontation and decision issuing in a new life of spiritual and moral consistency. Theologically Baxter was a Calvinist and felt that the great issues had been settled. In his

preaching he made frequent use of the fear of hell as a
method of arousing concern. Indeed, the mark of a genuinely
inward Christian was one who set his mind on his heavenly
destiny rather than upon earthly responsibilities.[8] Religion, it may be argued, was made prudential. We are moral,
and thus responsible, in order to secure our salvation.
God in turn uses this service to achieve order in the world.

This is hardly to do justice to Baxter, who was a deep
and sensitive spirit. *Yet a subtle change has taken place
because concern for individual salvation begins to occupy
the centre of the stage whereas formerly, as in Calvin,
man's responsibility was the reflection of the glory of
God throughout the whole of life personal and social, individual and corporate.* Baxter does admonish men in *The
Christian Directory* to love one's neighbour as oneself, yet
he scarcely ever sees beyond direct personal relations. So
much time is spent on inward introspection rather than outward social responsibilities and the problems arising from
them that the emphasis supports a growing individualism in
the interpretation of the Christian faith. This was especially true in Baxter after the Restoration and may well be a
reflection of the objective fact that by then the dissenters
were forced out of positions of social responsibility.

For a generation after the Restoration the leadership
of a person with the stature of Richard Baxter meant that at
its best dissent had spiritual depth and fervour as well as
a fairly strong theological base. There was no question,
however, that "faith" rather than "reason" had the upper
hand here when the two were in conflict, or rather, appeared
to be in conflict. The Independents and the Baptists, the
latter most especially, as well as the Quakers, were suspicious of anything that might lead to intellectual pride.
The relative moralism, reasonableness and lack of emotion in
the approach of the Cambridge Platonists held little meaning

and less attraction for them. From the standpoint of morals the "gathered meetings" were antilegalist in the sense of the Epistle to the Romans. They were not legalistic as is sometimes erroneously suggested of the early "puritans." A banal moralism tended to characterize the position of the traditional churchmen. The general narrowness of dissent, however, brought on by persecution as well as by inadequate intellectual depth led to petty bickering and made those who might have sought understanding with them impatient of what seemed of little consequence frequently disputed on questionable intellectual grounds.

Moreover, the rise of interest in the natural world as a result of the work of Newton and the thinking of Descartes foreshadowed a period of great confidence in human reason. It militated against the "sense of sin" so real to an earlier generation of "presbyterian-puritans" whether they were to be found in the Anglican or the Presbyterian faction. It made the middle of the road seem both more reasonable as well as morally acceptable. One did not have to practice the moral abandon of the king's court, on the one hand, nor discomfit himself perpetually over the wiles of the devil on the other. One had only to be sober, discreet, and reasonable. Indeed, this was what the Lord himself required according to Tillotson! Perhaps the poor needed "enthusiasm," the wealthy would seek adjustment, but the wise would walk between!

Some understanding of what was happening in the final half of the seventeenth century in the broader field of the history of ideas is essential here. C. B. MacPherson has coined the phrase "possessive individualism"[9] for that idea which was of growing importance from Hobbes to Locke and on to the present. It stated that the individual possessed certain basic rights but with qualifications. The individual must *possess* something. In Locke he is considered a possessor of his own talents and faculties which give him a vested interest in man's common lot. But for Hobbes, as well as Locke, this is extended to the idea of property. Both of these thinkers interpret man as essentially economic man. Now Tawney has already suggested that the fact of an impersonal cash nexus together with a growing international market was something new under the sun. It was inevitable that this fact should eventually affect the world of thought.[10]

Along with the conception of impersonal forces of supply and demand in the economic sphere came the Newtonian conception of impersonal laws at work in the natural world. To this emphasis on the impersonal in the economic and the scientific areas Hobbes had added another such emphasis in the political. He had said that unless some central authority is recognized by men and obeyed, man cannot enjoy *his freedom to life and to ownership*. That is why man must and does create the state. Power itself is impersonal and indifferent. *But one thing alone is certain--unless there is agreement among men as to who is to hold it and unless that agreement is sanctioned by the great majority there can be no peace and no freedom.* Here, as in the economic order, there is an agreement, a "contract," between men. As long as power was held effectively for the creation of order Hobbes was not too concerned who held it, though as MacPherson points out, it would have been unthinkable for Hobbes to have agreed that unless individual property is protected the purpose of the state as he conceived it is viable. Harrington saw the property holding classes, especially the newly rising merchants, as the ones who alone could hold effective power, and thus he wrote in support of them. Locke exalted these ideas of individual rights and freedom into a new interpretation of natural law reflecting in turn the impersonal natural laws of the universe.

*If these included life, liberty and the pursuit of happiness they also included the inviolable rights of private property.* It was only a step further for Adam Smith to claim that each man acting in his interest would thereby create the greatest common good. A far cry from New Testament teaching as Tawney correctly observes! In fact these conclusions were a compilation of non-sequiturs hidden from many.

The striking thing here is the apparent conjunction between the conception of impersonal laws in natural science, in economics and in politics as well as in philosophy. It is not surprising that Locke, following Descartes, found logic as used in mathematics representative of the proper way to think. It is thus no accident that the dissenters most concerned with the new utilitarian science and the new rules of economics and political science should have fallen so easily into rationalistic deism and legalistic moralism which easily accompanies a strong faith in "objective" natural law.

The final decades of the seventeenth century gradually saw the disappearance of a time when the great majority of intellectuals wrestled seriously with the implications of faith in a Christian God expressed in traditional terms, simply because they felt they were finding out so much about the universe on their own. The laws of the new science seemed to be quite clear, objective, self-evident, and straightforward. Those not yet known simply awaited discovery. In the political and economic realm "laws" seemed quite of themselves capable of establishing an authority that needed nothing other than themselves to give them authenticating power. It was not surprising then that Hobbes and Harrington found little place for God at all, and even Locke found it unnecessary to ascribe to God anything more than an originating power now that the Deity was no longer a necessary explanation for anything of critical importance to mankind in this life, if not in eternity.

It was far more than a man of Tillotson's stature, especially with his ecclesiastical burden, could do to stem such a tide. He succumbed to it. Nor was this fate reserved for the established church. As we have said, deism proved attractive to the dissenters especially since their new academies took to the new learning much more easily than did the traditional universities from which the dissenters had been excluded by law. This was not all loss by any means for the important distinctions between religious faith and empirical science were made in the academies. This in turn made a great deal of modern technological progress possible. But the depth, the mystery, and the majesty of a vital reformed faith had been ushered out to be replaced by a God small enough for the minds of men and an understanding of human life noticeably lacking in depth and complexity.[11]

When we turn to an analysis of the political situation in this period, the clue to an understanding of it lies in the role of the various parties and persons who brought off the Restoration. Here the most significant and powerful group was the great merchants and bankers of the city along with those gentry who found their economic interests in league with them. However, both of these groups needed at least the tacit agreement and emotional rallying power of the crown, and the moral authority of the church. The City had been opposed to the absolutism of Charles I and the ecclesiastical power of Laud, but now they were desperately concerned over the radical, democratic egalitarianism of the Levellers and the still more radical left. They were regarded by their social superiors, the landed aristocracy, at least as "the middling sort of men." Yet they were to hold decisive power in the days ahead and already held greater economic power than any other social class. The older landed gentry maintained their place in society only through alliance in economics or marriage with them.

It was ironic that Baxter, who supported the establishment in all save its view of episcopacy *de jure divino*, should have been forced further and further into the ranks of dissent though it may have been well for the vitality of the larger church. He saw the dangers of an affluent society; one in which the Christian no longer knew what it meant to suffer for one's faith.[12] He reasserted the fact that through his calling a man must serve God and his fellows. This made sense since those who listened to him during the period of persecution following the Restoration were primarily small tradesmen confined by law to trade and excluded from government and wider society!

Tillotson's world, in contrast to that of Baxter, as a servant of the establishment, continued to be that of those who really held power in the present and who were not disposed either to share it or to give it up again if they could possibly help it.

Neither major faction in the church at the Restoration was for a fully democratic, egalitarian society. Baxter, like Calvin and most orthodox Christian teaching, claimed an equality of all men before God but a functional inequality among men leading, within society, to greater responsibilities with great rewards for some and lesser responsibilities with lesser rewards for others.[13] A man was to rest content in his calling seizing the opportunity to serve others in it as to Christ.[14] It is possible, says Baxter, for a wealthy man with great power to serve Christ. Yet it is all but impossible! Poverty is not to be desired, but *a way between* is that which gives sufficient to live upon but keeps a man's mind set on things above.

Inadvertently Baxter had given up serious criticism of

the social order. Other radical sects, save for the Quakers who had themselves become relatively quiescent, had disappeared not to return again until the movements for social reform in the mid-nineteenth century. Baxter seemed quite unaware of the influence of the great new impersonal forces in both politics and economics, the rise of the authority of common law and the new uses of money. Certainly he did not see the influence these forces could have on the lives and on the conduct of individual men who were either benefactors from them or the victims of them. His message, in its lack of a vital social dimension, was in striking contrast to the outlook of Preston fifty years before.

At the Savoy Conference of April 15, 1661, Baxter had hoped that there would be real concessions to his ecclesiastical views and to certain changes in the Prayer Book. He was mistaken. The restored episcopacy won out completely though certain minor changes were made in the Prayer Book. The Act of Uniformity of 1662 called for the restoration of the Prayer Book in the traditional form. Those not ready to comply were forbidden to act as clergymen. According to Cragg, over two thousand refused to do so.[15] Hard on this victory the various impediments of the Clarendon Code, the Conventicle and the Test Acts, deprived the dissenters not only of freedom of worship but the right to serve in any political office. The acts not only asserted the king's supremacy in matters ecclesiastical but contained express penalties against any act of disloyalty toward the crown. They were directed not only against the dissenters but against the papists.

The Act of Uniformity of 1662 was based upon the premise that one comprehensive church was still really a possibility. The Act of Toleration of 1689, on the other hand, while a recognition of the failure of comprehension, was a

# The Pivotal Period

victory for limited religious toleration. The dream of one uniform faith for the nation was of necessity given up because there was insufficient ground for agreement between dissent and the establishment.

Had the dissenters not persisted, the Act of Toleration would never have come about. The Conventicle Act of 1670 could ruin with fines any dissenter of substance. Yet many such men were regarded as necessary to the economic life of the nation by those in power. Charles II recognized this and in view of it, as well as a result of his sympathies with Rome, was not for continued persistent persecution. The church was dissatisfied with the attitude of the king but without the cooperation of parliament could do little. The House of Commons was for putting down dissent more forcibly because it was afraid of any recurrence of the instability of the Commonwealth period. However, Commons was distracted by its preoccupation with the struggle for power between Commons and the House of Lords. As a result of this distraction dissent had time to entrench itself and could not thereafter be dislodged.

In 1672 Charles II proclaimed a Declaration of Indulgence. He also declared war on Holland. The latter was a sop to the business community and thus to Commons while the former was an effort to protect those who were sympathetic to Rome. The dissenters took the opportunity to secure licenses to preach and to hold meetings. The period of persecution had lasted long enough, and was to last long enough in the days ahead, to consolidate their ranks while the periods of lack of persecution gave them opportunity to deepen and to grow. Thus, as a result of the tension between king and parliament, as well as the tension within parliament itself, dissent was able to take advantage of the failure to enforce the restrictive acts according to the letter of the law. Moreover, at the time of the plagues in the sixties and the great fire the dissenting divines entered the city when others left. They won great sympathy in this way from the general populace. People were unwilling to persecute those who meant good rather than harm, and the informers who were necessary to enforce the acts against the dissenters became more and more unpopular among the general public. As a result of the interrelationships between these complex events dissent was able to persist even though it lost those who were after cultural power and acceptance.[16]

Dissent from its own political point of view was sympathetic to the rising Whig party and its leader the Earl of Shaftesbury who wanted restraint on the king. The reaction of Charles was, of course, further persecution of the dissenters and a revival of the conservative Tory forces in church and state after 1672. But then these same Tory forces were strongly supported by James II after 1675 who, like his predecessor Charles II, wanted greater freedom for the followers of Rome. This the tory Anglicans would not tolerate. Therefore, the king turned to Acts of Indulgence again. On this occasion even dissent feared the return of the power of Rome, and a greater warmth arose between the established church and dissent.

Those in parliament, who were in any case for greater parliamentary power, who were opposed to any resurgence of Rome as well as Canterbury and the other leading bishops of the church, made common cause with their old enemies, the dissenters, some of whom were men of wealth in the city and upon whom many in parliament depended financially. Thus "the Glorious Revolution" took place in 1688 with the invitation of parliament to William and Mary and the humiliating exit of James II.

The Act of Toleration of 1689 was the result of all this. Unfortunately, deep divisions of a theological and ecclesiastical kind had made comprehension an impossibility.

No doubt institutional interest, rather than strictly spiritual concerns, brought about the toleration, but it also ought to be said that at a deeper level, in spite of disagreements, religious motivation surely played its part. Were this not the case, there would have been greater indifference to the reentry of the Roman Catholic cause. Of course, parliament itself was not ready to have this happen not only for religious reasons but because of political considerations for Roman Catholicism now represented the political and economic power of France against which English trade was struggling. Nor was it prepared to see a real resurgence of the power of the crown at its own expense, nor to see a renewed power of the church. It displayed little interest in the religious issues that separated dissent and the church. It was rather determined, and succeeded in its determination, to keep the church in subjection to itself, to use it and its offices for political patronage and in order to maintain social stability through the church's exertion of moral influence on society at large.

It is not surprising therefore that a broad view toward strictly religious matters, a rather indifferent moralistic view in the attitude of those who held decisive power, which is what "latitudinarianism" came to mean by the end of the seventeenth century, won out.

Moreover, as between the church and dissent the last decade of the seventeenth century was marked by fierce theological debate of a narrow doctrinal kind. This was especially true on the part of the dissenters. As long as a man like Baxter with some range of intellectual power gave leadership, pettiness was on the whole avoided. But just as he began to leave the stage, rationalistic latitudinarianism began to take over in the established church. This movement had, without the intention of its founders such as the Cambridge Platonists, become shallow and moralistic. The established church was further divided in its own house by the resignation after "the Glorious Revolution" of the nonjuring bishops who upheld the divine right theory of the monarchy as well as strong views concerning both the disciplinary authority of the institutional church and the necessity for a strong personal piety. The non-jurors made the left-wing groups such as the Baptists more suspicious of "reason" than ever. When this narrowness was joined with the latter's social deprivations, it was no wonder that their "enthusiasm," as their enemies called it, was looked upon as unattractive.

Some of the dissenters themselves were equally hostile to what they considered religious narrowness among their own number as they came increasingly under the influence of impersonal economic laws in their business activity and the attractiveness of the new Newtonian science. It was there that deism began to make its influence felt among the "gathered churches" of the Independents and Presbyterians. Thus, dissent itself was divided, and the cold light of an over-simplified empirical rationalism began to have its day.

While the cause of non-conformity flourished in terms of new meeting houses in many parts of the nation, according to John Owen, with prosperity came shallowness, a lack of zeal, a new sense of propriety. On the brink of a new century the old fires burnt low both within the established church and among the dissenting churches.

We must not leave our discussion of the role of church and state on the eve of the eighteenth century without further reference to the role of Convocation, because its loss of political power was extremely significant for the future use of power itself in England. During the middle ages diocesan and archdiocesan government had ruled much of man's life. The church had power to tax as well as to discipline spiritually, and as the greatest single landlord it vied for both political and economic power with the king and the lords. The Act of Submission during the reign of Henry VIII had placed the government of the church and its councils, especially the national council, or Convocation, made up of an upper house of Bishops and a lower house of the Lower Clergy, under the king as head of the church. Thereafter the king had to consent to all making of canons, and the Convocation could only be assembled by the king's writ.[17] After the Restoration and the earlier experience of parliament with Convocation when it had supplied funds for James I and Charles I even though parliament had refused to do so, Convocation lost all power of taxation and, with it, its political power. The situation became one in which canons passed by the Convocation were not considered binding on the laity. Thus, in reaction to the misuse of power on the part of the church, including Laud's attempts at coercion through the Star Chamber and High Commission, the church lost what direct power it had.

Right after the Restoration, Convocation did have an opportunity briefly to re-establish itself, but this opportunity was lost because there was such a struggle within the church over the powers of the upper and lower houses. The lower clergy hoped to improve its lot economically by sharing the wealth of the church with the bishops to a far greater extent that it had before, but the bishops were in no mood for this to take place. The king as well as parliament was doubtful of Convocation's ability to agree even on minor matters, and this gave Archbishop Sheldon good excuse not to call it at all. Thus it met only on rare occasions, as in the reign of Queen Anne, and when it did it was hopelessly ineffective. For over a century it did not meet at all! *What changes were made henceforth, including of course ecclesiastical preferments, were all made by lay leadership in parliament and not by the church itself.*

Sykes is convinced that the church was hamstrung during the eighteenth century in any plans it might have made to meet the great changes taking place in all walks of British life by the clergy's enslavement to parliament.[18] It was in the interest of parliament to keep things this way. Church appointments meant patronage. Control over the church also made for the limitation of the effects of religious differences as between the established church and dissent and so, from the point of view of the politician, meant peace. At the same time the maintenance of religious tests kept dissent reasonably unattractive while it tempted those seeking success into the church.

None of this made for depth in spiritual life. The resolution of things then in the religious, the political and the economic realms at the end of the seventeenth century was not conducive to an age of greatness for the Christian faith and its influence in human society. As we have seen this loss of influence was far more complex than the inability of men like Laud and Baxter to assess aright what was happening in the economic realm alone, as for example, with the uses of money as Tawney and Yinger would seem to suggest.[19]

The single most important political factor in this period is that power accrued to parliament and to the emerging parliamentary parties of Whig and Tory. After "the Glorious Revolution" even the executive power that had formerly rested in the hands of the King and his Councillors passed into the hands of "Cabinets" chosen by the King's chief minister. Cabinets were in turn responsible to the Commons as well as to the King. By the end of the eighteenth century even George III could not manage to overcome the opposition of the ministers to his most beloved policies. He could only delay and obstruct as a century earlier the parliaments had been able to delay and obstruct the crown, but he could not determine and carry out policy by himself. The basic reason for this development was that by 1660 neither the crown nor the church could tax directly, so that both were fundamentally dependent on parliament. The transfer of power was carried forward by "the Glorious Revolution" which dealt the *coup de grace* to the theory of divine right. Both factors issued absolute monarchical power out the door. By the time of "the Glorious Revolution" people were in no mood for further religious persecution. Thus broad churchmen under the lay power of parliament, a parliament still landed and aristocratic, geared to the country, not to the rising cities and towns, held the prerogatives left to the established church as well as the power it had garnered from the crown. After the "Bloody Assizes" the courts too fell increasingly under the more rational control of the legislative branch. By the beginning of the eighteenth century the Act of Settlement of 1704 made it clear that it was parliament and not God that decided who should be king.

Parliament thus came firmly into control of effective political power in England. It was a parliament of landed gentry, yet many of these supplemented their income through trade increasingly as the century wore on. This was all the more important because by the Treaty of Utrecht in 1713 England had defeated not only Holland but France as well for dominance in the arena of world trade.

As soon as parliament began to take over power after the Restoration, that body began to divide into factions which formed the first political parties in England. Throughout the eighteenth century these parties were little more than clubs of the aristocracy who debated the legislative questions which now had to be decided by parliament. After 1699 the rule of law, including especially the rule of contract, had a growing place in the sharing of power and in making power responsible. The Bill of Rights of 1689 conferred greater freedom upon the common man than he had ever enjoyed before, though it was limited not so much by political realities as by economic ones, that is, property became the measure of the man. Trevelyan has this to say:

> The Whig Party founded by Shaftesbury (in 1685) remained, until long after the Reform Bill of 1832, the party of the underprivileged dissenters, and of the mercantile and middle classes arrayed under a section of the higher aristocracy. The Tory party, alike in the days of Danby, Pitt and Peel, was in its heart of hearts the party of the landowners and of the Anglican Clergy and their adherents, though often with strong allies in other classes.[20]

Except for a brief period under Anne and another brief attempt in the 1750's until the younger Pitt rose to power at the end of the eighteenth century, the Whigs rather than the Tories were the dominant party.

The significance of the rise of the nation state under a government of men finding its sanction in "natural contract," in common law, rather than in formal religion and its institutions was a new thing under the sun as Tawney, Figgis and MacPherson have made clear. The state

> appeals to no supernatural commission, but exists to protect individuals in the enjoyment of these absolute rights which were invested in them by the immutable laws of nature.[21]

Among the most important of these was the right to private property. This new theory was far from the corporate view of society held during the medieval period. It begins to usher in a modern, secularized conception of the world. *This change, which affected not only politics and the economy but social morality as a whole, meant that the old order in which medieval, functional, organic social teaching, regarded as normative in theory if not in fact, passed away.* This was due not only to the changes in the economic order as such and the failure of Christian social theory to take them into account, as it should have done if it was to guide such change; it was also due to genuine reaction against the abuse of power by the institutions of religion, whether under a Laud or a Cromwell, under Cavalier or "presbyterian-puritan."

The church as a whole had been so involved in the abuses of the old order, attacked at the outset by Wycliffe, and then had sought through the theory of the divine right of kings added authority to stem social change through enhancing the authority of the monarchy, that she was incapable of carrying over leadership into the new order. On the other hand, it was natural that dissent should have allied itself with forces that were also seeking a new day in English society.

Nevertheless, it was the failure on the part of professional religious leadership on the whole which, as much as other factors, accounted for the growing appeal at this time of "political arithmetic," which was to be exemplified, *par excellence* much later on in the thinking of Adam Smith as a viable alternative view of reality to that of the Christian. The concept that natural self-interest automatically served the common good, as Tawney has said so well, made the necessity for a Christian social and ethical theory superfluous. The difference was between the functional medieval view of society in which each man had his place and that of a mechanistic view of society in which each man has his function in an economic process. The former more personal; the latter, vast and impersonal. The one tended to promote a sense of individual interdependence or, if you will, social solidarity. The other made for fuller individualistic self-expression, especially where it was accompanied by material wealth which in turn made the development of such self-expression culturally productive and personally enriching. Where it was not so accompanied, individuals were reduced to cogs in the machine or were regarded by the social order as non-productive burdens which had to be borne. One thing is clear--the idea that economic factors left to their own devices would naturally serve the moral ends of man would have appeared completely irrational and immoral to medieval man.[22] Just as, in the political sphere, theories such as Locke's exhalting the rights of the common man of property appeared to justify what had happened there, so in the economic sphere the vast new processes set in motion by the new mercantilism and then the newly emerging industrialism and finance were eventually justified in theory by Adam Smith.[23] The new economy was to raise the standard of living over the long pull immeasurably; whether it was to lift the quality of human life and human relationships in like measure is a matter for further reflection.

The factors which led at the end of the seventeenth century and the beginning of the eighteenth to the increasing emphasis on little central government were complex, involving the world of thought as well as that of politics and in particular economics. One of these factors was the rising strength of the new merchants, and later on the industrialists who, as England became more and more dominant economically, were for less and less government protection or control. Many of these were dissenters who were happy to be left to the pursuit of trade and to the personal, or rather *private*, discipline of their own consciences. Tradesmen were ready to accept the protection of military and naval forces against the Dutch and the French, but the memories of the military during the Commonwealth and the divided loyalties of the forces during the reigns of the Stuarts made them skeptical of any military force of any size.

Justices of the peace and the militia exercised local authority at the close of the seventeenth century and throughout the eighteenth, but the central government exercised relatively little control over them. It hardly wanted to do so because the Commons was controlled by the same people who were running things in the countryside, if not in the rising towns. Indeed, the brief periods of "toleration" under Charles II and James II had only served to confirm the fears of the country gentry of "papists" and "puritans," and so they were determined to keep things in their own hands.[24] Thus it was the Pitts and the Foxes, the lesser gentry, who were to dominate England for another century and a half in the name of a dying landed class. Yet even they had recently inherited their wealth from trade. Sir Nathaniel Herne, Sheriff of London, had observed when the Bishops had wanted to imprison the dissenters in 1674 "that they could not trade," said he, "with their neighbours one day and imprison them the next."

We turn then to economic considerations. On the foreign scene, since "the City" had the decisive hand in affairs not only at the Restoration but also at "the Glorious Revolution,"[25] it saw to it that there was a great expansion in shipping and in the navy after 1688. Until well after the turn of the century protectionism was the government's policy as it sought to export all it could and to import as little as possible. "By 1714 London had succeeded Amsterdam as the centre of world trade." The dream of men of 1650-57 had been realized.[26] Wages were kept low to force the poor to work. To some extent this did increase production and eventually raised the general standard of living as an unintentional by-product.

Internally, as a result of the increased enclosures and the decline of the yeomanry and small masters in the trades, a large landless working class developed. Over against them was an oligarchy which held land and also derived wealth from business. On the whole, after the Restoration, dissenting businessmen were increasingly excluded from this group and found their place in trade based on new industry. Most economists thought in terms of a great pool of labourers working for subsistence wages as the *sine qua non* for the conquest of world markets.[27] Since the market internally and externally was as yet poorly organized, this led to extremes of poverty in the early eighteenth century which the old parish Poor Law system could not handle. When such poverty was combined with mercantilist economic theory, it led to great suffering and neglect for at least half the population of England according to the statistics of Gregory King.[28] That is, one half of the population was dependent on the other "productive" half. There were 1,300,000 "paupers" in a population of 5,500,000.

After the Restoration we must clearly understand that it was the city bankers and merchants who really held the dominating influence both in politics and in economics over both crown and church. They were prepared to tolerate crown and church but the latter recognized their dependence upon those who paid the bills. Many of the Bishops, for example, would have been glad to support the Tory party where they felt their interests in the long run really lay. They could not do so because appointments were in the hands of parliament and parliament was in the hands of the Whigs, and that meant in the hands of the City and their cohorts among the gentry in the countryside. Parliament and government were run through Boards and Committees much as they had been in the days of the Commonwealth. After the Restoration old

Royalists never did regain much of their lost property or their lost prestige.

The intimate relationship between religious, political and economic factors is clearly reflected in the social structures of post-Restoration English society. Baxter and other religious leaders exhorted upper class gentry, or, if you will, the upper middle class who had lately been businessmen or still were, to accept the social responsibilities commensurate with their station. These responsibilities included government office at every level from local Justices of the Peace to Ministers to the King. A man like Baxter, in the early post-Restoration days, could call such men to repentance. The fact, however, that men like him were silenced and deprived of much of their influence as clergy at this time partially accounts for the fact that the counsels of Tillotson were much milder and less forbidding. Schlatter clearly outlines the class to which both spoke:

> The theory of the gentleman was a mixture of patriarchal and bourgeois, corresponding to the actual gentleman of 1660, half aristocrat, half businessman. No doubt men of birth were still grouped together as a distinct order in the social hierarchy. They had definite, personal functions to perform... they could not justify their position, as some moderns do, by claiming that they served the function, merely by existing, of saving money and providing capital like human banks. On the other hand, there was a bourgeois element in the teaching that gentlemen should avoid, as sins, conspicuous leisure and conspicuous waste...sins especially disgusting to the busy thrifty man of affairs who never has sufficient capital to take advantage of all the opportunities that beckon.[29]

Right after the Restoration when stability was the

concern and mercantilism still the policy of dominant financial interests, it was no accident that government control and church control met together and walked hand in hand. Both suspected those who wanted "liberty" and "toleration" as asking for freedom to do as they pleased in the marketplace. This, in fact, was the case. The pre-Restoration monopolies interfered with progress in new trade and industry, while it was in precisely the latter area that the dissenters were chiefly at work. After the Toleration Act, which recognized the growing power of the new economic interests, the older mercantilist monopolies could not have it all their way. *Laissez-faire* and "toleration" in religion, politics and economics did, in fact, together serve the interests of those who were to captain the industrial revolution.[30]

A consideration of the life of the poor at the end of the seventeenth century clearly supports Tawney's thesis that the denial of the personal in human relationships of any kind, including the economic, requires an opiate.[31] The poor were not considered persons in the fullest sense of the word because they did not contribute to the gross wealth of society and because they had no standing or function within it. We have already alluded to Gregory King's figures which reveal, in so far as they can be depended upon, that half the population was dependent on the other half. If we include both those in the armed forces and the poor as nonproductive, then these figures are not exaggerated. One third of the nation was exempt from the Hearth Tax on grounds of poverty.[32] Though the Poor Law was run more efficiently after the Restoration and though the amount used for the Poor Rate was half the entire revenue of the crown, it amounted, nevertheless, to only 3 pence per week for each pauper and cottager.[33]

According to the Act of Settlement of 1662 the poor

were required to stay in the parishes in which they were born if they were going to make claims on the Poor Law. This fact, plus the growth of the idea that there must be a great reservoir of cheap labour, led to a worsening in attitudes to the poor by the end of the century. Labour should be bought as cheaply as possible. In 1696 Commissioners for Trade and Plantations deplored the dearness of labour. How could France and Holland be challenged effectively if the poor were not available? One author wrote,

> In a free nation where slaves are not allowed of, the surest wealth consists in a multitude of laborious poor....We have hardly poor enough to do what is necessary to make us subsist.[34]

It was taken for granted that the poor would not work unless they were sufficiently hungry.[35] Increasingly, parishes wanted to get as many of their poor off the welfare roles as possible. They attempted to find ways to disown them. This contributed to the growth of "the mob" in a city like London where the poor would drift, thinking to find work in rising industry. In an age of growing individualism it was insisted upon that the poor were poor because they wanted to be; because they failed to exhibit the virtues of thrift and industry. After the Restoration the voice of social protest disappeared and the clamour for social justice, or even for equal opportunity, was lost for more than another century. The poor were considered less than human, and if some of them were "deserving," the majority of them were regarded as not. The poor came to regard themselves as society regarded them. They had to be restored to the dignity of manhood through a recaptured self-respect.

If great changes were taking place in the other structures of society during the seventeenth century, this was no less true for the family. It had traditionally been patriarchal and extended. It continued to be so until the industrial revolution brought about the emergence of the nuclear family. Nevertheless the changes in class and status, as well as political power, that were taking place in the transition from the medieval to the modern period were very much reflected in marriage customs. In the middle ages marriage had been used as an institution for the preservation of political and economic power by the ruling classes and as a concession to the weakness of the flesh among the secular orders. Mutual love and affection undoubtedly had their place in spite of these purposes, but the latter largely prevailed. On the one hand, the view of the church toward marriage was more negative than positive, and, on the other, chastity was more honoured in the breach than the observance.

In a patriarchal, authoritarian society in which status is static the position of the family is always more important than the wishes and feelings of the individual. The other side of the coin is that there is a double standard. A great deal of illicit lovemaking goes on. The dissenters attacked the latter, a fact so often remembered. What is more often forgotten is that they had a very positive view of the goodness of God's creation, even though man's sin perverted it. They thus taught that marriage was a positive good and that sex was not to be denied within the monogamous family. The wife was still to be in subjection to her husband, but the husband was to love his wife "as his own body." This undoubtedly was the emerging middle class view of the family, yet it also led to a far more positive view of the use of this world as the arena of service to God and of a resulting measure of joy on the part of vast numbers of men and women, as well as children, within the bonds of monogamous marriage and family life.

Yet there is a cloud in this picture, especially among those in whom the religious interest was at best secondary.

# The Pivotal Period

Status and economic interest were not altogether forgotten. The father was enjoined to see that the interests of his family prevailed, that its status improved rather than fell. Personal feelings were to be subordinated to this end.[36] Christopher Hill has a brilliant analysis of Samuel Richardson's novel, "Clarissa Harlowe and Her Times." In it he shows how the conflict of interests between Clarissa's desire for a lover for whom she really cares and her family's plan that she should marry one of the wealthy gentry, in this case a rake who has rank while Clarissa's family had wealth, come into conflict with one another. In the end, the purity she has to give is taken from her by force at the behest of "our gentleman." She knows that society will not forgive her because she has had taken from her, though by force, that which she "owns" and which gives her "worth." Appearance, not motive, counts. It was her virginity she had had to sell in exchange for family rank. That was her dilemma. It was also part of "our gentleman's" desperation that he had somehow to rescue the family's fortunes and so was expected to lose his freedom, to settle down with Clarissa for good. And so they were married! Status and wealth would have their day. Even here "contract" won out.

Nevertheless, the affirmation of family life at least in the lives of the actively religious and many of the humble poor as a positive good, with mutual love and affection playing a large role, kept the personal factor alive in this area of social life when it was being extinguished from others.

III

The period we have just reviewed must be regarded as "a pivotal period" because it marks the turning point from all that had to do with the world view characteristic in any sense of the middle ages to one that ushers us into the modern age. The former was characterized by the role which traditional religious faith normatively played of providing, at least formally, an overall interpretation of the meaning and significance of human existence. But from the post-Restoration period on, formal religion was no longer granted that opportunity. After the Glorious Revolution, in particular, it was taken for granted that vital religious faith was a matter of personal, voluntary preference and the authority formal religion had previously had was taken over by the predominant forces in political and economic life. Those forces, however, had their own theology which has been correctly identified as that of "possessive individualism" which, while more than incipient in the last decades of the seventeenth century, was to rise to its heights in the eighteenth and early nineteenth centuries and to go virtually unchallenged until the middle of that century at least.

At this important turning point, then, we may come to the following conclusions:

(1) From the first to the second generations after the Restoration we move in the established Church from the depth and breadth of the Cambridge Platonists to the cultural moralism of Tillotson, which reflected the use to which the church was being put by those in political power. The period reflected as well faith in a prevailing logical rationalism.

(2) In the same period dissent had moved from a sense of the Sovereignty and Glory of God, as reflected in the thinking of Calvin, to a prudential concern for individual salvation with its accompanying individualistic piety. Religion for the dissenter had been removed to the inner life and was to be expressed outwardly in the moral integrity of individual relationships. The laws of the marketplace as

well as those of science, indeed like them, were objective and self-validating. They supported the stance of "possessive individualism." They worked to separate the life of individual religious faith and moral responsibility from the life which the same man might live in the marketplace. Indeed, he began to accept such a state of affairs as normative. These views were reinforced by the actual empirical situation into which dissent as a movement had been forced as a result of the period of persecution and the failure of comprehension. The dissenter was forced out of responsibility for public and civic life. It was therefore easy for him to come to the conclusion that such had nothing to do with his responsibility as a Christian. The state became his enemy, and this further reinforced his desire to be left alone in the marketplace, free from the restrictions of the state. His sense of corporate responsibility was thus weakened on both fronts.

At the same time we must insist that the dissenters who remained loyal to the cause illustrate forcibly the fact that self-conscious religious faith may be determinative. They had only to return to the establishment to be rid of their disabilities, as indeed many did. A great many, especially among the smaller tradesmen, however, did not. They suffered economically and politically as a result. Because they were faithful, they were able to increase their numbers during periods of indulgence and to do so noticeably after toleration was granted. They were also witnessing to a conviction which modern man is just now beginning to understand, that is, that a man must not, indeed cannot, be coerced in matters of ultimate allegiance.

(3) The impersonal laws of the universe as disclosed through Newtonian science gave an added authority to the impersonal laws of the marketplace, and these in turn were related to the moral laws "self-evident" to man's reason as

advocated by Locke. However, such laws were related to the rights of property more than to the needs of men. The "man of property" emerged as the truly human man. The sanctity of property prevailed over the sense of corporate human responsibility. Both Tillotson and, finally, a majority of the dissenters succumbed to a rationalistic moralism which reduced profound religious faith to a rational, social utilitarianism in the former and a cold, lifeless deism in the latter.

(4) In the political realm parliament prevailed over both crown and church. Henceforth the crown could not act without parliament because the latter held "the power of the purse." The crown still had some gifts in its own right which gave it a certain leverage in relation to parliament, but the church had none. The power of appointment was entirely in the hands of parliament, and parliament proceeded to use the offices of the church in the Lords for political advantage and to regard the church as an instrument whose duty and function it was to maintain social stability. Just as the lower clergy continued to be dependent on the higher, so the hierarchy was dependent on the patronage of parliament for appointment itself.

The whole system of patronage in the church was still dependent upon the feudal privileges that went with the land. Parliament meant to continue to use it to further consolidate its power, a fact which left the church hardly in a position to relate itself to the changes that were taking place in the political and especially economic realms with any degree of freedom and creativity. The religion of the majority of gentry in Commons really rested upon the sanctity of "title to land" and of "contract." This was disclosed even in the basis upon which many a marriage was contracted. To a great extent the self-interest of one segment of society, the propertied classes, was sanctioned by the power of law.

(5) The economic life of the nation during this period was in a state of transition from the feudal order through mercantilism, now at its height, to industrial capitalism, which was to emerge in the middle of the eighteenth century. The impersonal market had begun to take over, especially in overseas trade, and the national market had begun to develop a complexity which was to become more characteristic as intermediate steps between producer and consumer were introduced. In all this the poor were regarded either as a burden on the economy to be dealt with through the Elizabethan Poor Law or as "hands" to be used for the development of overseas markets, giving one's nation a favourable balance of trade.

(6) Perhaps the most significant development of all was the passing of the old, organic feudal order with its measure of corporate responsibility. The new authorities displacing church and crown were the impersonal laws of nature, of the marketplace and of the state, supposedly "self-evident" to the reason of man but strangely indifferent to the welfare of vast numbers of them.

PART II

THE GREAT TRANSFORMATION: THE EIGHTEENTH CENTURY

CHAPTER THREE

## THE CONTEXT OF CHANGE
## POLITICS, ECONOMICS AND SOCIETY IN THE EIGHTEENTH CENTURY

It is impossible to understand the nature of the religious life of eighteenth century England unless we bear in mind the momentous changes that were taking place in the political and most especially the economic and social life of the nation at the same time. Since much has been written of the latter, we will try to resist detail and draw broad, though we hope, defensible strokes. We shall deal only with those major events and general trends which had the deepest cultural significance and which therefore affected the other structures of society including the religious.

The first and second halves of the century stand in clear contrast to one another. This is true whether we are dealing with internal or external political or economic matters. The external struggles of the first half of the century were primarily related to questions of monarchical succession which also had economic overtones. Those of the second half had more strictly to do with whether France or England would win out in the struggle for the raw materials of North America and India. The internal life of the nation was more stable in the first half of the century than in the second. It was not until the second half that the incipient factors which brought about the "industrial revolution" began to be felt with anything like their full force. The first half of the century was in many ways an unexceptional and unexciting time. It was a "time between" the upsetting changes seemingly resolved at the Glorious Revolution and the coming age of British supremacy in the nineteenth and early twentieth centuries. Walpole, the principal political leader of the first half of the century, saw his task as one of "balancing interests." It is not surprising that in such a time the life of both church and state could hardly be described as either dynamic or creative. In the second half of the century fateful economic changes with great political and social ramifications both internally and externally were well underway. These forced response within all the other structures of the social order.

Throughout the eighteenth century the political life of England was governed by the compromise reached at the Glorious Revolution. Power was "shared" between the crown and parliament. Neither could do without the other. Neither could dominate the other. The cabinet, or more correctly, if we are to avoid confusion with present day realities, the king's ministers, sometimes called his closet, was the link between the crown and parliament. Maintaining the tension between them without an explosion was the particular skill required of the leading political figures throughout the century such as Walpole, Pelham, and both the Elder and Younger Pitts.

Just as the king's closet cannot properly be identified with a twentieth century cabinet, neither can Tory and Whig be identified with contemporary political parties in the sense in which they exist in modern England. They did not have strictly defined platforms upon which they fought an election and which they sought to forward in the houses of parliament. They were alliances held together only by the broadest tendencies. Men taking similar stands on a particular issue could be found in both parties. Tory designated the fact that you were for maximum power in the monarchy short of a compromise with Roman Catholicism which might threaten the established church and signal the return of divine right. In the brief period the Tories were in power between 1711 and 1715, during the reign of Anne, they passed the Occasional Conformity Act of 1711 and the Schism Act of 1714. The first of these made it impossible for a Dissenter who took communion only on occasion in order to qualify for public office to do so.[1] The second made it necessary for every school opened to have the consent of the local bishop. This was aimed at the dissenting academies which were gaining an enviable reputation in the country and provided the only access to an education open to Dissenters. A Tory might even be willing to risk the return of a Stuart. He would be more likely than not to support the high church party. As a result, the Tories were rarely in favour with the Hanoverian Succession, and this helps to account for the long domination of the Whigs during the greater part of the century.

The Whigs were broad churchmen and were more tolerant of Dissent. The smaller gentry in the closing years of the seventeenth and early years of the eighteenth century tended to be Tories because they suspected a link between the city merchants and the Whigs. In this they were only partially correct. One of the ways Walpole maintained his power was by keeping land taxes low. While this favoured the smaller gentry, it also favoured the great landed peers who were gaining increasing power. The latter, generally Whigs, were roundly disliked by the smaller landowners who found the new agriculture hard to introduce on their lands because their holdings were small. In reality, the link the small landowners feared should have included the great landowners.

Throughout the first half of the century, ending with the events of 1745, there was always the "threat" of trouble from the Pretenders. This strengthened the Whigs, but it also made for a shallow latitudinarianism in religious matters. The great majority were willing to avoid the religio-political controversies of the seventeenth century at almost any cost. Such a context provided a situation very much in need of the religious renewal which came through Wesley and others. At the same time the church became an arm of government, so deeply were her offices used for purposes of political patronage. The appointment of bishops was one of the methods used by Walpole and others to maintain a policy in and through the Lords. If one played along with government policy, a bishop was translated to a more lucrative see. If he did not, like Richard Watson, he was kept in the poverty of a poor Welsh diocese. All of this was aided by the fact that the extreme right, represented by Roman Catholicism, *was* linked with the political and economic interests of France, England's greatest rival.

The Church of England was weakened from within because its own governing body, Convocation, even when it did meet, which occurred only twice during the century, could not agree. The economic interests of the higher and the lower clergy did not coincide, and thus they differed on what the national policies of the church should be. This tendency was accentuated as the century wore on because the wealthy landed families found the benefices of the church to be a highly lucrative source of income and influence for the younger members of their families. Inevitably changes in the relative power of church and crown led gradually to a strengthening of the power of parliament at their expense. The power of parliament over the church led in turn to a failure in moral and spiritual leadership on the part of the church. The men who held the balance of political power were those who kept the interests of crown and parliament, as well as of church, in precarious tension. That was the task of the king's closet and most especially of that particular man, the chief or prime minister, who held at any given time major power in that small group.

Thus the role of the national government in eighteenth

century England must be understood essentially in terms of the balance of power between the king and parliament. Since the balance was delicate, it meant that no one interest could be secured at the expense of the other. This made politics a matter of agreements, of compromises between personalities and factions. It meant that except for particular crises, such as the ending of the war in 1713, the Seven Years' War and the whole question as to what was to be done relative to the American Revolution, politics had to do with the serving of special interests. At the outset it was Walpole's great genius that he understood this and kept himself in power for so much of the first half of the century. For him the way to govern was to serve particular interests and to keep them in harmony, to rock the boat as little as possible, to keep everyone happy. Unless a person or group represented some real power, Walpole had little time for them.

The major interest of those who had power at the beginning of the century, especially at the local level, was to maintain and strengthen the power of those who held property. Landed property was the basis of the social structure. The power of the national government lay in the fact that it had local patronage and thus local power to dispense. The "political machine" of Walpole and Newcastle was built on the utilization of such patronage.

The monarchy was dependent for any extensive funds, such as those necessary to wage war, on parliament, even though it had a civil list which provided income as well as patronage. It could use it at its own discretion. The king's household thus provided one, though only one, centre of influence and power through patronage. The king could grant the privileges of office to those who pleased him and the most prominent of these could join the galaxy of stars in the closet, were they able enough. At the same time, those who aspired to such heights also had to be able to manage the passage of policy in parliament, to which the king agreed often reluctantly. When this was not so, the system was brought to a stalemate and so broke down.

This division of powers served the majority of those who had any measure of power well, according to their light. It meant that local government remained relatively strong and that central government was unable to interfere with the use of property as its owners saw fit. Huge areas of economic life which were emerging as a result of the industrial revolution were able to do so without "benefit" of obstruction from the planning of an overall agency. "The less government the best government" was coming to be the attitude of those who possessed both political and/or economic power. Inevitably it was an age of individualism. This, in turn, meant that the policies of government were often reduced to pettiness, to competition for the spoils of office, to the skilled manipulation of a Walpole who could sense the ebb and flow of power from one side to another and through anticipation could ride the tide and stay in power. As a result, almost everything was reduced to banality. The church was "used" in this process and fared no better than other pursuits. It is amazing that there was as much creativity in her life as there was. Men like Law, Berkeley and Butler could hardly be described as banal. The strength of the Walpole regime, as well as the Pelhams which followed, was also their weakness. They were able to cope with stability but not with dynamic change and growth.

The link between national and local government was the patronage which the crown had to dispense. This was countered at the local level by the fact that the great landed families dominated the voting powers of their tenants so that the crown, which also had to contend with the Commons, was forced to work to some extent through the landed nobility and the local structure which the nobility controlled. In this fashion politics was kept local and "in the family." Plumb points out the important fact that the British peerage in 1726 numbered only 130.[2]

The parish was the unit of local government. Its unpaid officials were elected by the inhabitants. These were the church wardens, the overseers of the poor, the surveyors of highways and the constables. Above them were the justices of the peace. Most of them throughout the eighteenth century were local squires. Sometimes they were clergymen. In any case, their powers included the supervision of all local matters, including the poor laws. Since the justices of peace were so closely linked to the landed class, they were naturally unfavourable to those without land, whether they were the new industrialists or the poor.

The principal officials above the justices were the lord lieutunants of the counties. They were the highest county officials. They had considerable power because they dispensed power at the local level, which was available only through the crown. The Duke of Newcastle, who became the expert *par excellence* on the dispensing of patronage, was lord lieutenant of the three counties where he had large estates. As such, he appointed justices of the peace and doled out all manner of appointments and pensions that were a part of traditional royal power. In exchange, he received the promise of votes from those in the area. Thus a political machine was built up, and eighteenth century politics became the struggle it was for the spoils of power among those who could by themselves, or through combination with other "clans," build up great centres of influence.

The First Lord of the Treasury, a position which Walpole held, was a powerful post, for, while the king could operate much as he pleased through the funds voted to him

under the civil list, this amount was fixed by parliament
and anything extra was subject to its power. Thus, while
national government was related to local government through
the justices of peace and the lord lieutenants, it was a
two-way street in that the central government also depended
on the goodwill of the landed gentry and the great peers who
controlled the local electorate. As Dorothy Marshall
points out, it was a situation in which neither the king nor
the landed peers had sufficient strength to do without one
another.³

It made for a static situation, since each side was unwilling to concede any more than it could help for fear of
losing its grip. The Septennial Bill (1716), which prolonged the life of parliaments for seven instead of three
years, made any change even more difficult. This meant that
the new towns such as Birmingham and Manchester, still considered parishes, were virtually without representation
while those who were in control of the "rotten boroughs,"
that is, old corporations related to the past but with
little relative wealth or rising economic influence and
population, intended to keep things as they were. As the
cost of electioneering grew and the price of office was inflated by competition for the right or patronage, the great
peers won out at the expense of the smaller gentry, *and so
an economic aristocracy based on land emerged* by the middle
of the century as the centre of power over against the king.
Neither the poor nor the rising industrialists of the new
cities, *unless they also possessed land,* had a political
voice in the England of 1750.

As the first half of the century drew to a close, then,
the government of the land was in the hands of a landed
aristocracy small in number. Its power was balanced by the
interests of the crown which were not always those of the
landed aristocracy. The former might have an interest in

# The Context of Change 91

foreign intrigue, but the latter did not. They were interested in what was going on in their own localities. Increasingly, many of the great peers did become interested in forwarding Britain's colonial empire because they were able to supplement their fortunes that way. Also, those who were interested in joining the landed classes often did so through fortunes earned abroad with which they purchased land.

Both king and peers sought to keep the church politically subservient as a source of wealth and power and also of moral influence over the people, which could be used to keep them loyal to the status quo. The Hanoverians were firmly Protestant and, while the Occasional Conformity Act could be repealed, yet Dissent could not be fully recognized for that would have conceded too much to the rising industrialists.

In the whole scheme of things the poor, that is, the landless, had no voice because they were not men, not men of property that is, so they lived and acted out the role they were given as human beings outside of society, as its outcasts and therefore its enemies.

As the economic interest of the nation forced government into a more active role during the second half of the century, especially at the local level, the new industrialists insisted upon freedom for the marketplace to control its own destiny. *When the government was used, it was used to free those who held property from responsibility for those who did not, that is, the labourers and the poor.* If there was an attempt to control the moral life of the nation as there was through the Association for the Reformation of Morals, the morals to be reformed were those of the poor who had no power to resist the encroachments of the government on their personal behaviour, as did the rest of society. The privileged did not understand, or if they did understand did not care, that the despairing, often dissolute, life of the poor was owing to the fact that they had no stake in the social order. Says Dorothy Marshall, in a comment on Pelham's ministry at the end of the first half of the century,

> A careful perusal of the statute books during Pelham's long ministry would reveal a steady interest in the fostering of the economic interests as well as the social morality of the country as a whole.[4]

Yet, she comments,

> Many of these men, women and children were pitiable objects, (referring to the poor) the product of evil social conditions which had given them no chance. Discipline from without could do no more than contain the evil and the eighteenth century seemed to lack those resources which could lead to the cure imposed by self-discipline.[5]

Certainly it was a period in which any sense of social solidarity, of mutual responsibility was almost entirely absent from society as a whole.

If there was one person who was aware of what was going on in society at large at mid-century, it was William Pitt, later Earl of Chatham. While he had served in Pelham's Cabinet, he was never happy with George the Second's interest in Hanover and in internal struggles for succession in Europe. As a result, he was not popular with the king. *He sensed, rather, that Britain was on the eve of great expansion in trade and that the age immediately ahead could open up for her economy all kinds of possibilities if she were wise enough to lay hold of the opportunity with a manifest sense of destiny.* Pitt knew that it would no longer do simply to take the interests of the great landed peers into account. The City and the new industrialists could not be ignored. He was prepared to go all out for British interests, but he knew, too, that a price would have to be paid in terms of heavier expenditures of funds if Britain's goals were to be realized. To a point, merchants and industrialists were ready to cooperate because they knew their interests depended upon safe trading channels at sea and ready markets abroad. The gentry, however, was alarmed because it meant a rise in taxes with no necessary benefits for them. Inevitable changes were in the air, and they were to be ushered in in a severe and costly war with France.

Europe was in an almost constant state of upheaval for the last half of the century as the rivalry between the rulers of France, Austria, Prussia and Russia vied for a balance of power that would leave each of them and their dynastic, as well as national, interests intact. Pitt did come to see that European markets were increasingly important for England as the years went by and that therefore England did have a stake in what happened on the Continent. Yet his chief interest, and the wider interests of England, as he well knew, lay not in Europe but in the Americas and India. Until the French Revolution, the three major events which affected England abroad were the Seven Years' War and its outcome, the change in British relationships with India and the American Revolution and its significance.

While Pitt was an expansionist at others' expense, he did see that the future course of events was to belong to the trading and industrial interests and not to the crown and the landed interests. He was convinced that arbitrary authority, whether of crown or of parliament, could not prevail either over the colonists or the industrialists. George the Third and his cabinets did not understand these realities. As a result, they lost out in North America and eroded the authority of the crown. While the exploitation of India went on apace, constant war with France as well as

the uncertain nature of economic enterprise in the early
days of the industrial revolution made for both economic and
political instability until well after the French Revolution
and the close of the Napoleonic wars. In spite of all,
Britain emerged after 1815 intact and with a future brighter
than anyone could have imagined.

But the most significant *political* fact of the last
half of the eighteenth century was that the economic power
of the rising industrialists was beginning seriously to
compete with that of the landed classes. This meant that it
was increasingly impossible to ignore them in the political
structure. The attempt was made, but it was as great a
blunder on the part of the king and his councillors as was
their policy in relation to the United States. In both
instances what occurred involved the redistribution of
actual power as a result of economic realities as well as
the rise of new ideas about the nature of political power.
Whether the rights of men as men were to be respected or not
was not yet decided, but men of increasing wealth meant to
see that their rights were not only respected but that those
in authority were accountable to them. Both George III and
Lord North were acting on the basis of a view of authority
that was no longer shared by powerful groups of men.

The basic contest, then, was over the extent to which
power would come to be shared by new interests. Here a
whole spectrum of possibilities was disclosed. It began
with the affair of John Wilkes. Wilkes was an M. P. of
rather dissolute character. He was strongly opposed to the
policies of George III in the Seven Years' War and openly
attacked him in an article in "The North Briton." He was
arrested at the order of the king and his ministers. The
courts threw out the right of the crown so to act. Later
the crown as well as the house attempted to make it impossible for Wilkes to take a seat to which he was repeatedly

elected. In the process, the populace as a whole was whipped into an enthusiasm for popular representation. Public petitionary meetings were held which introduced into English political life a new method for putting pressure on the government. *It was widely used from this time forward by all manner of reform groups.*

Wilkes, himself, was hardly an exemplary character, but his case provided the focus for reform. One of the first reform groups to emerge was within government itself. This group, known as the Rockingham Whigs, led by Shelburne, himself chief minister for a time, stood for moderate reform of the worst abuses of the government. Among the group of "rational dissenters," as J. H. Plumb calls them, were Priestley, Price and Bentham, together with Edmund Burke who, at that time, was still among their number.[6] They were prepared to prevent all civil officers from taking part in the House, as well as all those who held government contracts of any kind. In 1782, when the Rockingham group came into power, they put these reforms into effect. But they were not prepared to modify in any basic way the resolution of matters as constituted at the time of the "Glorious Revolution," which they regarded as sacrosanct and as representing the proper English constitutionalism. They *modified* the power of the king's household but did not go beyond that.

Though Pitt the Younger attempted a more radical reform in favour of the new cities and the rising industrialists when he came to power in 1785, he was defeated on the issue. Throughout his period of office he kept a precarious balance between the old powers of the crown and those of the new day.

Charles James Fox continued to represent a more radical reform of the House and a wider extension of suffrage. He had based his policy on the hope of regaining Whig power through using the franchise of the new industrialists once it was given to them, yet through his constant political opportunism, he lost even their support.

More radical reform groups represented by the labouring class, led by certain middle class leaders, were not to be satisfied with piecemeal reform. The Association Movement under the leadership of men such as James Burgh, John Cartwright and Chrystopher Wyvill organized groups which planned to form one huge National Association to take the place of parliament in London if parliament failed to radically reform. They organized for the election of 1781. However, the Gordon Riots intervened in 1780. These riots were brought about as a result of the Catholic Relief Bill which parliament had passed and which sought to give some civil rights to Catholics. The riots were ostensibly against such a measure but, in fact, were the reflection of the profound discontent of the poor and the labouring classes in view of their own distress and the losses which the government was suffering abroad.

These riots put the fear of the mob into those in power and along with the French Revolution did a great deal to push back the timetable of reform in English political life. The French Revolution was at first idolized by reform groups in England, but it made reactionaries out of other men, such as Edmund Burke. Through his influence parliament passed the Treason and Sedition Acts and the Combination Acts which suppressed efforts at both political and economic reform in the years 1795-1799. The Reform Bill of 1832 was to await the arrival of the middle class "radicals" who sought privileges for the new industrialists. Justice for the labouring class was still further off.

While it is true that certain political decisions were fateful for the future of Britain, for example, the loss of the United States and the final success of England against

France, it is still true to say that the dynamic nature of British life in the eighteenth century was not as a result of either leadership from, or changes in, her political life. From the beginning to the end of the century, from Walpole to Pitt the Younger, politics was reserved for a select few who served the interests of the crown and the landed nobility and gentry. This meant they served and affected directly only a minority of the people. If this was less true on the local scene, it was more so on the national. The very fact that both the interests of crown and Commons as then constituted had to be served led to a certain paralysis of creative leadership. A positive leader like Pitt the Elder could stay in office only during periods of crisis. Politics reflected, it did not direct, the dynamic, transforming activity that was going on in other sectors of society, especially the economic. In the field of religion, too, politics stifled, it did not free, the established church because of the political use of patronage related to the church.

The economic sector put pressure for change on English government as well as on society at large. That pressure was reflected in the intellectual life of the nation as, for example, in the work of such men as Smith and Bentham and Priestley. The drive toward an open economy, to free markets, to *laissez-faire* indicated the growing self-confidence of the economic world. Its heady individualism permeated political as well as religious and philosophical thought. That much of the leadership in the economic arena was debarred from political responsibility because it adhered to Dissent made even more pronounced that fact that creativity was so little found in political circles.

Of course, we would not overlook here, though we will take it up in another place, those political reformers such as Wilberforce who did effect some important social reform.

Even they did so, however, in spite of, rather than with, very active help from such powerful political figures as Pitt the Younger and Charles James Fox, the latter of whom did sympathize with their cause. Dorothy Marshall, in a final comment in her brilliant work *Eighteenth Century England*, confirms what we have said as she reflects through the eyes of one who looked out on English life after the American Revolution:

> Only if he had read the works of Adam Smith and visited the new industrial areas of Lancashire, the Potteries and the Black Country would he have realized that a new England with new interests and new capacities was coming into being. Beyond her shores the same thrust into the future was apparent....It was not at Westminster that the shape of things to come was most evident when the new Parliament met on the 18th of May, 1784. [7]

II

Until the middle of the eighteenth century British overseas trade still reflected a residual mercantilist approach. It was a period of great overseas expansion for the British Empire. The drive behind it was for the purpose of securing raw materials to be processed in England and then sent back to the colonies or to Europe. The idea was to buy as cheaply as possible, to protect one's markets as much as possible through government monopolies granted by the government to particular trading companies, and then to sell at competitive, yet profitable prices, outside the domestic market. It was thought imperative to have a large pool of labourers willing to work for little on the domestic front so that the nation could have a favourable balance of trade.⁸

General prosperity was to be kept up by the government and the nation earning as much as it could abroad. According to contemporary economic theory even the ability of the electorate to pay taxes in order to pay the Poor Tax, into which a major part of government revenue went, could be fostered only in this way. The thought of establishing a domestic market which would have the purchasing power to use much of what was produced did not occur to people at that time; it awaited the actual increase of a population with some ability to buy as a result of factory wages reaching the hands of large numbers of people. This did not even begin to occur until the end of the eighteenth century.⁹

If mercantilism was still characteristic of the external market in which Britain participated in the first half of the eighteenth century, the manufacturing system was most characteristic of her internal economic life. This system was quite different from the old domestic guild system of industry of the middle ages when basic manufactures were carried on under the domestic jurisdiction of a master and in which the whole operation of manufacturing textiles, for example, was carried on in the home.

What had happened in the meantime was that a group of merchant manufacturers had arisen. They did so in order to answer a particular economic need. As city centres became larger, and as domestic markets abroad expanded, there had to be someone to act as entrepreneur between these centres and those doing the manufacturing. No such person was needed when most goods were consumed where they were manufactured. A growing disparity between production and demand had developed as, in an unplanned way, orders came in and great quantities of goods were produced until over-production took place. Contraction then set in too late. The new merchant entrepreneur was the one who could and did benefit in this situation. When the producer over-produced and prices fell, he frequently could not pay wages and his previous gains were wiped out by losses. Unless he could turn to agriculture as an aside as some did, he either lost his enterprise or went into debt to the merchant entrepreneur who supplied him with new raw materials to get started again when new demand arose. Frequently the producer actually sold his machinery to the entrepreneur who then hired the producer. Mantoux outlines the process and defines what came to be known as the system of manufacture, the system that preceded industrial capitalism, in the following way:

> Manufacture itself implies the separation of labour and capital....The artisan who previously worked for himself in his own house and with his own tools had become nothing more than a tenant, paying rent for the use of tools which no longer belonged to him. The manufacturer then went still further. He kept the tools, and organized workshops under his direct supervision whilst the artisan sold him only his labour, for which he received a wage.[10]

Capital was also available to the entrepreneur because until this time he had not had to risk it as had the producer. Capital hereafter was also separated from labour.[11]

Division of labour had in fact become more complex. Small retail tradesmen received their merchandise from the entrepreneur so that there was a separation of at least two removes between the final market and the producer. A change in the method of distribution toward complexity had taken place. Some of these merchant entrepreneurs gradually built up larger and larger shops. A few began to use machinery to increase production. As the age of industrial capitalism arose, some became the new "captains of industry."

One aspect of the economic change which took place in

# The Context of Change                                                     101

this period was the way in which economic changes brought about a change in law and in turn a change in the relationship between government and the economy. In the old guild system there was a great deal of legislation which not only dealt with the quality of goods but most especially with the labour regulations under which they could be produced. In other words, the guild system was written into law. There were long periods of training involving special steps in processes which were restricted to apprentices, or journeymen, or masters. As new methods of production were introduced, replacing the old-fashioned skills, these regulations stood in the way of change. Merchant entrepreneurs had little interest in such laws. They were chiefly concerned with producing as much as possible and selling it for as much as possible. They were ready to work with anyone who could help them do this. This attitude became even more prevalent as machinery was introduced in the last half of the century. Workmen, on the other hand, accustomed to the old system were concerned to keep the regulations for the protection of their jobs. They fought the effort to get rid of them, though it was a losing cause.

The era of *laissez-faire*, then, was dictated by what was considered economic necessity, by the new type of economic organization that had come into being and which would eventually have to be regulated in its own way. *The period of radical change from the guild system to the factory system can be measured from the time when the old regulations began to crumble, which was as early as the late seventeenth century when dissenting tradesmen and merchants in the city wanted no interference from the monopolies, to the gradual re-introduction of new regulations related to the new system beginning with the earliest factory act of 1802.*[12]

While these great changes were taking place in trade and industry, merchants and merchant manufacturers through their wealth frequently became landed squires. The fact that they sought to do so indicates that agriculture and the land still dominated much of the thinking as well as the life of England.[13] Right up until the twentieth century in England the way to power and to influence was to own spacious lands, even though these may have been unrelated to the real source of your own personal wealth or to the national wealth. They were *symbols* of status and prestige and the passport to respectability and frequently to a voice in political affairs.

No estimate of the eighteenth century can fail to take account of the tremendous changes that took place in agriculture. As a way of life it changed remarkably. This was due not only to the improvements in agricultural techniques but to the great increase in land redistribution. This redistribution began with the English Reformation in the sixteenth century. Enclosures were common then and throughout the seventeenth century, but they began with a fresh intensity in the reign of Queen Anne and reached their height in that of George IV, in the early years of the nineteenth century.[14]

As Mantoux shows, the enclosures of the latter part of the eighteenth century were an effort to do away with the old open field system rather than to simply enclose the common as had been the case earlier. The great landlords wanted larger tracts of land so that they could undertake crop rotation and employ the new methods of agriculture which began with the work of Jethro Tull in 1731. The new methods meant that the nobility and the landed gentry could recoup some of their lost wealth and power relative to the merchants and the rising industrialists. They were, therefore, very anxious to utilize them. Since they had power in parliament, it meant that enclosure acts were passed easily. That in turn meant that the small farmer, the yeoman, either

# The Context of Change

lost out completely or took his little gains from the sale of his land and tried to get started in industry. If he lost out completely, he joined the ranks of those who were swelling the ranks of labour for the new factories.

After 1760 the new industrial system was well on its way while in agriculture a great rationalization had taken place. Fewer persons were producing more food for greater profit, so that even here the new capitalist system had taken over. The fact that the established church was still oriented to an agricultural society did not matter so much in the first half of the eighteenth century, but, because of the critical changes that were under way by the beginning of the second half, it made a very great difference indeed. *It simply meant that the established church was not physically equipped to meet the alarming needs of the people as they moved in a completely unplanned way from one physical location to another and as they entered an entirely new way of life.*

The gentry during the eighteenth century were in a favourable position so long as they managed to keep up with changes that were being made or were able to afford the enlargement of their lands through enclosures. Since the squire was frequently the justice of the peace in his area and usually sat on the Review Boards for the Enclosure Acts, he seldom lost out. His place, of course, could always be taken by a city merchant who could buy him out if he were in debt and so the merchant joined the landed gentry himself. Sometimes his place was taken by a former yeoman who had successfully taken up the new agriculture and was prepared now to rent land as a professional farmer using technical methods. Thus the old gentry either lost out or moved into a position of greater economic strength as a result of carrying on agriculture on a larger and more scientific scale.

We cannot stress too strongly the fact that the

merchant tradesmen were those who were gaining both economic power and social prestige through acquiring land on the side or through marriage with those of the nobility and gentry who were in danger of insolvency. The future in every respect belonged to this class who were one with, or were linked with, the new industrial capitalists.[15]

The yeoman class, which had held free title to its land, was either forced to sell out to the larger landholder who could practice the new methods of farming more efficiently or, because the exceptional yeoman happened to make it financially especially in times of food shortage, managed to hold on until his numbers declined rapidly after 1825. A few who had sold their lands earlier were able to use the funds to set themselves up in business and in time to become "captains of industry" as did, for example, Josiah Wedgwood, the great pioneer in the pottery industry. The majority of them simply joined the ranks of the labouring man.

Beneath the yeomanry were the labouring classes. In the first half of the eighteenth century, as we noted earlier, the labouring classes organized as journeymen and apprentices under the old guild system were gradually reduced to ordinary labourers as the skill required to operate weaving and spinning machinery lessened. At the same time, the merchant manufacturer reduced the old producer-master himself to a dependent employee. It was such changes as these which formed the basis of labour's resistance to the new technology, which led to the efforts to destroy machinery as well as to employ old laws to protect privileges no longer meaningful in the new situation. The fact that the woollen industry was protected became the occasion for its falling behind in modernization. Therefore, whether one belonged to the old master class or to that of the journeyman-apprentice, resistance to change only spelt disaster. The old order was changing and the new labouring class was to become

# The Context of Change

a *necessary* adjunct to the machine, a fact which was to give them whatever power they were eventually to possess.

Beneath the labourer was the great mass of poor. King's statistics claimed that they made up one half of the population at the beginning of the eighteenth century. That is, one half of the population, the productive half, actually kept alive the other half! Some of these were in the armed forces, but the great majority had no occupation whatever. They were completely dependent upon the poor law for sustenance. This burden used up the great majority of the national treasury's income. Moreover, since the law required that the poor remain in the parish in which they were born, it meant that the mobility required for employment in the new industry was hampered and that all kinds of abuses, such as the effort of one parish to disown a child, or a woman, especially an expectant mother who was dependent, became a common practice. Sometimes a parish would pay another to take dependent children and the new parish would then put them to work, or their employers would do so as hands in their factories, to make sure that whether they were bought or sold, they earned their keep. It was this situation which brought about the tragic child labour conditions which prevailed, especially during the last half of the century. It was the opinion of everyone, including those who believed that they had the best interests of the children at heart, that the children would be kept from evil if they were forced to work long hours. They would learn thereby to be dutiful and to possess that degree of humility which their station required. Even the basic education that was given by the dissenting academies in some cases, or in schools like Kingswood founded by John Wesley, were frowned upon by some for fear that they would make the children rebellious. It was the availability of this "pool of labour" which was one factor which made the new technology and the factory system a workable possibility.

With the increased division of labour the role of labour changed drastically, and the labouring man not only had to find a new dignity on a new basis, but he had to rediscover the basis of his power which would make the importance of his role obvious to this fellowmen. This took a century-and-a-half. It was not even on the horizon in the middle of the eighteenth century. Instead, labour was fighting to maintain the old order largely unaware of the momentous changes taking place all around it.

In any assessment of the economic life of eighteenth century England the time factor must be carefully born in mind. The inventions of a mechanical kind that so revolutionized industry did not take place, or in most instances their influences if they did take place in the first half of the century were not felt, until well into the century's second half. The first factory in England appears to have been built by Thomas Lombe on an island in the Derwent in 1718. It was built to house silk-throwing machines, but it was exceptional, until men like Arkwright, Boulton and Wedgwood organized factories on a serious scale. This did not occur until the 1760's and '70's. While John Kay's flying shuttle invented in 1733 was the earliest invention in the textile industry, other necessary improvements came with Hargreaves' spinning jenny and Arkwright's water frame, the first significant use of other-than-human power. These took place in 1765 and 1767. Their official patents were taken out in 1768.[16]

The organization of industry on the basis of the factory system meant a whole new method of marketing goods had, in turn, to be established. "Contracts," agreements for purchase and sale, had to be worked out that were much more complicated than anything that had gone before. "Thus the manufacturer," says Mantoux, "being at the same time a capitalist, a work manager and merchant, set a new pattern of the complete businessman." This breed, full blown, did not make its appearance until men like Arkwright, Boulton and Wedgwood were upon the scene in the last quarter of the century.[17]

> The object of all industry is the production of goods, or to be more explicit, of articles of consumption which are not directly provided by nature. By 'factory system' we therefore primarily mean a particular organization, a particular system of production. But this organization affects the whole economic system and consequently the whole social system, which is controlled by the growth and distribution of wealth.[18]

As Mantoux points out, the following elements go into the making of the factory system: greatly increased production as a result of the use of machinery, the use of other-than-human sources of power, a vast work force, complex organization of both production sales and purchases, strict division of labour, huge amounts of capital and the desire for profit which continually spurs the system on to greater growth. This system could not come into its own before the invention of the machinery that made it a necessity. Therefore, it did not really appear in English society as a manifest force until the years 1760 to 1800. *This system affected every aspect of English life.* For example, it shook the old class structure to its roots for the new system divided men into two basic classes, those who possessed capital and managed the system and those who had nothing to sell save their labour. It also brought about a vast change in the numbers and distribution of the population of the country, which it is vital for us to understand.

Though there are no exact figures, the most reliable

estimates indicate that during the century the population increased at least by 60%-75%. In 1700 the population was 5,135,000-6,122,000 and was 9,156,000-9,287,000 in 1800. It is estimated that the rate of growth from 1750 to 1800 was four times as great as in the preceding period.[19] What is of equal importance for us is that after the middle of the century the population centres which continued to grow were in the north and west; the centres of the mining and metal-working, the textile and port cities such as Birmingham, Leeds, Manchester and Liverpool, and in the northeast, Newcastle. Only London, as a great commercial and trading centre, remained densely populated in the south and east. In 1785 Arkwright's factory was the only one of any size in Manchester, but by 1800 there were at least fifty mills in the city. Thus the industrial revolution was bringing about not only a change in the organization of economic life but a vast increase in population as well as determining *where* the centres of that population would be. This was a fact of great significance for every other aspect of British social life, including the religious.

The changes taking place in the economic life of the nation also affected the relationship between the economic and the political sectors. We have noted above how the old guild regulations disappeared while the labouring classes tried to use the regulations of that system to protect them in and from the new. At this juncture the new manufacturers who had been against the old regulations, as representing government interference in industry, were now ready to use the government to pass new regulations *against* the combination of labour. In 1782 and in 1799, through legislation against combination, the manufacturers banded together against their workmen in representations to the government to restrict any effort of workers to combine in their own interest or even to seek government help to put in effect

# The Context of Change

laws for the protection of labour which had been established in the earlier period. Thus while *laissez-faire* was the spirit of the day and free trade was definitely in the interest of British industry, the General Chamber of Manufacturers formed a powerful lobby to use its economic strength to influence the government in order *to do away with restrictions that hampered their interests*. They succeeded completely except for such new measures as the Factory Act of 1803, which was minimal, to say the least. The Reform Act of 1832 finally meant the triumph in government of the new "captains of industry," whose power was based on industrial wealth as over against both the old landed aristocracy and the new labourers. The political order fell to the domination of the economic.

The new interest in *laissez-faire* economic theory was a reflection of the actual economic state of affairs that had come into being. It was an empirical fact that a great new period of economic expansion was underway and that a minimum amount of responsibility for its direction was in the hands of those who happened to have political rather than economic power. It was a period which called for individual initiative and imagination. Both of these, combined with the great expansion made possible by revolutionary changes in techniques, could scarcely help but lead to a period of individualism in which there appeared to be enough for everyone and in which, or so it could easily be believed, everyone acting in his own interest could best contribute to the welfare of all. *So ran the theory of Adam Smith, as much the reflection of objective events as a theory of their proper direction in the economic sphere*. It was no wonder that the economic order dominated all the other areas of human culture at this time, because it was in this area that revolution was in fact taking place.

When we turn more specifically to a consideration of

class, status and power in eighteenth century England, it is obvious that the landowners, including the hierarchy in the church, still predominated. It is true that in the second half of the century they were being challenged by the new industrialists, but the latter had to achieve what influence they did through landownership. The landed hierarchy could stem the tide of change even it it could not prevent it.

The upper class consisted of some one hundred and thirty titled families with great holdings in land. They wielded political power through the House of Lords but in firm coalition with the landed gentry in Commons. Through justices of the peace and the lord lieutenants at the local level they could put together an unbeatable political coalition in parliament. Just as there was an apex in income distribution in their favour, so there was a political apex in their favour which increased after the middle of the century. This was at the expense of the crown as well as other interests, especially those of the new industrialists and the new centres of industry. Elections then as now cost money and they were in a position to buy both votes and patronage.

The gentry, the country "squire," belonged to the upper middle class. His cooperation was needed both at Whitehall and among the landed families, because he shared in the control of votes which sent men to the House of Commons. He was usually the justice of the peace, at that time the single most powerful political office in the country because government had become so highly de-centralized. A justice of the peace was usually joined by an "Overseer of the Poor," who might be a clergyman of the Church of England, and a constable who was most frequently a freeholding yeoman. These three made up the local unit of government.

Mobility into the gentry, though relatively slow in the first half of the century, increased in the second half. It came from those bankers and merchants whose growing wealth made it possible for them to own the suburban dream of the time, namely, a country estate. It was through land ownership that such interests were able to make their voices heard in government circles.

The bankers to a very large degree continued to control the growing wealth of the nation. These men were necessary to the new industry and helped provide the capital for it. Merchant traders were also necessary to market the goods of the new system. The newest ones to join this class were the "captains of industry," whom Mantoux describes in the following way:

> Between the man who owned and used this capital and the wage earner whose labour he bought for a low wage, between the man who directed the whole undertaking and his humble helper kept to one narrow groove, the gulf was becoming almost impassable. The manufacturer now was so high above his workmen that he found himself on the same level as those other capitalists, the banker and the merchant. He needed them both, one to give him credit and the other customers, while in return he provided the one with investments and the other with goods, but he never merged his own individuality in theirs. He had his own special work, which was to organize industrial production, and his own special interests, to the aid of which he very soon learnt to turn political power. With the factory system a new class, a new social type came into being.[20]

Some of these new industrial leaders were the manufacturing tradesmen who earlier had replaced the masters of the old guild system, but the majority of them were not. Mantoux has made a convincing case for the fact that most of these new leaders were formerly part of the yeoman class who

had been forced off their land by enclosures and either sank
into the labouring class or through personal ingenuity were
able to wed their former experience in the towns to the
rising industry. They became the new management. Among the
most conspicuous were the Peels, the Wedgwoods and Matthew
Boulton.[21] Once they had gained power in this way they then
became country gentlemen again, buying up large tracts of
land. Their skill was in their ability to organize efficiently both capital and labour. With notable exceptions,
such as Wedgwood, they themselves were the inventors of
very little, and the originators of less, but they raised
what had come to them into efficient patterns of organization. They refined the contract, for example, until everyone was aware of his degree of responsibility and enterprise
and thereby became the more efficient and profitable.

The most outstanding men of this class, like the
Wedgwoods and Matthew Boulton, took a wide interest in
religion, philanthropic and cultural interests. The latter,
like Benjamin Franklin, was more of a moralist with a utilitarian bent than anything else. Frequently their community
activities were also self-rewarding. Mantoux claims, however, that the men we have mentioned were exceptions to the
rule. The majority of the new captains, he says, were interested in one thing only, their own personal profit and
the acquisition through it of large personal fortunes.

> Their consciousness of power made them tyrannical,
> hard, sometimes cruel: their passions and greed
> were those of upstarts. They had the reputations
> of being hard drinkers and of having little regard
> to the honour of their female employees. They were
> proud of their newly acquired wealth and lived in
> great style, with footmen, carriages and gorgeous
> town and country houses. But their generosity was
> not proportionate to the luxury in which they lived.

At the beginning of the nineteenth century 2,500 pounds were collected for the foundation of Sunday Schools. The total sum contributed by the chief cotton-spinners of the district, who employed about 23,000 people, was 90 pounds.[22]
Apparently the evangelical revival of the time did not get through to them!

Though the new industrialists had not been "accepted" as men of influence and thus of high status in wider society, in the industrial counties they were men who were increasingly looked to for leadership and counted as of great worth by the general populace.[23] As a result of the industry of one of their numbers, Sir Robert Peel, his own son rose to the height of political power within one generation. It was the Reform Act of 1832 which marked the arrival of this new branch of the power elite in whose hands, and not that of the landowners, the future of Britain was to lie.

If the ranks of the upper middle class were being swelled by the rising industrialists and financiers, they were being joined, at a slightly lower level, by a host of new professionals. New thought and more effective techniques drew men into medicine and the numerous changes in land title, as well as the development of business contracts, meant that lawyers were increasingly needed. With the growing number of academies and also of parish schools, more teachers were required, though, if one is to judge by salary, like clergymen, they could hardly be counted among the "middling sort of men." They must be included at best with skilled labourers.

The bulk of the middle class were yeomen, landed freeholders and copyholders. It was they for whom life was to become increasingly uncertain. Enclosures and improvements in farming, requiring large tracts of land in order to compete, did not hit them critically until after 1760, but when they did, some yeomen were able to transfer funds from their land into new enterprises and thus joined that group to which the immediate future was to belong. Or, even though they were copyholders because they were good farmers, they might rent "improved" lands. If their fortune was good they might in turn purchase land on a scale adequate for a good living. Yet the great majority, having lost their land, joined the ranks of the new labouring class.

Small tradesmen and artisans, or skilled labourers, made up the remainder of the middle class. Their position was very uncertain during the first half of the century because markets were uncertain and methods, especially in the textile industry, were changing which meant that new locations became better than old ones. For example, the south and west lost out to Lancashire and the West Riding.

It makes little difference whether we rank skilled artisans and labourers in the bottom of the middle class or at the top of the lower class, since these terms are always relative. If the emerging factory system waited for the appearance of efficient managers and administrators capable of giving leadership to large organizations, it also waited upon the appearance of labour willing to accept the responsibility for regularity and efficiency in fulfilling the particular tasks created as a result of the growing division of labour. *It was these two requirements which more than any others account for the increased vertical mobility of the period.* Responsible labour was at a premium, and where ability appeared among such labourers especially in the second generation, that is after 1800, when the sons of a Wedgwood and a Boulton, for example, had to give greater attention to the organization of their works, managers and foremen were required. These roles were filled with such labourers of ability so that eventually a man could move from poverty to a small fortune and at times even to large.

# The Context of Change

Though a number of Methodists filled the ranks of large and small industrialists, by far the bulk of them came from those who possessed special skills and so gained a real degree of economic security. *New capacity thus met new opportunity so that hope born in the souls of men through faith was met and reinforced by the new success they had, even in this life.*

The farm labourer and the unskilled labourer, along with the destitute poor, lived a life scarcely above and, at times, falling below the subsistence level. In the rural areas such folk frequently live in mud huts, or cottages hardly better. Both were usually overcrowded. They were situated on commons gradually being put under cultivation which meant that they were driven from them to join the ranks of the wanderers only some of whom provided the "hands" for the new factories. In the city the poor lived in cellars and overcrowded garrets. They lived chiefly on bread and cheese with small amounts of beer of which more was always desired. If fortune shone, they ate meat once a week. With rising prices toward the end of the century, their situation grew worse rather than better. The poor were tossed from pillar to post, from one parish to another, if they were unwise enough to leave the parish in which they were born and in which they had poor relief rights. This meant that those who needed work had to take a great risk when they moved out to those areas such as Lancashire of the West Riding or the northern mines or perhaps to London to find the work they so desperately needed. Vast numbers of them did move and swelled the numbers pouring into the new cities such as Birmingham and Manchester which were utterly unequipped to handle them. Out of such stuff riots were made and criminal behaviour encouraged.

The plight of the poor during the latter part of the eighteenth century has been described many times elsewhere so that we will not go into detail here. When there was a shortage of male adult labour it was taken up by women and children. Many male labourers hated the factories. Compared with the old cottage system of industry, or with work as a farmer, the factories seemed like prison houses. Along with their wives and children they were driven by the constant threat of destitution. Sixteen hour days were not exceptional. A twelve hour day for the children was not insisted upon until the first Factory Act of 1802. Prior to that it was still lengthier. Physical, as well as moral, conditions were indescribably bad in the factories well into the nineteenth century.

The factory worker belonged to the dispossessed. He enjoyed neither status or power. If the new industrialist was the most powerful economic figure ever to have arisen, the factory labourer, especially if a woman or a child, was the most powerless. These conditions were at their worst at the end of the eighteenth century, suggesting that neither the evangelical revival in general nor the Wesleyan movement in particular had been able to do anything of consequence to alleviate them. They were, of course, a new and unexpected phenomenon and given the "cultural lag" to which humanity seems prone when it comes to the alleviation of the sufferings of the dispossessed, it is not surprising that it took decades to begin to cope with them. It must also be said that it was men such as Wilberforce and Shaftesbury who, religiously motivated, did move to do something about them.

Though statistics of the roughest kind only are available, T. S. Ashton estimates that at the outset of the century temporal lords had an average income of some ₤2,800 while the poorest eeked out an existence on some ₤6,10s per year. One quarter of the national income was shared by 3.5% of families. One half of the national income was shared by 18% of them while three-fifths of the total population lived on one sixth of the national income.[24] The figure given for the population of England at the beginning of the nineteenth century is 9,168,000. If we use Colquhoun's estimates based on the returns of 1801 and 1803, we discover that there were some 2,005,767 "artisans, handicrafts men and labourers employed in manufactures of all kinds" and that they had an average family income of only 55 pounds per annum. Since there was great fluctuation in the economy, people at this level were constantly facing the threat of unemployment and/or the workhouse in which to end their days. There were some 450,000 seamen whose incomes were still lower and who were frequently the victims of press gangs and another 200,000 common soldiers whose pay amounted to 29 pounds per year. There were over 1,530,000 domestic servants and farm labourers whose income amounted to some ₤31 per year while 130,000 miners and canal workers earned forty pounds. All of these groups could drop into penury at any time with nothing but parish poor relief to rescue them. Over a million paupers were able to earn no more than ten pounds per year, while another 220,000, including those in prison, lived completely off the poor relief and received some ten pounds from this source. If, then, we can say that there were one million and one quarter persons in abject poverty, we must also say that there were another four million who were on the fringes of it and who could lose all at almost any moment.

It is interesting to note that perhaps the most significant factor to come to the rescue of child labour was not the early Factory Act but the fact that, as machinery became more complicated, the system of hiring parish apprentices, that is pauper children, had to be given up because they were inefficient in the handling of such machinery. Though every technological change brings about suffering with the adjustments that must be made to it, and though there were occasions when industrial leaders were ready, if not forced, to find employment one way or another for those put out of work by the new machines, nevertheless, the record is one of great inhumanity on the part of the vast majority of the new industrialists.

It can be shown that in spite of a standard of living that would seem intolerably hard to a twentieth century person, that standard did improve gradually for the first two thirds of the eighteenth century. It was in the last quarter of the century, as a war economy began to take over, compounded by frightful overcrowding in the industrial centres, that inflation brought about such wretched conditions that even the wealthy became frightened at the prospect of riots among the poor. This explains the ruthlessness with which the Gordon Riots were put down in 1780. At the same time, because the purchase of child labour was increasingly expensive to the industrialists during a period of inflation, both the sale of such children from one parish to another and the ban on the movement of the poor, which was part of the poor law structure, were done away with in 1795.

The change which took place in the administration of the poor laws was undoubtedly motivated by a degree of deep human concern. In the midst of the depression at the end of the century, indeed as early as 1782, an act initiated by Mr. T. Gilbert in Commons and called Gilbert's Act gave local authorities the right to find work for the impoverished. When that was insufficient, they were permitted to supplement their wages with relief grants. The Act, however, never really went into effect until the Berkshire magistrates of the village of Speenhamland actually set a minimum income for a family below which their income would be supplemented by a grant from the poor rate. The motivation was excellent, and it did meet the needs of the poor in many

# The Context of Change 119

places throughout England when the device was taken up during the distress of the Continental War. It may well have saved England a French Revolution as many have suggested, but in the long run it worked against the interests both of the poor and the general public. The reason for this is that industrialists frequently kept wages down, knowing that the poor would have their income supplemented and thus would not actually starve. Moreover, the poor rate was paid by the community at large. Thus the industrialist profited at the expense both of the poor and the community.

The new industrial system tended to drive society into two extreme groups, those with almost unlimited power who owned the means of production and those who had nothing but the labour of their hands to sell. Yet small shopkeepers and a growing clerical army formed a small but swelling middle lower class between the two extremes. Just below them were the foremen in the mills who could maintain their families in some respectability. Moreover, since it was a period of rapid industrial expansion, in spite of sporadic depressions, upward mobility could take place for those prepared to discipline themselves to take advantage of it. Those who responded to the evangelical and Wesleyan revivals were often to be found among these groups.

While suffering of the labouring class had a long future ahead of it at the end of the eighteenth century, we must not overlook the spirit of charity which, at least in some of the new industrialists, expressed itself in support of Sir Robert Peel's Factory Act of 1802. Many of those who supported it were either of "the evangelicals" like Wilberforce or among the Dissenters like Wedgwood, Boulton, Dale and several of the Quaker industrialists. It was a serious piece of legislation which, though not meant to interfere with the spirit of *laissez-faire*, was rather an act of sheer goodwill. It provided real machinery for enforcement and did bring both better conditions and shorter hours. Peel, however, meant that that should be the end rather than the beginning of such legislation. Shaftesbury was to prove before long, and the course of history has proven since, that Peel was fortunately wrong. The balance of power and of justice had to be redressed. It says something for the influence of religious factors in a time when a doctrine of unbridled freedom had become a dogma that the consciences of some men of power would not permit them to follow its consequences to its logical limit.

CHAPTER FOUR

## IN THE WORLD AND OF IT:
## THE ESTABLISHMENT IN DISTRESS

The single most important fact to be stated about the established Church of England from the reign of Henry VIII until the legislation following the report of the Ecclesiastical Commissioners in 1835 is that in creed, liturgy, discipline and government she remained, in form at least, unchanged. The abuses arising out of the Henrican and Elizabethan settlements, such as nepotism and pluralism, were with the church in spite of numerous efforts to correct them until the reforms of the 1830's. The crisis of the commonwealth period, the continuing challenge of the Dissenters, as well as that of the Methodist and Evangelical revivals, all came and went, but the establishment remained essentially unchanged. Her wings were clipped from the Restoration onward by the invasion of parliament into her prerogatives. The laity now dominated the clergy. The amazing thing is that she continued to serve the religious needs of the nation as well as she did. As Norman Sykes has said,

> In all fairness if we are to remember Wesley and Whitefield and their contribution to the religious life of England we must also remember Law and Butler.[1]

We must also recall that in countless parishes throughout the country the sacraments were administered and the pastoral needs of the people met through counsel and sermon. Nor was the responsibility of the bishops for ordination, confirmation and visitation of their dioceses by any means thrown to the winds, though the former was done more decently and in order than the latter two.

The tragedy of the Church of England in the eighteenth century was not that she was unfaithful but that the degree to which she was was simply inadequate to meet the challenge of a new day, of a rapidly changing society, before which an essentially unchanged, rural church was frequently helpless. The crisis which the Christian faith faces in English society today is not unrelated to this earlier failure.

It is not our purpose in this chapter to deal with theological and doctrinal developments. We will do so later. We only want to say that for better or for worse the Thirty-Nine Articles were left intact, including loyalty to the three Creeds, the Apostles', the Nicene and the Athanasian, in spite of onslaughts of rationalism and unitarianism.

The most fateful factor for the church after the Restoration was that the power that Laud once attempted to wield on behalf of the church and its discipline was almost completely taken over by the laity. It was they who really determined the nature of the church's institutional life and who, crying clericalism, turned a deaf ear to the reforms suggested by at first Edmund Gibson and then by Richard Watson. The Establishment was used as a complement to government for the purpose of maintaining the *status quo*. It thus became a reflection of the prevailing culture. Reform was hardly to be desired if it was to cut down on the freedom with which the monarch and his chief ministers used the church and its appointments for their own patronage. The king and his ministers as well as parliament, with all the lay impropriations which it represented, wanted continued control of the church not reform of it. After the Restoration, Convocation was unable to pass canons which had any authority over the laity without consent of parliament.

When Gibson seventy years later challenged this complete stripping away of Convocation's power, Lord Hardwicke, the principal juror of the day, found it convenient to level the charge of "clericalism" against him, while remaining utterly insensitive to the intrusion of parliament into the institutional life of the church. After the ruthlessness of Laud, the suffering caused by religious conviction during the Commonwealth and after, it was perhaps natural for a reaction against religious bigotry and partisanship to set in. Indeed, it was a primary characteristic of the outlook of the eighteenth century Englishman. However, it was unfortunate that on the whole, with the exception of persons like William Law and Bishop Butler, the result was not a sharing of religious concern but a cynical use of the power which naturally arises from the institutions which religious interest creates for the selfish aggrandisement of those who held economic and political power. It was this fact which made it so difficult for the Church of England to be the church during the eighteenth century, and which made it an expression of the grace of God that other churches were able to supplement her work.

I

The structure of the church remained what it had been. The King was her supreme governor. The Convocation ostensibly paralleled the Upper and Lower Houses of Parliament with the bishops and higher clergy making up the upper house and the lower clergy, the presbyters, the lower. Because so much power had been taken from Convocation even when it came to enforcing matters in its own right, for example, excommunication, marriage and divorce and the like, which now had to be backed up by the civil courts, the clergy had little to do save to quarrel among themselves. That they proceeded to do. Even so strong a Convocation man as Atterbury insisted that the lower house had the right to initiate action and that it could meet on its own. This insistence upon the rights of the lower clergy was not only an expression of the similar power of Commons relative to Lords in parliament but also a reflection of the tragic distrust between the higher and lower clergy as a result of the tremendous gulf in their economic status as well as the power of the bench to dispense patronage at will. Thus when Convocation did meet, it was unable to transact business and only reflected for all to see the dissension in the church while achieving nothing of lasting value. Convocation ceased to meet, therefore, after 1717. It was called once in 1741 but had to recess without any positive accomplishments whatsoever. It did not meet again until the middle of the nineteenth century. This meant that even matters of doctrine were finally settled by parliament rather than by church courts, as the Feathers Tavern Petition of 1771 illustrates. The laicization of the religious establishment was complete.

The greatest abuse of the century so far as the church was concerned continued to be what it had been ever since the Reformation settlement, that is to say, pluralism. While it is true that the lords spiritual, the bishops, held discretion over great lands and numerous appointments, they were nevertheless shared by the crown and the laity. With the increased power of parliament, even over the monarchy after the Restoration, it meant that the prelates themselves, while sharing power to some degree in parliament, owed their appointments to the King and his ministers, who were themselves increasingly subject to parliament.

Many of the sees were wealthier than others. Under George III, Canterbury possessed revenues of ₤7,000, while the first report of the Ecclesiastical commissioners showed

that the see rendered ₤19,182 in 1835. At the other extreme
was Llandaff with only ₤550 and ₤924 respectively.² This
revenue represented patronage received from the multiple
holdings of chaplaincies, (based upon tithes due to each),
cathedral prebends, rectorships and curacies. Shared also
with the crown were appointments to deaneries, archdeacon-
eries and the like. Many of these were held in plurality at
various levels, while the actual services were rendered
either nominally or by a lower clergymen who served in the
appointed clergyman's stead. It is true that the bishop's
revenues were taxed for firstfruits and tenths, that he had
to undertake large hospitality, and had to spend much of his
time and expense in travel between his see and London.
Nevertheless, there was a great gap fixed between the wealth
of the higher clergy and the lower. A parish priest was
well off indeed if he had revenues to the tune of ₤300 as
did Parson Woodforde. If he were a beginning curate, as
John Wesley once was, his salary amounted to ₤30 per annum.
Throughout the eighteenth century at the level of the lower
clergy there was a glut on the market of candidates, especially when many of these offices were taken by relatives of
those who had the power of appointment but who enjoyed no
other qualification for the office.

However, it was not only among the lower clergy that an
undignified scramble for office and search for privilege
continued. Because of the wide disparity of income between
the episcopal sees, a bishop who was appointed to Llandaff,
for example, soon sought translation to a more lucrative
diocese. At times, this translation took place even before
the incumbent had made one visit to his former see. Moreover, the Bishops were kept subservient to those in power in
parliament because they were beholden to the ministers for a
new appointment. There was a profound economic dependency,

then, of the clergy on the crown and its ministers, as well as upon the laity, and of the lower clergy upon the higher.

The hierarchy in the church reflected the hierarchy in society at large. Just as there was a great gulf fixed between the lord of the manor and the peasant, so there was a great gulf fixed between the lords spiritual and the humble curate. Many thought it was a happy arrangement. The higher clergy, it was assumed, because of their station, enjoyed the respect of the higher orders and could thus serve them while the poverty-stricken curate was close enough to the poverty-stricken farm labourer to understand him!

> We may divide the clergy into generals, field officers, and subalterns, wrote Addison in *The Spectator* of 24 March 1710-11. Among the first we may reckon bishops, deans, and archdeacons. Among the second are doctors of divinity, prebendaries, and all that wear scarfs. The rest are comprehended under the subalterns. As for the first class our constitution prevents it from any redundancy of incumbents, notwithstanding competitors are numberless. Upon a strict calculation, it is found that there has been a great exceeding of numbers in the second division, several brevets having been granted for the converting of subalterns into scarf officers; insomuch that within my memory the price of lute string is raised above two pence in a yard. As for the subalterns they are not to be numbered.[3]

And Sykes has this to say,

> In each corporation the higher grades of preferment were generally the preserve of the aristocracy, whilst the common soldiers, recruited largely from a lower social order, contend fiercely for the

minor occasions of advancement presented with infrequency. Within the Church the division between the privileged minority and the depressed majority was deep; and the gulf was widened by the agglomeration of pluralities upon the fortunate favorites whose feet were set securely upon the ladder of preferment.[4]

It was taken for granted that there were at least two types of clergy. The first gained his preferment largely by family connection. Not what he knew but who he was was what counted. Certain sees such as Durham and Winchester, Salisbury and Worcester appeared to be granted on this basis. Little in the way of spiritual or intellectual leadership was expected from them. But as for Canterbury and York, London and Ely, more depended upon them; therefore men of greater dignity and wisdom, ability and learning were required to fill such bishoprics. Thus it was possible for a second type of clergy to emerge, though even here they had to have had some connection with the great, either as chaplain or tutor, to be brought to their attention. They were sometimes men of humble birth, as were Edmund Gibson, bishop of London, and Richard Watson, bishop of Llandaff, who, because of sheer ability, domonstrated, usually at the outset of their academic performance at Cambridge or Oxford, that they could be relied upon to give serious leadership to the life of the church. The Church of England during this century would surely have failed completely without such men! It was through them that what degree of dynamic spiritual vitality there was in the establishment was kept alive in spite of the vice-like grip that the whole system of patronage had upon the church. The spirit was not utterly quenched even though the church was used for purposes which reflected the vested interests of those in political power.

Thus the church was thoroughly embedded in the culture of the day, though not completely determined by it.

Rectors and curates, the lower clergy, were divided according to rank and role. The parish priest was not only better educated but was much better off financially than the curate. His style of life was that of a country gentleman, and it was thought appropriate that he should be able to socialize with the squire. While he was greatly aided in the conduct of worship by the Book of Common Prayer, it was assumed that he knew both Latin and Greek to a degree. He was expected to preach an acceptable sermon at least once, if not twice, on a Sunday. He might be assisted, especially if he had more than one appointment, by a curate and perhaps even an assistant curate. At times the curates could scarcely read the service. At other times, especially if the parish priest held his office because of family connection rather than any real qualifications by training, he might use his better equipped curate to do his preaching. The level of performance, then, among the lower clergy varied immensely. Their offices were more frequently than not carried out responsibly within the framework accounted acceptable. The parish clergy were part of a social order based upon land in which "the man of property" was "the man of power." *The country squire was the man to be envied and his style of life emulated.*

Not only was the squire at once the Justice of the Peace and often the most powerful person in local society, but he frequently held the power of appointment to the "living" related to his lands in his hands. This meant that the clergy were so involved in, so indebted to, either their landed superiors or their political superiors, that they could buck the system only at the risk of courting ejection from it. Bishop Watson was simply ignored by the powers that be as a result of his independence of mind and spirit as well as his suggestions for the reform of inequities. The great majority of clergy had no desire to protest because they believed so thoroughly in it themselves.

It is estimated that one quarter of all the Justices of the Peace, by the beginning of the eighteenth century, were clergymen. As the century wore on and threats to the *status quo* increased as a result both of the Industrial Revolution and the growing storm approaching in France, the office of parish priest was regarded as more and more important for purposes of social control. Thus, while there was a strong anticlericalism among many of the affluent, encouraged by the religious ferment of the seventeenth century as well as by the jealousy of the "men of property" over any encroachment upon their preserves by churchmen, later on in the eighteenth century the parish clergy were regarded and respected as allies for the preservation of a way of life threatened by the winds of economic and political change.

As the century wore on, the Whigs came to represent more and more the new industrial class, including the Dissenters, and they moved farther and farther away from an earlier alliance with the landed men. The country parson then came to represent the interests of the countryside as opposed to the interests of the growing cities and industrial towns. As Tories, both country parson and country squire then found "a most happy alliance!"

The condition of the poor curate remained largely unchanged, even though Queen Anne's Bounty strove to do its best for the relief of their penury.[5] G. F. A. Best's exhaustive study of the Bounty and its work entitled "Temporal Pillars" establishes the fact beyond doubt that all the economic inequities characteristic of the church of the sixteenth and seventeenth centuries were continued into the eighteenth. The suffering of vast numbers of the lower clergy was excruciating. Nothing of consequence was done about it until the appointment of the Ecclesiastical Commissioners in 1835. They then came to the aid of those who had been trying to do something through Queen Anne's Bounty which could not of itself possibly meet the need.

Before we leave this consideration of the structure of the established church we ought to say a word about theological education in the eighteenth century. According to Canon 41 of the canons of 1604, persons who were to preach were required to have a Master of Arts degree. As we have indicated, there were ways for a parish priest to get around this, but, in view of the fact that there were many more candidates than offices, one could usually find the services of one so equipped if it were lacking in oneself. However, every gentleman was expected to have been at the university. There his education was classical, no matter what profession he was to follow. This meant that both clergyman and gentleman had the same basic education and that a clergyman simply went on in his graduate studies to do some theology. On the whole this was regarded as a strength rather than a weakness because both clergy and laity had the same basic education. This minimized the gulf between them sometimes raised by the serious study of theology.[6] The weakness in this was that it rarely led to the doing of creative theology. Paley was an example of its poverty and Bishop Butler an exception to it. Nevertheless, the colleges were kept close to the church not only in that various chairs were supported by particular church livings but in that professors of Divinity were needed for the training of the clergy. It also meant that the educational system, because it was not open to the dissenting clergy, was a further means of separation. On the other hand, the dissenting Academies, freed from the classical background of the Universities, were more open to the demands of the new science and thus to the new day.

## II

The economic base of the ecclesiastical structure was land. The Church of England continued to be tied to the land lock, stock and barrel. This was the basis of its wealth and the source of envy directed toward it by laity who professed to be friendly to the church but who were quick to seek legislation to curb its power through parliament whenever they could. Thus when the Commissioners for Queen Anne's Bounty received considerable sums as gifts through the probate of wills for the relief of the poorer clergy, they were charged with threatening such persons on their death beds. Parliament then passed the Mortmain Act of 1736 which made properties inalienable. The excuse was that through this means the church was seeking to extend its power unduly. The ghost of Laud was conjured up to give force to the argument.

Tithes had always been the means of support for the church. Because a non-voluntary means of raising funds has always made enemies for the church, the fact that the ecclesiastical courts frequently had to force payment or undertake eviction in earlier centuries, and now used the secular courts to do so, did not make the people love her. Yet, like every other human institution, she had to survive. Apparently, toward the end of the century, the church benefited both by enclosures and by the improvement in agricultural methods. The see of Durham, on the other hand, increased its revenues because its lands provided coal used increasingly in the new industry. The Commissioners of Queen Anne's Bounty might have been in less trouble, as G. F. A. Best suggests, if they had put some of their earnings into the newly capitalizing industries rather than into land. The suspicion of them would at least have been reduced.

Of course the offices of the church carried with them certain obligations. The bishops had to provide firstfruits and tenths to the crown. They had also to maintain their properties and to provide hospitality on a large scale, though frequently this did not filter down to those who needed it most.

The rural base of the church was the chief factor which made it impossible for the establishment to be free to meet the challenge of a society that was on the move from farm to city. The fact was that a new parish to accommodate the shift of population could not be created without an act of parliament. This meant that traditional patronage would be upset and so the chances of success of such bills were nil. While it was true that at this time the society was still overwhelmingly rural, and that a church which was to serve the whole people should therefore have been expected to be related to the land, it was also true that the established church, because of her bondage to the land, had no means of responding to the changes that were taking place in society at large.

### III

Every ecclesiastical system has its method of church discipline. After the Restoration, church courts were recognized but were not to pass any legislation binding upon laymen without the consent of parliament. For all intents and purposes, with the lapse of Convocation, statute law took the place of canon law relative to the life of the church. Even though the ecclesiastical courts had jurisdiction of the matters special to her, such as excommunication, marriage and divorce, even here they had to be backed up by the actual force of the civil courts. The latter were frequently used, as we noted above, to force reluctant ratepayers to come through in the payment of tithes. This intrusion of the civil into the authority of the clerical was challenged most effectively by Edmund Gibson's great study of canon law entitled *Codex Iuris Ecclesiastici Anglicani* or *The Statues, Constitutions, Canons, Rubricks and Articles of the Church of England methodically digested under their Proper Heads*. This was an effort to claim the legitimate rights and authority of the church to govern its own life and to supervise the lives of its communicants. Lord Chief Justice Hardwicke, however, regarded it as a usurpation of the powers rightly belonging to parliament. In any case, Gibson's work, even though he was the principal advisor to both Newcastle and Walpole on church matters, got no farther in practice than the paper upon which it was written. The laity continued to have the upper hand both through the courts and the parliament.

    Frequently Christianity was regarded as being one thing while the church was another. One could be for the former but opposed to the authority of the latter. Indeed the writings of Bishop Benjamin Hoadly himself appeared to confirm this stance, much to the horror of William Law and Bishop William Warburton. On the whole the church was regarded as useful for the purposes of maintaining order and for the fulfilling of the basic rites and rituals of religion. This above all meant concern for the eternal destiny of the soul. It did not enter the imagination that the church should be free to transform the social order! Of course she had proven in her time in as great need of perpetual reformation and renewal as any other institution sharing in power, and the memory of this fact on the part of the laity was the basis for their fear of "clericalism." The laity were now free to prove whether they could handle power while remaining aware of the "whole duty of man."

In this they were hardly more successful than the clergy had been.

Though their sees were far too large, the bishops did manage to carry out their duties of ordination, confirmation and visitation with some semblance of order. Frequently there was no means of knowing whether those being confirmed had been instructed with any adequacy because their numbers were so great. It was suggested that suffragans should be appointed in order to aid the bishops, but these, like so many other suggestions, were swept aside. This meant that there was a great measure of religious illiteracy among the people.

Throughout the countryside the standard public worship was Morning and/or Evening Prayer along with a sermon on the Sabbath. Except in London and Westminster it was hardly possible for the full complement of services, either on the Sabbath or weekdays, to be carried out though, because of the attraction of the city for those of unusual training and ability, even extra lectureships were sometimes well attended. Thus, while there was much neglect of offices basic to her task, such as orderly and regular celebration of the sacraments and the instruction of the people, there was also much accomplished when it is considered that the church was attempting to serve the whole people. Even the sick and those who were poor were ministered to in some measure as the diaries of Parsons Cole, Woodforde and Skinner testify.[7]

In terms of conventional piety, then, the church fulfilled in faithful measure its duties among the people in the context of an age that took both riches and poverty for granted, and that sought adjustment to the world rather than transformation of it. To be a good citizen was thought to be a good enough Christian, and if the offices of the church could afford one reasonable assurance of safe passage to a world of bliss beyond, what more could be asked of her?

## IV

When we turn to a direct consideration of the relations between the church as an institution and the state, we discover the point at which the established church was changed in this period, not by reason of reform from within but rather by reason of what was done to her from without. In reaction to Laud, and in memory of the Commonwealth, the restored parliament under Charles II made certain that no canon law, unless confirmed by parliament, was to hold over the laity. Then, not even at the instruction of, or with the permission of, Convocation, Archbishop Sheldon in 1664 gave over the right of the clergy to tax themselves, which meant that parliament could institute new taxes on the church without her collaberation. There was, therefore, no necessity for Convocation to meet in order to supplement the revenues of the crown or parliament. Because Charles I had used the Convocation in this way for his own purposes, parliament wanted to make that an impossible course for the crown to follow again. This was simply another instance of power being taken over by parliament which had previously belonged to both church and to crown. The church to some extent had no one but herself to blame for the demise of Convocation and thus for the almost inevitable rise of the influence of parliament over the government of her life. Apart from the Commissioners of Queen Anne's Bounty and again after 1835, the Ecclesiastical Commissioners, the church had no central executive body of any kind that might have governed her overall life until Convocations were called in the middle of the nineteenth century. It was the enmity between the upper and lower houses of Convocation that led to the primates feeling it was the better part of valour not to call Convocation at all than to display the church's inner dissension.

The nadir of the church's power even over her own life is best illustrated in the Feathers Tavern Petition of 1771 wherein a number of the clergy petitioned that they should be asked to subscribe to the Bible alone, as the source of the divine truth, and not to the Thirty-Nine articles. Many of the clergy had reservations to the articles (because of their Arian or Unitarian beliefs). However, the petition was refused by parliament. The man who argued most eloquently that it should be refused was none other than Edmund Burke. Thus, even in creedal matters, the church's doctrine was decided by parliament rather than by itself. Not even the greatest idealist could thus picture the church as an equal along with the state under a common head, the king, as she was pictured to be but in fact was not.

It is not surprising that Edmund Gibson should seek to defend the church legalistically through an exposition of canon law rather than theologically. The attack upon her prerogatives was legal, not theological. What is so important about the new relationship obtaining between church and state was that it made all suggestion of reform of the church an impossibility. When Gibson suggested that the size of disceses be changed so as to be more manageable and that reassessment of church tithes should be made in view of the new value of money, as usual, the cry of "clericalism" went up in parliament. Though he himself was allied with the Whig party, his suggestions got nowhere.

No one better represented, and therefore was more favoured by parliament in the early decades of the century, than Bishop Benjamin Hoadly. His view of the church was that it was of two kinds, visible and invisible. To the nature and structure of the visible church he was essentially indifferent and felt that it was an institution under civil law as were other institutions within the state. This extreme Erastianism pleased parliament but displeased his clerical brethren so much that consideration of his heresies was the occasion for the prorogation of Convocation in 1717. For Hoadly it was the invisible church which mattered and which was known to Christ alone. He had left no authorities to usurp his direct relationship between himself and the believer. Parliament had no right to coerce in matters of conscientious religious belief, but had every right to interfere if religion disturbed the peace of the realm. As Hoadly saw it, sincerity alone mattered in the religious sphere. He was effectively opposed by William Law who,

> proceeded to build up a constructive apologetic for orthodox Christianity conceived as a corporate society exercising authority over its members in matters of faith and morale.[8]

It was William Warburton in his *Alliance between Church and State*, published in 1736, who best demonstrates the thesis that what first exists empirically frequently elicits theories in its defence. We have seen how this was true with respect to the doctrine of *Laissez-faire* in the economic realm. His purpose was both to defend the established religion and to justify the Test Law against Dissenters. In view of the fact that his position eloquently defended the *status quo*, his book found immediate acceptance. On the one hand, he insisted, with Gibson, that the church had her own inherent rights of government, of ordination, and the like which were peculiar to her in her own proper sphere. No government had leave to interfere with such. His claim was that even though the magistrate had to confirm the liberty of the priest to act, no government was capable either of making a priest or should desire to do so. On the other hand, with Law, he insisted upon the corporate nature of religion. A visible church had always been and would always be necessary to Christianity. While the state's concern was with things temporal and with the use of religion to maintain order, the church existed for an eternal purpose. *Thus while the state had the right to compel conformity to a religious establishment for the sake of its own health, it did not have the right to coerce in matters of ultimate individual religious commitment.* This was the business of religious bodies. He was therefore able to justify both the established church and the right of non-conformity within certain bounds. The established church, along with other churches, alone had the freedom to excommunicate. The power of the state ought not to be used to enforce complete *religious* conformity. Thus, in essence, he justified the state of affairs as it had grown out of the settlement of 1689 and the Act of Toleration. Moreover, he was convinced, and was able to convince others in a day when "natural law" was the most popular final court of appeal, that the English religious settlement more perfectly represented the natural universal political state of affairs which should exist than did any other.

William Paley went even farther in that he insisted upon the separation of the final purposes of religion which were peculiar to itself from the means whereby it was propagated and the utility of its services for the public good. It was he who so eloquently defended ranks and orders in the church as happily corresponding with social classes in the wider social order which meant that each order could serve its corresponding status group on the basis of equality!

> A religious establishment is not part of Christianity it is only the means of inculcating it....The authority of a church establishment is founded in its utility.[9]

When vested interest found such a happy intellectual defence, it is not surprising that those who disagreed, who felt that church reform was long overdue, were swept aside. Richard Watson, who rose from obscure circumstances to the bishopric through sheer diligence and intellectual acumen, was left at Llandaff without translation from the time he was appointed until his death. The fundamental reason for this was that he made concrete suggestions for reform within the church which would have dealt with the tragic disparity of income between the higher and lower clergy. It would also have solved the problem of frequent translation by making the income from the sees more equitable. Watson suggested that,

> A half or a third part of the income of every deanery, prebend, or canonry of the churches of Westminster, Windsor, Canterbury, Christ Church, Worcester, Durham, Ely, Norwich etc. to the same purpose mutatis mutandis as the first fruits and tenths were appropriated by Queen Anne.[10]

However, nothing of this kind was done for another two generations when the spirit of political reform swept over into that of religious reform as well. Watson was also liberal in his theological opinions and was essentially in agreement with Locke's reduction of the Christian faith to a belief in the divinity of Christ based upon his miracles and the quality of his life. He was thus in favour of the Feathers Tavern Petition.

It may be that the church was better off because it was impervious to every new wind of doctrine as a result of the interference of the state, but there is little doubt that she would have exercised a far more transforming spiritual and moral influence upon the life of the nation in the latter part of the century if she had been free from the fetters of parliamentary control, free to recognize and correct her own abuses and thus free to respond to the changes that were so rapidly taking place in the economic realm and which were the cause of so much human suffering.

It is true that in the last third of the century there

was a renewed interest in the establishment of parish schools and Sunday Schools, in the founding of hospitals, and in 1797 even a society for the Relief of the Poor as well as the establishment of missionary societies. These testified not only to the growing influence of Wesleyan and Evangelical revivals but also to the genuine recognition on the part of a wide segment of the public of the general worth of religious faith. It was a much more positive attitude than had prevailed since the Commonwealth. On the other hand, such activities were very paternalistic and, in the light of the French Revolution, sought to use religion for purposes of "social control," for keeping Britain safe from the upheavals taking place in France. In the earlier part of the century church leaders like Archbishop Wake were opposed to the calling of Convocation for the purposes of church reform because they thought the mood of the public, as well as the parliamentary leadership, was so unfriendly to the church that it was better to let sleeping dogs lie. What parliament might have ended up doing to the church would make its last estate worse than its first! Later on in the century when there might have been some support for genuine reform in the church, the clouds from revolutionary France began to bank on the horizon, and with the help of eloquent conservatives, like Burke and Paley, who thought of England's "green and pleasant land" as the best of all possible worlds, the hope of reform once again faded.

> The Georgian church corresponded well with the unreformed parliament and with the regime of privilege and patronage in the civil administration. Nor did the temper of the eighteenth century seek innovations in any established institution. When to its natural conservatism and dislike of change there was added the sinister example of revolution, alike in religion and politics, in the neighboring kingdom of

France, suspicion of reform hardened into abhorrence and repudiation.[11]
So it was that the established church, like parliament itself, based itself upon a way of life unresponsive to the tremendous changes that were taking place all around it. Great shifts in population, new types of industry and new ways of thought went largely unheeded.

V

What, then, was the final result of this absence of reform in the life of the church?

In the first place, while the church remained what she had been in form since the Reformation, she had in fact lost not only significant political power but even power over her own life and destiny. This power had been taken over by the laity in parliament. While she had only a minimal share in political power, she was part of the political structure and had to suffer the criticisms levelled against it. The price of her establishment was her erastian position. Even at the local level the church was heavily involved in vested political and economic life in the countryside, either because the squire was the lay impropriator of the living which a clergyman might enjoy, or because the clergyman himself was a local Justice of the Peace. It could hardly be expected, therefore, that a church so identified with the prevailing order could also be its reformer. The church had a deep stake in the patronage and nepotism of the whole structure.[12] The church was, in this sense, "*in* the world and *of* it." The very participation of the prelates in political activity meant that they had to spend precious time at great expense in London attending upon parliament that might better have been spent in the supervision of their sees.

In the second place, the immobility of the established church meant that she continued to be related to the land, to rural England, and that she was unable to express her concern for the new urban centres filled with defenseless and poverty-stricken labourers by the thousands. Those who had freedom of movement could meet that challenge. Thus the Methodists were strong precisely where the established church was weak. The poor the Methodists gained had already separated themselves from the life of the church. Even Wesley could not bring them back to it, try as he may. The voluntary but highly disciplined class meeting of the Methodists was superbly suited for the needs of the anonymous urban poor. Through the organizing genius and commanding personality of its charismatic leader, John Wesley, the Methodist movement was able to make a coherent impact upon the abuses of the day while the cumbersome, essentially powerless, established church was unable to do so, in so far as she affected the *individual* lives of the poor.

Further, Anglicanism was imbued with the old pastoral, rural virtues whereas Methodism was filled with the spirit of "the Protestant ethic" and in this sense, too, was closer to the dissenting communities. It meant that the people called Methodists were prepared to share in the life of the rising bourgeoisie and indeed, especially after the death of John Wesley, came to be identified increasingly with the privileges of this new class.

Yet, while the established church failed to comprehend in its own life both the possibilities for order and of change that are always present in human life, we must give her credit for maintaining the former, if missing the challenge of the latter. As we have seen, many of the most important concerns of the church were carried out faithfully by her. She did uphold many of the positive values in the culture, thus promoting stability and order. She took part not only in the administration of Justice but also in the administration of parish poor relief which came to have more and more significance toward the end of the century.[13] In many ways she was filled with the works of the Spirit. These cannot be taken from her. Yet the fact that reform waited so long in her life, that men became used to using her for secondary purposes and regarded her so frequently as irrelevant to so many of the central concerns of life--such attitudes as these were the beginning of a set of mind that has not yet spent its course and the consequence of which is still being profoundly felt by the established church in England. To this day the established church has not been able to make vital contact with the labouring class. For years Walpole made a habit of playing both ends against the middle in religious affairs. On the one hand, he was for the repeal of the Occasional Conformity Act; on the other, even though he found ways around them, he knew enough not to attempt the repeal of the Test and Corporation Acts. So the religious establishment was considered a good and sometimes useful thing to have around so long as it neither took itself too seriously nor was taken too seriously by the people at large. The prophetic spirit disappeared from her life and with it that tension between church and state which must prevail if the community of faith is to help maintain those things which ought to be maintained and to change those things which must be changed if life in this world is to be fully lived.

## Chapter Five

## THE EXTENT OF DISSENT

Our purpose here is to try to measure the extent of Dissent in the eighteenth century. Among other things we want to discover its strength in simple numerical terms relative to the establishment. While it is true that one can never measure the vitality of any movement, especially a religious movement, in terms of numbers, they cannot be altogether discounted. Unless one has exceptional charismatic power and is in a position of unusual strategic importance, he is unlikely to be able to influence others in a way that is absolutely out of proportion to the numbers of persons involved. He may be such a religious genius, but even so his influence is likely to be felt after his lifetime rather than during it. If we discount numbers, we discount persons and their importance. This is as unsound theologically and philosophically as it is sociologically. Numbers, therefore, have their legitimate importance, and we shall take them into account.

However, we will want to go beyond this and ask, "Who were those who belonged to the dissenting communities? To what social class did they belong? How did they organize themselves in order to make their influence felt?" We shall leave until later the deeper questions with regard to the theological issues which separated the established Church and Dissent, as well as the effort to measure the degree of change which those who were involved in the evangelical revival were able to bring about during and immediately beyond the eighteenth century.

A word must be said about the prevailing mood at the

opening of the century if we are to catch the spirit of the age.  Gerald Cragg writes:

> The closing years of the seventeenth century had no place for arrogance or dogmatism, but they opened an era uniquely confident and self-assured. Enthusiasm was suppressed and passion carefully controlled, but this made it all the easier to believe in the neatly ordered regularity of life. Man was a noble creature (though never in an extravagant way):  the universe was marvellously contrived (yet not as yet so vast as to dwarf man by its immensity), the political order was securely established, and liberty (reasonably limited) was a part of the firm structure of society.  God, the ultimate ground of this stability, remained discreetly in the background as a kind of honourary president of the universe that he had made.  The influences which had recently been shaping the character of religious thought had combined to create a mood of dangerously complacent satisfaction and Addison, the spokesman of the coming age, could invite his readers to consider the world in its most agreeable lights.[1]

It is not surprising that with this confidence and the world opening up all around them men should look upon new disclosures in the realm of thought as having more authority because more novelty than the old, and/or that "natural religion" should have come into its own as well as the authority of pure reason.  Nor is it surprising that the logical skepticism of Hume should follow.  For many, man was finally free, finally "enlightened," to use the world as he saw fit without the shackles of religious superstition which, along with his ignorance of the universe, kept him in bondage. Men were beginning to do new and marvelous things with the world in terms of agricultural and industrial technology, opening the doors on the modern world. Who could wish for more? There were others, however, who were not as certain that the world was friendly, that man could be fully human while his destiny was reduced to nature of which he was undoubtedly a part.

The extent of human callousness, of man's inhumanity to man within the social order of the English nation alone, must be read and known to be believed. The cold light of reason seemed unable to deliver men into a kingdom of social righteousness. Indeed, the reverse could be argued forcibly in light of the evidence. By the standards of the twentieth century, life was still short and for the vast majority, brutish. Understandably, men, whether of high or low estate, had a morbid fear of death which was never far away.

There were those during this century who though hardly opposed to the real gains which man had made yet believed that man's reach did exceed his grasp; that there were still levels of understanding with regard to human existence that human reason alone had not laid bare; that the destiny of man was greater even than the measure of the world with all its marvels. There were some such from the very beginning, Watts and Doddridge, then Law and Berkeley and Butler as well as Whitefield and Wesley and the sensitive evangelicals of the established church. These were not all of one mind by any means, but they represent the challenge to the predominant attitudes of the day and in their persons account for the renewed vitality of religious faith which seemed at the beginning of the age to be at best a smouldering ember.

Let us be clear as to why we include Methodism in Dissent. Even though Wesley, as well as the Countess of Huntingdon and Whitefield, strove to contain their movements within the Church of England, it eventually became impossible because of irregularities with regard to ordination.

As a result, churches under the direction of Whitefield and the Countess of Huntingdon registered under the protection of the Toleration Act in 1781, and Wesley reluctantly took this step for the Methodists in 1787, though he still refused to officially countenance separation from the established church. There were reasons at a deeper level, well expressed by Horton Davies:

> Close as the affinities of Methodism appear to be with Anglicanism, its evangelical passion and experiental religion were a revival of Puritan religion without the latter's austerities. Its deepest affinities lie with the older Nonconformist Churches, for all are united in claiming that the Church is the servant of the Gospel not the Gospel the servant of the Church. 'Puritanism,' says J. R. Green, 'won its spiritual victory in the Wesley movement after the failure in the previous century of its military and political struggles.'[2]

For purposes of analysis the century falls into a familiar division. The first period lies between the Act of Toleration of 1689 and the end of Queen Anne's reign in 1714. It was a period of accommodation to toleration. The second, from 1714 until the beginning of Whitefield's preaching in 1736, which inaugurates the official beginning of "the revival," was a difficult time for religious faith of every description and of all religion in its organized expression; the years 1736 to 1791, that is until the death of Wesley, represent the formative, creative years of the renewal of religious faith. The years beyond them, until the final repeal of disabilities against the Dissenters in 1828, represent a period of continuing growth which did not reach its peak until the last half of the nineteenth century.

# The Extent of Dissent

I

Though accurate statistics in the modern sense are not available for the population of England at the end of the seventeenth century, the estimates of Gregory King and of W. Cunningham put it at about five and one-half million. From 1700 to 1760 it increased another one to one and one-quarter million while in the last forty years of the century another two million were added. Before 1751 the increase per decade was approximately 3%, from '51 to 1780 about 6%, in the next decade 9% and from '91 until 1801 approximately 11%. At this rate the total population in 1801 is estimated at about 8,892,536 persons. This means that within the century the population increased some sixty percent with the great bulk of that increase taking place in the last few decades. Moreover, the great shift in density of the population took place in the new industrial areas in Lancashire, the West Riding and the Midlands in general, as well as in the area surrounding London.[3]

It is estimated that at the beginning of the century there were some 250,000 to 300,000 traditional Dissenters,[4] but after the first quarter of the century until its close their numbers tended to decline. In the first full bloom of toleration hundreds of new chapels were rented or built and congregations established with some 143 permanent licenses being granted in the two years 1688-90. This declined to 21 built from 1731-40.[5]

Actually the "Three Denominations" as they began to be called, the Presbyterians, Congregationalists or Independents, and the Baptists, had much in common. At the outset, immediately after the Act of Toleration, this issued in what was known as "The Happy Union" between Presbyterian and Congregationalist churches in and around London. They banded together to help needy ministers and new congregations striving to be born. Before long theological strife brought denominational divisions, but in church organization all three denominations were essentially congregational in that their central authority was the local church itself. The Presbyterians stumbled into this because their scheme of national church government had failed years before with the Savoy Conference, so that the actual authority finally fell into the hands of lay trustees. Since the majority of them were of the merchant class, which in turn was deeply affected by the "new learning," the inroads of pure rationalism and Unitarianism among the Presbyterians were strong. They ended up a far cry from the traditional Calvinism of the Presbyterian churches of Scotland.

Calvinism, where it was preserved, was to be found in certain Congregational churches. At the outset it was true that Congregational churches went along with their Presbyterian friends in recognizing a loosely bound presbytery, but this was given up before long as was the attempt at Synodical organization.

Of course the Baptist groups were strongly set on local autonomy and dissipated much of their strength in arguments over open and closed communion.

The Society of Friends was moribund. It had lost its great leadership in the person of men such as Fox and Barclay and was not to recover its vitality until the latter part of the eighteenth century. Part of their difficulty was that they lacked any effective means of organization as well as clarity of theological insight into their early origins. Their preoccupation was primarily with such minor things as niceties of dress. The revolutionary vision and fervour of their founders had disappeared.

It may be said of all of the dissenting groups that they tended to turn in upon themselves, to be preoccupied with details of their own thought, behaviour and

# The Extent of Dissent 151

organization, with their own civil rights, but that they had lost any hope of reforming the religious life of England, or of restructuring the Church of England along lines more consistent with their understanding of the Christian church.

We have already noted the important role that the merchants of London as Dissenters played not only in the Restoration itself but in the resolution of things at the "Glorious Revolution." The class orientation of traditional Dissent continued to be essentially the same throughout the eighteenth and indeed the nineteenth centuries. By the year 1700 there were two distinct strata in this orientation. There were the wealthy merchants and professional persons, lawyers and doctors, around London. Then there were those out in the country, especially in the villages, who were yeomen of the lower middle class if not among the poor. Because there were those who did have wealth and therefore a certain amount of influence in London, they were able to seek legal redress even for those who were poorer among them in the countryside when the property rights of the latter were illegally attacked. As Manning's "The Protestant Dissenting Deputies" makes clear, that body at the outset was made up of London lawyers and merchants.[6] In the 1730's Walpole based his policy on trade and "the Dissenters were the backbone of the trading interests," according to him.[7] It was the wealthy Dissenters of London who, in 1742, were subjected to nomination to offices in the Corporation of London and then, because of the Corporation Act, were fined because they did not, and could not, take office. Because of the continuing influence of the landed classes supporting the established church, even Walpole could not bring about the repeal of the Corporation Act.

During this period of accommodation to toleration many of the more affluent among the Dissenters could see no further point in resisting the establishment. Since they had to suffer stigma as second class citizens and could not enter fully into the political life of the nation and, in any case, were anxious to find points of agreement with the Anglicans, they passed over into the established church. The great majority nevertheless persisted, even though a cold intellectualism settled over them and deprived them of most of their fire. That both richer and poorer among them did persist is attested to by the fact that so many of the dissenting leadership were merchants and professionals and were willing, later on, to bear heavy fines on behalf of their faith. They had influence, but they did not have sufficient influence to prevent the passing of the Occasional Conformity Act in 1711 during Anne's reign or even the Schism Act directed at the dissenting academies at the time of her death. Anne was strongly for the established church. On the other hand, their support of the Hanoverian dynasty was significant enough in the eyes of both crown and parliament that at least these Acts were repealed in 1719.

Another very important basis for the development of Dissent throughout the century was the provision which was made for the training of a ministry and indeed for an education for the children of Dissenters who were kept out of the universities of Oxford and Cambridge because of religious tests. This was accomplished through the setting up of what became known as dissenting academies. Both Philip Doddridge and later on Joseph Priestley were outstanding tutors in these schools. Because they were free from the restrictions of the older universities, they were able to enter into the "new learning" both in terms of science, of philosophy and theology. They provided the best education in the country in that day. Two dozen of these academies were established before 1688 while thirty of them were begun between 1690 and 1750. It was against their influence that the Schism Act was directed. It debarred anyone from teaching who was not

# The Extent of Dissent 153

a communicant of the Church of England on penalty of imprisonment. This would have deprived a great many children, many of the poorer classes in the villages, of any hope of education. It would also have done away with an educated ministry for Dissent. However, the Queen died the day it was to take effect and it was repealed without ever having been enforced.

While it may be true that the years following the Act of Toleration introduced a period of prudential religion exemplified by Tillotson, there were nevertheless a number of religious societies in existence which sought to relate religious faith to social concern.

> In London and Westminster the count of them sprang from thirty-nine in the beginning of William's reign to close upon a hundred just before its close; while they spread also to many other large towns in England and even across the Irish Seas.[8]

Samuel Wesley was a member of such a society and the Oxford "Holy Club" was patterned after their example. To some extent they were the watchdogs of public morals, as, for example, was the Society for the Reformation of Manners begun in 1691. Both the Society for the Propagation of Christian Knowledge (1698) and the Society for the Propagation of the Gospel (1701) were formed during this period and contained in the roster of members adherents both of the Church of England and the dissenting communities. A number of charitable organizations also came into existence at this time. While their vision was limited, the societies testify to the fact that vital religious faith was not altogether dead.

While there was a loss of creative faith during this period among Dissenters, nevertheless, there was a quiet persistence among the great majority of them. Isaac Watts and later Philip Doddridge gave exceptional leadership. So did a man like Howell Harris who anticipated the evangelical revival. Formal growth in those early decades was significant, even though it may not have represented the depth of religious fervour a half-century before. However, as Queen Anne's reign proved, there had not yet been any real affirmation of toleration which amounted to more than a political compromise for mutual political advantage.

II

The years 1715 to 1736 were especially difficult ones for Dissent as they were for all of the Christian churches. All of the authorities testify to the low state of morals at this time in the nation as a whole. It was the age of Robert Walpole when political expediency reigned supreme and infected every segment of public life. It was also the period in which political power was transferred exclusively to the king and his ministers on the one hand, and the parliament on the other, the latter gaining immeasureably through the reign of the first two Hanovers, though restrained by the reign of George III. There was the continuing fear of Roman Catholicism, represented by the attempt of the Old Pretender in 1715. Once again at that time the cooperation of Dissent was called for to ensure the Succession and, indirectly, the established church as well. But the Anglican Church was not prepared to go further in toleration than the agreements of 1689, and, therefore, the Dissenters tended to act with parliament against what a man like Edmund Gibson thought to be the best interest of the church and of the Christian faith.

Among the Dissenters themselves theological differences became more and more acute. At Salter's Hall in February and March of 1719 a division was forced between those who subscribed to Calvinist views and those who did not. The majority who did not were Presbyterians together with some of the General Baptists. Those who remained firm in their Calvinist convictions tended to be Congregationalists. Later the Presbyterians moved from Socinianism and Arianism to form the backbone of Unitarianism. In spite of exceptions like Law and Butler, Watts and Doddridge, the spirit of the times then was inimical to creative faith.

Though statistics for this period are scant, the fact that little growth took place is confirmed in a survey of 1731 of Presbyterian and Independent chapels in and around London which showed that there was only a difference of one between 1695 and that year. At least fifty nonconformist ministers went over to the established church between 1714 and 1731. Among them were such men as Bishop Butler and Richard Watson.

After the Salter's Hall Convention and the differences which took place there, each congregation decided whether it would subscribe or not. What this meant was that so far as church organization was concerned the congregational principle won out. The Presbyterian system was completely denied. Their congregations were taken over by their own lay trustees who ran them as they saw fit. It is true that there was a measure of cooperation among them for purposes of relief from political persecution so that the "Three Denominations," the Congregationalists, Presbyterians and Baptists, formed an organization in 1727. By 1732 this began to develop into the organization known as The Protestant Dissenting Deputies, a group of ministers and laymen from the congregations within a ten mile limit of London organized to defend and extend the civil liberties of the Dissenters. They were called on year after year to do so not only in their own interest but in that of their less influential fellow believers in the countryside. However, this cooperation was purely political and was concerned with legal and legislative matters alone.

Though the Whigs and the Hanovers were much more favourable to Dissent than Queen Anne and the Tories had been, nevertheless, the best that could be won by Dissent in their own favour was the repeal of the Occasional Conformity and Schism Acts and an almost negligible relief from certain aspects of the Test and Corporation Acts in 1719. When Walpole returned to the ministry in 1721, he instituted a *regium donum* in the interest of the relief of the families of poor dissenting ministers, something after the example of Queen Anne's bounty. Many have interpreted this as a sop in lieu of the inability of Walpole's ministry and parliament to repeal the Test and Corporation Acts. In 1727 Walpole saw to the passing of the Indemnity Acts which had the effect of cutting the ground from under the Test and Corporation Acts, though they had to be passed every year by parliament and so were hardly a guarantee of security to Dissent. The annual Indemnity Acts made it possible for Dissenters to hold political office by special act of parliament.

In the end Walpole gave up any effort to have the older acts repealed, taking it for granted that the *regium donum* and the annual Indemnity Acts were the best compromise that could be achieved. Yet this whole question and its handling is a beautiful illustration of Walpole's political method of expedient compromise. On the one hand, he got the cooperation of the traders whose help the country needed so badly and who were primarily Dissenters while, on the other hand, he did not upset unduly the established order in church and state based on the land, so necessary for the maintenance of political peace and social order.

As we have said, the years 1715 to 1736 were ones in which England in general and its religious life in particular were at best in a state of quietude, at worst one of morbidity. In the economy the rapid pace of change did not really begin until the last half of the century. In politics not even the best leadership was able to achieve any kind of reform because it was assumed that things as they were were best. In the church Warburton, not Gibson, prevailed. In Dissent even Watts and Doddridge were atypical, and in politics Walpole, the consummate compromiser, was the man of the hour. Stability, not change, was cherished. Such a society, however, is always on the brink of decay. Fortunately for England, not only in the economic realm but in the religious as well, there was to be a new day, the effects of which were to create a radically different and unanticipated future.

III

We may take the dawn of the "Great Revival" as beginning with the preaching of George Whitefield in 1736, even though it was not until two years later that Wesley himself experienced his own renewal. Together they led the whole of English Christendom into a new day. Though its effects were felt well into the nineteenth century and even beyond we may assume that its most creative period ended with the death of Wesley in 1791.

It took a remarkably short time for the influence of these men to be felt in terms of concrete organization, for Wesley was a genius in this respect. Wearmouth[9] estimates that from 1740 to 1770 some one thousand persons per year were added to the Methodist Societies, from 1770 to 1780 some two thousand per year and from 1780 to 1790 three thousand. In the last twenty years of the century it doubled its membership. The total membership in 1788 was approximately 80,000, while there were four times as many persons attending services. By 1800 the number had risen to 109,000, and, if one includes all adherents, it is estimated that some 500,000 were touched by the movement. This would include about one in every sixteen persons in the England of that day. One has to recall, too, that membership was pruned regularly according to Wesley's discipline.

The renewal, of course, spread into the dissenting churches and especially among the Calvinist Congregationalists. Their chapels were almost empty at mid-century, but by its end they were full and there was a vigourous program for building new chapels afoot. The Society of Friends and the Unitarian Presbyterians were only slightly affected, but new life was felt in the Church of England, some of which was directly to be attributed to the influence of Whitefield and Wesley and some of which developed independently of them. Wearmouth claims that by 1788 over five hundred Anglican clergymen were under Wesley's influence.[10]

The increase in the Wesleyan movement was felt precisely in those areas of the country where the population was increasing. They were the same areas in which the industrial revolution, with its accompanying social change, was most deeply felt. Elliott-Binnes is right when he claims that the Wesleyans hardly made up a number by the end of the century to deeply influence the total life of the nation.[11] On the other hand, we have to remember that those who were participating provided the labourers for the new industry, labourers made sober and stable. Those who were affected by the wider evangelical movement were frequently the "captains" of the new industry. Thus the role they played in the total life of the nation was not insignificant, even if politically their day had not yet arrived. Certain elements of Dissent, such as those led by Priestley, were little affected by the evangelical movement. Indeed, they

# The Extent of Dissent 159

caricatured it as anti-rational. Presbyterian leadership on the whole was untouched because it resisted the "enthusiasm" and "anti-intellectualism" of the evangelical movement. Congregationalism, however, as we have said, was affected both directly and indirectly, while the Church of England was stirred by those clergy who responded to it even though they were unprepared to identify with it to the extent of breaking with the established church.

Wesley had had the experience of participating in societies for religious purposes. It was not surprising, therefore, that he soon hit upon the expedient of establishing small groups of persons for the purpose of mutual support and spiritual discipline. The "societies" divided into "classes" of about a dozen persons with a particular person chosen as leader. Eventually the societies were organized in circuits and into districts and conferences. All this did not happen overnight, but by the time of Wesley's death it was in smooth operation under his decisive leadership.

It was to his organization and its implications that the Church of England objected. So long as Wesley sought to relate his societies to the Church of England, little objection could officially be made. Yet when he was forced to ordain in order that his following might have the sacraments, this was a different matter. At that point he had to identify his movement with that of Dissent.

Moreover, those whom he influenced, the new industrial poor, had been largely neglected by the establishment. They could feel little or no attachment to the established church. Horton Davies mentions the fact, however, that the principle obstacles were the irregularities in church order practiced by Wesley, such as field preaching, the use of extempore prayers in preference to set forms, the appointment of lay preachers, the establishment of societies, synods of lay preachers, the establishment of societies, synods, and conferences and, the greatest offense of all, the ordination of preachers in North America.

As Wearmouth points out, while Wesley had a deep sense of the worth of individuals and was able to convince the poor of the profound love which God had for them and thus gave them a new sense of self-respect, a new hope, he had no idea of reforming either the structure of English society or the structures of the Church of England. Methodism was out to reform the nation but this meant primarily, almost exclusively, the individual citizen. While there was a deep sense of social solidarity in "the ecclesiola" which Wesley established among his followers, there was little insight into the way in which social practices enter into and affect what we are and what we do. Wesley can hardly be blamed for failing to understand the shortcomings of the new industrialism, since they came into being in the later years of his life, but one wishes his churchmanship had extended to the use of his influence in bringing about the much needed reform of the established church. This may well have been impossible because of his deep and right identification with the poor who were outcast and who took so much of his time. He could hardly be all things to all men. Even the influence of the evangelical movement within the Church of England, which was made up of the upper and especially middle classes, was not felt until the end of the century. The attitude of that movement to the poor was that they were deserving of charity and that they would do all in their power to help them as individuals. They did not entertain the thought that the "station" of the poor in society could be changed. They did not understand the reality of social structures and the relationships of individuals to them. "Systemic violence," though of great magnitude, was largely unrecognized.

The Extent of Dissent                                           161

Meanwhile the very "captains" of industry were frequently among the leading Dissenters of the day and were to some extent responsible for the tragic conditions of the labouring poor. Even the leadership of Methodism after the death of Wesley, through the person of Jabez Bunting, became conservative and served the purposes of the middle classes. Methodists were among the best militiamen called out to maintain order in riots at the end of the century. They elicited the praise of the conservative Burke in their support of stability against rabble rousers like the Dissenters, Wilkes and Priestley. This servility to the powers that be would have enraged Wesley who, though a Tory himself, had a profound sense of equity. Later on the conservative mould of Bunting's leadership was to bring about great losses among Methodists as the poorer among them saw their interests deserted.

When one considers the overall conditions of social life in the eighteenth century, even at its close, one wonders what real social influence the evangelical movement had. Policies instituted by the government particularly in the '30's and '40's led to famine amongst the people. It was accepted that the poor would not work if they were not hungry. Yet by 1780 the Gordon Riots were also set off by conditions of famine among the dispossessed. The penalties for stealing in order to protect the "men of property" remained terribly severe.

> The year 1785 was probably the blackest in English judicial history; nearly five hundred were sentenced to death, many others were sent across the seas.[12]

As a result of the reaction to the French Revolution, the whole spirit of reform was set back in church and state and society at large. It is to the credit of the "Clapham Sect," made up of those who had been influenced by the evangelical movement, that they fought on against slavery, even in this atmosphere. We also recall the spirit of renewed concern among the Society of Friends in such persons as John Howard and Elizabeth Fry. Moreover, the Speenhandland approach to the poor law and the early Factory Act of 1802 were attempts to be sensitive to the needs of persons through social legislation. A balanced view would have to recognize that it was probably too early to see clearly the immoral aspects of a *laissez-faire* economic order which served almost exclusively the vested interests of the propertied classes while it also made for a slow rise in the general standard of living. Even those affected by the evangelical revival had not really come to see the significance of the relation between the sovereignty of God, on the one hand, and the total life of man in society, on the other. Christians had a far less comprehensive view of the significance of the Christian faith for the whole of life than had been the case either during the Middle Ages or until the end of the creative period in "presbyterian-puritanism" marked by such a man as Richard Baxter.

# Chapter Six

## FAITH, THOUGHT AND LIFE: THE VITAL ISSUES AT STAKE

In every period in human history there is a profound relationship between thought and action. What is thought influences what is done, but what is in fact done in turn influences what is acceptable thought. In the economic realm the thinking of Adam Smith was as much a reflection of what was already beginning to be done in the economy as it was an effort to outline in theory the way in which it ought normatively to be done. Had Smith advocated the continuance of a protected mercantilist market, or a planned socialist one, it is unlikely that we would have heard of him today. Instead, he advocated the kind of market which was already coming into being and thus his thought, in corresponding to experience, gained a hearing among the public.

This is not the whole truth because it can be demonstrated that thought not only reflects accepted behaviour but **also** initiates novel behaviour. While there is mutual reinforcement between thought and acceptable action, there is also some degree of creative tension as new thought and new ways struggle for acceptance. The time lag involved can be fateful for the good or ill of the human race in any particular period. Our intent here is to illustrate the way in which the *interaction* between thought and life in the eighteenth century illustrates the above thesis. We will trace the interrelationships between what was thought theologically and philosophically and the political, economic and social life of the period.[1]

The banality which was characteristic of the political and social life of the nation after the compromise of the

Glorious Revolution was also reflected in religious life. The reaction to "fanaticism" in the earlier period resulted in an indifferentism to profound though inescapable religious questions. The compartmentalization characteristic of modern secular life began to set in as the political theories of Hobbes, Locke and Smith tended to replace theological interpretations. The influence and authority of "reason" as opposed to "mystery" created a reductionism in thought in general and most especially in theology. The discovery of "natural laws" in science reinforced a similar, though not necessarily adequate, view of economic theory. In religion deism, in ethics moralism, was the result. None of these could deal in depth with the problems of evil and suffering. The ethos of the age like that of most ages was accepted unselfconsciously. Unintentionally the only challenge to the authority of "reason" came from what is popularly known as the evangelical revival. That movement's greatest lack was its failure to comprehend that social justice cannot be achieved simply by the reformation of the individual but must bring about social structures that encourage rather than frustrate justice.

As the century wore on and the limitations of the prevailing understanding of the nature of reason were attacked by Kant and the skepticism of Hume, one finds the latter so threatened by the implications of his thought that he became a conservative. He could conceive of no other authority to replace "reason" than prevailing custom. This was hardly an answer to the social injustice of the age. Even the intellectual radicals such as Paine had far less to say of the suffering of the poor than Wesley because even they were caught up in a general optimism about the possibilities for change which the dawning industrial revolution seemed to presage. The eighteenth century came to a close on a note of profound ambiguity so far as the general welfare of the British populace was concerned.

I

To grasp the atmosphere of eighteenth century thought we have at least to go back to Descartes who reversed the medieval way of looking at things. The latter is exemplified in Anselm's *credo ut intelligam*. I believe in order that I may understand. The former is expressed in Descartes' *cogito ergo sum*. I know therefore I am. What this meant was that henceforth faith was to be judged by reason, however defined, rather than reason enlarged by faith. We have already discussed the way in which the Cambridge Platonists permitted reason a large place in their interpretation of the Christian faith. The Platonists were sensitive to the fact that mature religious faith should lead not to fanaticism but to the best use of reason. It was this for which they stood. But "reason" as it came to be used during the eighteenth century meant orderliness, control, lack of contradiction, whatever was in accord with sensate experience so interpreted. Mystery, paradox and evil were ignored. Contemporaries did not take the time to really examine the word. Its meaning was taken for granted and its authority, because of the orderliness science was discovering in nature as well as the control humans were gaining over nature as a result of following the lessons of science, increased without question.

John Locke (1632-1704), as the founder of British empiricism and as such inadvertently one of the most influential thinkers of the past three, almost four, centuries, was convinced that our knowledge of the external world does not come from anything innate but rather from the contact between the external world of experience and the images which are imposed on our minds by that contact. On reflection, our mind arranges these in categories; this is a process arising from within our consciousness. He did, therefore, claim an inner realm. Moreover, he was so confident of the mind's capacity to order that he at once moved from that capacity to its ground which he claimed was God, the One who Himself had originated such order. Even though he claimed that our knowledge of things arose from external experience, our knowledge of God arose from within, from our inner capacity alone. The logical problems of this position which were later expressed by Kant did not seem to bother him. He felt that the ordering capacity of the mind should be applied to religious knowledge and that, when it was essential, religious beliefs were reduced by reason to very few. Among them were the belief in Jesus Christ as the Messiah, though not necessarily as one among a Trinity. Nevertheless, in his own eyes he remained a loyal churchman. He believed that Jesus' Messiahship, oddly enough, was attested not only by his own miracles but also by the miracle of the resurrection.

As Cragg and Stromberg among others have pointed out, undoubtedly the inconsistencies in Locke's thinking were overlooked by reason of two things. First, the fact that atheism as such was not taken seriously as a position, and secondly, because reason enjoyed such uncritical authority.

It was a period of growing affluence at least for those in power and for those who were about to inherit power. It was therefore inevitable that this confidence in reason should reach into the common religious life and search out what it considered irrational there. Men had not long to wait. In the early decades of the eighteenth century, and indeed lasting throughout it, there were three challenges to the Christian faith that could not be ignored in view of the new confidence in reason. They were Socinianism, Arianism and finally Deism. All of these were attacks on the traditional trinitarian position which it had always been claimed was critical to the whole scheme of Christian soteriology, or doctrine of salvation. The Socinian position was that Jesus was not pre-existent, that he was simply a good man with whom God was well pleased. The Arian position was less extreme and therefore had more currency. Its claim was that while Jesus was pre-existent he was created by God and subordinate to Him. The whole issue arose because the idea of the unifying, ordering capacity of human reason had such a grip over the minds of men that anything that was so against simple logic as the concept of the trinity could not possibly be acceptable. The whole dimension of "mystery," of man's reach exceeding his grasp, which had been so congenial to the Cambridge Platonists had been wiped out both by the atmosphere of the new day and the influence of Locke who insisted, as Dryden echoed, that beliefs be "few and plain." As a result of reaction to decades of theological contention and of a new interest in the physical world, men did not want to have the clarity of their minds confused by the deeper issues.

As a result, the orthodox first attempted to reply on the basis upon which they had been attacked, that is, reason. Men such as Waterland, however, were hardly successful and to their contemporaries were not convincing. Following Clarke's study of scripture a Dissenter like James Pierce took on the Arian position, and so profound a spirit as Watts remained troubled throughout his life by the issue. His hymns reflect the tremendous sense of orderliness and harmony he believed to exist in the universe as a result of the Newtonian influence over him.

The Dissenters were seeking some authority other than the church and, since the Bible at times seemed confusing, reason provided another resort. The laity especially were impatient of any kind of obscurantism. The divine and inevitable "decrees" meant little in an age when men felt they could begin to manage things. Thus the Predestination-Arminian controversy was put on the shelf and lost to antiquity, or so it seemed, at least for a season. It was estimated that by 1750 half of the Presbyterian congregations had given up faith in the doctrine of the Trinity.

The step beyond either Socinianism or Arianism was Deism, the position that the universe conceived as a vast machine was brought into being by a First Cause who has ordered its life both physically and morally. Jesus was indeed a wise man because he knew the moral law and taught it, a law based upon the impersonal source of all truth. Matthew Tindal began as a Socinian and ended up a Deist. John Toland at the end of the seventeenth century was a disciple of Locke's and from there moved into Deism. Anthony Collins (1676-1729) most ably defended Deism in *The Grounds and Reasons of the Christian Religion*. For reasons we shall mention below, the impact of the movement was largely spent by the 1730's, though its influence was potently at work in the Feathers Tavern Petition of 1772 which almost won the houses of parliament for the position that clergymen of the establishment should not have to subscribe to the Thirty-Nine Articles but only that the Bible contained all doctrines necessary to salvation.

Priestley and Godwin continued the Deist tradition, but the effect of the French Revolution was against them. Their idealism was not borne out by the inhumanity of the French Revolution which had demonstrated that nothing can be more inhumane than man's slavery to his own absolutized ideas. The same force in its infancy had helped Burke, more for political considerations than religious ones, to defeat the Feathers Tavern Petition on the grounds that a change in belief at that time would have disturbed the peace of the nation. The question was not raised as to whether there was any adequate ground for faith.

A further offshoot of the confidence in reason was the new interest in "natural religion." As the outside world was opening up to the Occident, men were discovering anew that there were other great civilizations without benefit of the Christian faith. Had God left Himself without witness among these men? Did they not have the law written upon their hearts? Indeed, this whole consideration strengthened the view that common sense religion had primarily to do with matters of morality, with obeying the "moral law." No charitable, God-fearing man could really believe that others were completely benighted and they could cite Paul's epistle to the Romans in their defense (Romans 1:18). Did this not make at least two things clear? First, that it was religion which mattered not the particular religion. Second, that there was a universal moral law open and apparent to all men who sought it. This reinforced the conclusion that the new rationalism had already reached, that there was a unifying moral source for truth, namely God.

These developments, then, gave credence to the idea that there was a moral sense quite apart from religious faith open to all men of reason. This in turn made the appearance of a new science of ethics possible. It began with Shaftesbury and Hutcheson, with Gay and Bentham. These in turn were related to the new science of "political arithmetic" which attempted to look at the world of economics in particular in terms of abstract "natural laws." Adam Smith found the ground for his theoretical convictions in this way of looking at things. The impersonal market of supply and demand, plus the principle of the division of labour, worked in such a way that production and consumption were automatically related to one another and thus through the exercise of self-interest based on man, both as producer and consumer, the good of all was advanced! No regulation of government was necessary because there could be no real conflict of interest. It would always be in everyone's interest to be related to the market in a way that would make either his labour or his capital, or both, productive for himself and for his neighbour.

In view of the expanding nature of the economy of the day, plus the reality of a developing market economy as well as the optimism of men concerning human nature, it was hardly likely that this happy interpretation would be challenged. *If there were immutable laws of nature which were clear to rational men, there must also be equally clear moral laws that are also discernible.* John Leland pointed out that this was a *non sequitur*, but his insight went largely unnoticed in a day when the only enthusiasm permitted reinforced the prejudice of this opinion.

Adam Smith was a man of deep social conscience. He was concerned about the common good, but he was made over-confident not only by the emerging successes of the economy of his day but by the theological and philosophical presuppositions of his time. As Tawney points out, Smith's theory is clean contrary to the Christian ethic, an ethic that had been given at least some real deference in relation to the economy in the past but was now brushed aside, except as philanthropy, by the paying, and the increasingly affluent, members of society.

It is not surprising, given the spiritual and intellectual context which prevailed at the end of the seventeenth century, that the accommodation arrived at ecclesiastically in 1688 was looked upon as altogether the most "reasonable" of all solutions. The leadership of the Church of England from Tillotson through Paley at the end of the eighteenth century was firmly of that conviction. This made it easy under the compromise and patronage system for Walpole to use the church increasingly to serve political and social ends. Hoadly (1676-1761) defended this in the Bangorian controversy, even though he horrified most of his fellow bishops by saying that true religious faith was a matter of the individual conscience and as such could neither be created nor defeated by fiat of government. Every government, he claimed, needed the services of an established religion, as for example in the state religion of Rome, in order to encourage peace and order. Since the religious faith of the majority of people in England was Christianity, it was perfectly legitimate for the state to use the establishment of this religion for its own purposes which were not, in any case, those of religious concern *per se*.

This piece of erastianism satisfied no one. It undercut the authority of the church because it failed to make any connection whatever between the visible and invisible church, as Calvin had been careful to do, and thus gave over the whole field to private conscience. This may have been acceptable to some extreme Dissenters but to no one else. On the other hand, it justified the use of the establishment by government much as it saw fit. This outraged the Dissenters as well as every sincere reformer within the church for it seemed to justify every prevailing abuse.

Warburton (1698-1779) recovered the situation by a highly rational defense of the *status quo* which strove to give a modicum of authority to the church within its own sphere. The state was to guarantee the faith of the majority of its citizens and to strengthen and to maintain the church's proper ends as a religious institution. This was not inconsistent with granting limited exemption to those who in good conscience could not conform because history had shown that in religious matters men could not be coerced.

He claimed that invincible ignorance brought about by our environment blinds the eyes of all of us to some degree.

On the other hand, the state had the right to require that the religious establishment not threaten the peace of the realm. He thus justified the exclusion of Roman Catholicism from any recognized privileges. At the same time, the religious establishment ought to forward the general moral life of the people in return for the help it received from the state. Religion for the great generality of men was considered a matter of common sense and of prudent morality, not something over which men should get excited, or, to use the despised word of the day, "enthusiastic."

While it is true that Warburton was in most respects in the tradition of Hooker, his was essentially an eccelsiastical rather than a theological resolution of the problem. It certainly did nothing to deepen the vitality and insight of the church at large but rather enabled her to settle for the *status quo*.

By the time we get to William Paley, at the end of the century, we have altogether lost any vision of the role of the church other than as a utilitarian agency to spread the knowledge of Christianity. The church was reduced to a moral agency for the reinforcement of the orders of society as then constituted. In his sermon entitled "A Distinction of Orders in the Church Defended upon Principles of Public Utility,"[2] he claimed that the threefold order of the ministry was a most happy arrangement since it provided a class of clergy for each class in society! We recall that it was just at this time that the church was being heavily relied upon in the countryside to maintain social control during a period when the heady ideas of the French Revolution were being introduced to England and when there was great social distress because of famine. Richard Watson was only in this company in so far as he was indifferent to theological issues on any other basis than Locke's approach. In other respects his desire for reform of the church led to his banishment from any position of influence. We must also claim for Paley, on the positive side, a sensitivity to the need for complete religious liberty.

What we have recounted here, of course, is the description of a function that religion is frequently called upon to fulfill in human society, namely that of a conserver rather than a transformer of it. Yet even in this respect those who represented this particular position failed. In the last analysis they gave in to an erastian conception of the relationship of church and state. Political interest gained the upper hand so that even when Edmund Gibson, through his *CODEX* in the 1730's, wanted to bring about a correction in some of the abuses in the church, his effort was frowned upon as an attempt on the part of the church to reassert not simply its independence but some measure of *direct* influence as in the days of Laud. This was a far cry from any realistic possibility. A further illustration of the predominance of political interest was the cynical refusal by Walpole of relief for the Dissenters in the same decade because he felt he had done enough for them to keep them content. No more was necessary. He represented *realpolitik*. He made no claim to statesmanship. Because the church was in the grip of political lay leadership that had little concern for its basic purpose and because it was led by those who were too weak on the one hand to challenge that leadership or on the other to defend the church itself, it was incapable of really creative and dynamic leadership throughout the remainder of the century.

This was not true of the whole church. The Non-Jurors along with some of their spiritual descendants such as Law and Butler and Wesley, as well as the low church evangelicals, must be excepted. The point to be made is not, of course, in the position they each represented but rather that they were clearly willing to give up preferment for religious conviction. Archbishop Sancroft after 1688 paid a price for his faith and this was exceptional among men in the post-Restoration period. There was a depth of piety among the Non-jurors which kept alive the insight that religious faith, if it is to be vital, must have a dimension that goes deeper than expediency. Both Law and Wesley's family roots were in this tradition. Religion, they had learned, was no trifling matter.

What eventually happened to this movement is important for an understanding of the Tory rather than the Whig position throughout the eighteenth century. When it became apparent that there was no hope whatever of the restoration of the old line of the monarchy, the Non-jurors had to find some justification for their earlier concern. Their claim was that from whatever source political authority may in fact arise when it does it is to be recognized as a gift from God and obeyed as such. For the gifts of peace and order are for the sake of righteousness among men and for the containment and eradication of immorality and its consequent anarchy and disorder. The only time constituted authority may be challenged is when it deliberately contravenes the Word of God. Then passive obedience is to be enjoined, and Christians must suffer awaiting the just retribution that will inevitably come to unjust rulers.

This was the attitude to authority that Wesley inherited from his non-juring ancestry and which he held until his death. Rulers are responsible not to the people but to God and God's Justice as well as His Mercy. This was a far cry from Hobbes and Locke who found power to originate among the people on the basis of contract for the sake of protection of property. It was also a far cry from radicals like

Priestley, Paine and Godwin in the latter part of the eighteenth century who found power to originate solely in the inalienable rights that had been granted to every man by his Creator. In his attitude to government Wesley was with Burke, but for the much more profound religious reasons we have mentioned above. At the same time, he had a profound sense of responsibility that rulers had to fulfill the will of God as reflected in the doing of justice and mercy toward all men *regardless of their station in life*. That point of view appeared to be something new under the sun. The point we wish to make here is that the Non-Jurors and their descendants represented one stream of religious life that was not simply a reflection of prevailing values in human culture but one which moved against the stream and later had some creative, formative influence within it.

It is no wonder that a church worshipping a God so domesticated came so easily under the domination of the state. The tragedy was not ecclesiastical but theological. The church as institution had proven itself open to the abuse of political power as much as any other human institution. Moreover, religious fanaticism *had* proven a danger to the welfare of the wider community. Locke's response to this in his essay "On Toleration" was to claim rightly that governments ought not to coerce the consciences of men. Therefore, in the final analysis, a man's religion must be his private concern. The institutions of religion must be separated from those of the state and there must be no *direct* interference of the religious institution in the affairs of the state.

One can hardly argue that this was anything other than an immense gain for British society. Yet the immediate effect of this approach was to weaken the influence of religious conviction in the political and in the economic arenas and to relegate religion to the realm of the purely subjective. Inadvertently this led to the tendency which prevails in modern secularized society to break life up into separate compartments, public and private, interior and exterior. Political, economic and intellectual life came to have an autonomy of their own. This has led to increased specialization and fascination with the detail of life. The strength of such a view is that it contributes to the complexity and richness of human culture. Its weakness is that it has been unable to provide a common ground, a depth dimension, upon which public and private interest might be reconciled and made to serve one another with a minimum of coercion. That common ground was lost because Locke and those who followed him throughout the eighteenth century failed to distinguish between the need for a common uncoerced recognition of the sovereignty of God over the whole of life, as an article of faith necessary to the integrity of human life as such, and its expression in and through the institutions of religion at any given time. In such a view the element of non-coercion does not have its justification in human necessity but is a reflection of the nature of the relationship between God and man. Of course, the strength of such a view must depend upon the degree of its acceptance in the ethos of any age. It was not the alternative chosen by those who shaped the life of eighteenth century England.

II

It would be an error to suggest that the "age of reason" as reason was generally defined in the eighteenth century resulted altogether in loss or that that definition of reason went unchallenged.

The new faith in man's capacity to reason along with

the concomitant rise of the scientific method was responsible for the growing control over his environment which, until recently, as moderns we thought we possessed.

But it is with the challenges to that concept of reason from within the period itself that we are here concerned.

Pascal (1623-1662) attacked that view and had he lived longer he might well have influenced the whole flow of seventeenth and eighteenth century thought more than he was able to do. He was convinced that man's reason was deepened and enlarged through faith rather than circumscribed by it, and that the narrow method of deduction introduced by Descartes was a tragic over-simplification of human understanding. He was to France what the Cambridge Platonists were to England. His voice was muffled, however, by the prevailing climate of the times.

William Law, in his *Case of Reason* (1731) was the first to attack the champions of rationalism on the English scene. His work was a reply to the deist Matthew Tindal who had argued that God's creation was perfect from the beginning and that man as the creature of God was granted reason to grasp both the perfection of God and of his handiwork. Why man had not done so long since, Tindal never explained. Law pounced on the inadequacies in Tindal's argument and suggested that God might be great enough to transcend the mind of man! Law himself was overcome by the majesty of God, but his sensitivity in this regard found little acceptance among his fellowmen.[3] His mysticism did have some influence among the Society of Friends and to some extent was the ground for their renewed vigour on behalf of social justice in the latter half of the century.

The next to do battle was Bishop Berkeley in his *Alciphron* (1732). He challenged Locke's easy transition from the thing perceived to the one who does the perceiving. In a pattern reminiscent of Platonic idealism he came to the conclusion that it is not the external thing but its internal image in our minds that alone is real. He argued that we are given this capacity to so order the external universe by the ordering power of God who is the source of all ideas and the most real of all realities. However, an age that took the empirical world so for granted, that was beginning to do amazing things with its natural environment, was hardly likely to believe that that world was anything but very real and intensely interesting. It paid little attention to Berkeley or to his criticisms of Locke's presuppositions.

A further attack was instigated by Bishop Joseph Butler in his *Analogy of Religion* (1736). He argued that one could not so easily infer from the discoveries of science that all nature was a harmony and he pointed out facets of it which denied this. He drew attention to the fact that other religions as well as Christianity had their dark as well as bright sides, and that man left to his own resources had proven quite as unreasonable, ruthless and immoral as he had at times shown himself capable of the opposite. He pointed out the mythological nature of the primitive man, the "noble savage" dear to Hobbes, Locke, and most especially Rousseau. Reason left to its own resources can establish only that which is not certainly but only probably true. If this is the case the probability of Christianity's truth, which cannot be proven, is just as great if not greater than any other alternative view. Butler, himself, proved that he was a man of his own age by conceding so much to reason. Nevertheless, through probability and analogy he presented a respectable alternative to the more prosaic views of the Augustan age.

The one who logically dealt the *coup de grace* to an unbounded confidence in reason was David Hume. With ruthless logic he pointed out that the easy transition from the thing perceived to the perceiver's perception could not be taken for granted. He was skeptical not only of man's capacity to grasp the phenomenal, but also of the reality of the noumenal, to use Kant's phraseology. For one thing, both what is perceived and the perceiver are in a constant state of flux so that "the knowledge" that may be meaningful or adequate at one moment is not the next. Everything and everyone, in a way reminiscent of Buddhist psychology, is in a state of flux. What does one moment does not do the next. Such were the limitations of reason! While Hume had nothing to offer in its stead, he identified the metaphysical problem, the split between subject and object, that has badgered western man ever since. This was an immense accomplishment, yet he was given little recognition, because men in that day did not want to hear it.

Moreover, Hume himself became practically frightened of the consequences of his own thought. Since man could be certain of so little, what was he to rely upon for guidance? The answer to that was that he was safest to rely upon custom, upon what had been found useful in the past. His thought, while radical then, was countered by his conservative attitude toward social practice. In that regard he was closer to Burke than to anyone else.[4] What better to do than what had always appeared to be best for the greatest number of people. Those numbers turned out to be strangely distorted in favour of those who already held power. Thus, while men such as Locke and Hume may on the one hand appear to be progressive in their thinking, that thinking as well as their influence tended to be thrown on the side of those who already held power and property.

Though strictly speaking Wesley and the evangelical movement in the Church of England in the latter half of the eighteenth century were not interested in attacking the basis for confidence in the sufficiency of human reason, in practice they did so. Wesley, like Law, asserted the traditional faith of the reformers wherein faith is regarded as trust, as response of the whole man to the challenge of the whole of life. Reason can never be abstracted from the stream of life but is always involved in it. Whatever may be the case with regard to the way in which we may understand the material world, in the area of human relationships, of moral choice, of purpose and meaning for life, the rules are different. Men must decide on the basis of a faithful or faithless trust in the reality and goodness of a God who is always more than we are. The note that Pascal had struck a century before was struck again. A note that was to be struck once more a century later by Kierkegaard. On this presupposition all men were the concern of God and therefore the poor were His concern. Amazing discovery! It made unwitting revolutionaries out of conservatives like Wesley and Wilberforce. Or so it seemed in the eyes of a true conservative such as Edmund Burke.

In Edmund Burke we have the final *tour de force* against the cult of reason. Those who had followed its path he claimed had divorced themselves from any sense of the past. They were the first "reasonable" men according to themselves and in their revolutionary call to liberty, along with their fellow travellers in France, they displayed how unwelcome and inadequate was their approach. Truly "reasonable" men would trust traditional custom; they would observe the moral and spiritual dictates of the past, if they were proper God-fearing men! The French revolutionaries had cried justice, but in a brief few years had proven themselves the most tyrannical and unjust of men. Decent men prefer order, with the trust, he claimed that justice would be done *gradually*. Freedom must at best be extended to others only over time.

So, as Cragg and many others have pointed out, the age that started out with what appeared to be a free field for the exercise and supremacy of human reason ended in a great retreat from it in the extremism of the French Revolution and the reaction to it in other European nations, especially Britain. This was to be followed by the rise of romanticism in Wordsworth and Coleridge and subjectivism in theology as represented by Schleiermacher. This is further to illustrate the close interrelationship between thought on the one hand and prevailing practice in the structures of the social order on the other.

To sum up, then, there were at least five different reactions to the age in which reason sought to reign supreme.

The first was a continuing, though superficial, confidence in the competency of human reason as Locke had understood it. This was reflected later in the thinking of William Paley who represented the official position of the church. In politics it meant a continued support of the Whig position at first through Walpole and at the end through a person like Charles James Fox. Church and State had their separate but complimentary roles to play with the church still regarded as the handmaiden of the state, as charged with a deep responsibility for maintaining order.

The second group who continued to base their approach on an undaunted faith in the limitless capacity of human reason was that small group of radical non-conformists, deists like Godwin, Priestley and Price. They challenged the accepted order in almost every way and would accept very little on faith. They regarded themselves as pioneers for freedom of conscience and as champions of justice for all men. Yet their ideas were too abstract, too far from those of the poor who needed justice most to be heard by them.

The remaining three positions are related to each other in that they represent reaction against the "cult of reason." The first of these is represented by Edmund Burke, who found tradition safer than reason, and who was convinced that order was more precious than freedom. He also felt profoundly that religion should be used by the state to stabilize society and so set himself steadfastly against change. Burke's influence set back the cause of justice and freedom extended to the labouring poor at least two generations.

A fourth position was that of Wesley and the wider evangelical movement. Even though they shared in a respect for a rational defence of their position, which is exemplified in the great majority of Wesley's works, they interpreted reason as the handmaid of faith, not faith as the servant of man's rational faculty. Their activity had at least as deep an influence for social justice as did that of the radicals, if not much more so.

The fifth position carries us into the nineteenth century and is reflected in the Romanticist movement. It, however, was highly individualistic and hardly capable of establishing a whole view of life that would include a view of the nature of God's sovereignty that embraced all men and all nature and called both for the widening of reason's horizons as well as man's concern for his fellowman, though Coleridge did indeed anticipate the Christian socialist movement.

III

It was not so much the theoretical battle over man's capacity to reason which brought into question those who had unbounded confidence in it but the continued realities of suffering and evil. Hume's response was obviously one of fear. The best the Deists and Benthamite radicals could offer was the hope that "in the long run" reason and justice would prevail. But the suffering of the masses was there for all to see, not to mention the tenuous and ambiguous nature of life for rich and poor alike. It was the nature of reality itself which challenged the more superficial claims for the authority of reason. It also proved the basis for the wide following which the evangelical movement enjoyed among the populace at large. We must, therefore, deal more directly with the basic presuppositions of that movement.

We have pointed out that earlier theological discussions concerning predestination and its alternative, free will, had been put aside by an age that found it impossible to believe that man had no part whatever in deciding his own destiny, both in this world and the next. Locke had been under Arminian influence in Holland and through his influence, as well as the temper of the times, even the modified predestinationism of Baxter had become unpopular.

Not only the freedom of man but the problem of evil was a baffling one to the men of reason. Indeed, if the rational, moral nature of the universe were as obvious as the Deists had said, why had men not discerned this truth and in their own interest followed it? On the other hand, could reasonable men believe that they were to be held responsible for evil they had not committed? Yet again, how could the God of Mercy of Love and Truth also be the deliberate author of evil? The concept of a self-limiting deity and of inherited social evil had not yet emerged as a possibility, partially because all were bound to a linear, literal interpretation of scripture. The only alternative to it at that time was allegory, which was still less acceptable to the rationalist mind. The concept of development was just emerging but had not taken hold.

However, the problem of evil was bound to arise as soon as religious faith was taken seriously again by a significant number of men. It is not surprising, therefore, that it was over this issue that Whitefield and Wesley divided. As early as 1738 John Taylor had seriously attacked the problem of original sin and could not bring himself to affirm it, yet found the alternatives equally unsatisfying. Whitefield took the position of double predestination, a position that has been held, some would claim, by Augustine, certainly by Calvin, but has never been a confirmed doctrine of orthodox Christianity. It is tempting to believe that Whitefield clung to this doctrine, at least in part, because his ministry was much more to the upper and middle classes than was Wesley's, though this was by no means exclusively the case. If it is believed, as it was by both protagonists, that all men are sinners and come short of the glory of God, then all men are equal in their standing before God and the equalitarianism that Wesley emphasized is the result. Yet, if *some* are elect, then on that basis they are entitled to special privilege. Indeed, it was the later "puritans," and the lesser ones, who began to identify their commercial success with their election. At least one could vindicate his privileged station in this way, as Whitefield enabled his followers to do. But if all men had the same opportunity, then it was possible for a man to change his standing in every way. That was the practical implication of Wesley's Arminian teaching. The offer of salvation was universal, and it was conditional only upon a man's acceptance of it and his willingness to bear fruit of its evidence in good works.

This view was congenial to an age which found it more and more easy to believe in the gradual perfectibility of man, to be optimistic about him either on the grounds of faith, as was the case with the Methodists, or on faith in "nature" as with Adam Smith. In a time of expansion and of the objective possibility of upward mobility in society this

was good doctrine indeed. At the same time, in view of the
remaining crudeness and inhumanity of man, evidenced in
famine, in general immorality, and in social injustice
brought about by the changes in the economic system, it was
equally impossible to believe, as Priestley did, in some
pure goodness in man. The truth lies between. It must be
said, in all fairness to the radicals, however, that,
together with those involved in the evangelical revival, it
was they who began to stir an interest in the latter part of
the century in social reform. Both believed that the world
could be different than it had been. Perfection was not
only a theological doctrine in which it was possible to
believe but a secular hope born on the wings of human
"progress."

  It is not our intent here to go into the theology of
this movement in depth. That can be achieved either by
reading the works of those directly involved or more suc-
cinct collections of them such as Outler's *John Wesley*.
Without doubt, the evangelical revival had the most transforming impact of any religious movement of the day on the
total life of eighteenth century England. We concentrate on
Wesley here not because he was the only one who contributed
to the movement, but because he was the principal one whose
activities continued to have a lasting effect upon British
society. This was largely due to his genius for organization, which brought the Methodist Church into being even
against his own intent. The movement had its followers also
among faithful churchmen like Romaine and Simeon, the Venns
and Thorntons as well as Wilberforce, to name only the best
known. All save the last were leaders in the Clapham sect.

  What Wesley, and those like him, did was to change
entirely the grounds of debate over religion. He was not
interested in interminable debate *about* religion, nor was he
interested simply in manners and morals as so many of his

fellow churchmen were. He was interested in a vital religious, we would say existential, faith which involved the whole man. He was not the descendant of Descartes but of Pascal and the Cambridge Platonists. Faith must be free to inform reason, but it is not irrational. Faith is complete trust in the object of its faith, which object is antecedent to that faith. It is its author in the sense that it makes the response of faith a possibility at all.

This is what Wesley meant by prevenient grace. We are continually surrounded by the activity of a God who anticipates our good and continually seeks it for us. That God has acted for our salvation made necessary through our sin, the abuse of our freedom first indulged by our ancestor Adam, through the gift of His only Son, who paid the price made necessary by the justice of God. In his doctrine of the atonement Wesley followed Anselm's ransom theory. But it was God's love for all men that made this act possible in the beginning. It is, therefore, God's love for all men that makes our salvation a possibility.

Wesley returns to the great reformation doctrine of justification by faith found in the Thirty-Nine Articles. In this he is the friend of Calvin, too, but he does not follow him when it comes to double predestination. We are invited to respond to others in terms of that same agapeic, other-regarding love of which God has made us the objects in the first place. God is thus the One who assures us that we are loved and sets us free, as a result, to love others. Through our renewal, which is the beginning of the life of sanctification, we move into a life which can grow into the image of God. We may also, according to Wesley, fall from grace. Thus we must not presume upon God or claim too much for ourselves. Wesley insists upon the fact that sanctification is a cooperative endeavour.

Moreover, he is unwilling to limit the possibilities of

God working His perfect will within and through us. This was the basis of his doctrine of perfection. It was not that a man could reach some final *form* of perfection, but that it was possible for a man to completely conform his will to the love of God and of his neighbour. A man might be in a state of perfection and lose it. He may aspire after it as Wesley did himself and confess like Wesley that he had never attained it. What this doctrine did was to accentuate the positive. In an age when men of affluence, then as now, found hope too easy and the poor found it impossible, the assurance of the latter that they were loved by God, that they could become different persons, not some time in the future but here and now, that they could at least begin the journey, brought hope to the hopeless. It actually did transform their capacity to deal with the world which was theirs rather than to be defeated by it.

Compared with Saul Alinsky, or even Martin Luther King in our day, Wesley was an organizer of the poor *par excellence*. Through his faith he was able to produce hope, and that hope was not disappointed, partially because the other factors in the equation, especially the economic, were expansive and thus supportive.

It is true that Wesley nevertheless had a strong doctrine of the elect. That is to say he believed, with the great majority of men in his day, in a literal judgment. Only those who responded to God's goodness within the span of their lifetime would enter into eternal blessedness while others would be completely excluded. He also believed that God willed that all should be saved--"Whosoever will." This meant that he had a strong sense of discipline and translated it into the organization of his societies. They were an *ecclesiola in ecclesia*. They were called out of the world for the salvation of their individual souls, but, at the same time, they were called to win others by the same expression of love toward them that God had displayed in Jesus Christ. Thus, while they lacked any sense of corporate sin and corporate salvation which accentuated the stress on the individual so characteristic of the eighteenth century view of man, they overcame it, at least within their own societies, because, as Warner says, *the individual will was socialized*.

There was a sense, however, in which Wesley himself escaped from this narrowness because he felt that he was only bringing into the fold of the church those who had been outside. In truth his perspective was not narrow, but broad and deep. He owed his faith not only to the Reformers but to the early church Fathers and so in his eclecticism was both catholic and reformed. In his faithfulness both to the Homilies, the Liturgy, the Sacraments and the Orders of the Church of England he was a loyal churchman. He would not, however, as he said, suffer himself or other men to be "half-way Christians." His understanding of the faith involved the whole man, head and heart, will and emotions. As Outler says of him,

> He was a creative theologian practically involved in the application of his doctrine in the renewal of the church. Few of his doctrinal views are abstruse and none is original. It is their sum and balance that is unique, that gives him a distinctive theological stance. The elements of his theology were adapted from many sources: the prime article of justification by faith from the reformers (Anglican) of the sixteenth century; the emphasis on the assurance of faith, from the Moravian pietists; the ethical notions of divine-human synergism, from the ancient Fathers of the Church; the idea of the Christian life of devotion, from Taylor, à Kempis,

Law (Scougal), the vision and program of perfection, from Gregory of Nyssa via 'Macarius.'[5]

There was nothing narrow, then, in Wesley's faith, though we cannot claim that either he, or even those in the wider revival in the church such as the members of the Clapham sect had aesthetic interests. In this they were descendants of the earlier "puritans." But it may also have been that they were simply too busy with the needs of men to have time for such. Moreover, Wesley's conception of moral good was not petty.

> By good I mean conducive to the good of mankind, tending to advance peace and goodwill among men, promotive of the happiness of our fellow creatures-- and by evil what is contrary thereto.[6]

He sought to "lessen men's sorrows" here and now, but taught them in accord with the Tory convictions we have outlined, "in whatsoever state they are, therewith to be content."

Yet the sense of worth and stability that not only the lower middle class of skilled artisans, who made up the bulk of his leadership, and the poor gained through the faith he interpreted meant that their this-worldly station was in fact frequently changed. While men like Hartley were arguing illogically that men were both totally conditioned by their environment and yet free to change it and thus encouraging men to strive, Wesley insisted on man's freedom to determine his destiny under God. In this regard, too, he was in harmony with the sense of control that eighteenth century man began to think he had over his environment and in large measure was beginning to gain.

Yet Wesley and others connected with the revival were in so many ways creatures of their time. At times incredulous, bound to literal interpretations of scripture, and sometimes impatient of sound hard thinking, dismissed because its practical value was not obvious.

Nevertheless, Wesley had a consuming desire to serve God and God's intent for man as he understood it. The immediate sense of the presence of God was the ground for his faith, but this was confirmed by the witness of church, scripture and his own experience. Its greatest weakness was the conviction that salvation was individual, so that the corporate nature of salvation was altogether lost. It was modified to some extent by the commitment that was expected of the individual believer to the welfare of his fellowman, even though the believer was "called out from among them," that is, from among unbelievers. The believer could not see that so long as he participated in social injustice he was to that degree himself at best only partially "saved."

For Wesley an overruling Providence was in final command both of ongoing history and of man's eternal destiny. There was "a force which makes for righteousness among men," and those in authority as well as those called upon to obey authority were finally responsible to the One whose Hand was over all. It was God who was responsible for the orders of creation and it was to God one must answer. The basis of political and social life was God's justice and mercy. It was this which tempered Wesley's lack of attention to political matters, since he considered himself a man with a religious not a political mission. On the other hand, he was ready to take the government on when he considered its acts unjust. Most frequently, however, he left the task of social reform, as for instance in the case of slavery, as well as of prisons, to others. Lesser men who followed him easily identified their own affluence with the will of Divine Providence and did little to deal with the problems of social injustice even within the fellowship of the Methodist Societies, which was a factor in their ending in division.

The fact that there was a deep equalitarianism within the Methodist Societies, while at the same time they lacked a theory of equalitarianism for society itself, led finally to the view that we must do good to others out of a sense of duty toward them. We must give alms. *There was no vision of a renewed corporate society whose structures would be at least more just than those which prevailed*. Even the Benthamites were convinced that as things were organized more and more would be included in the advancing wealth so that there was no need for structural reform. A radical like Priestley had no program save education for the poor until they could join the middle classes. With growing confidence in *laissez-faire* interpreted by Adam Smith, it could hardly be expected that anyone would regard the suffering of the poor as anything other than temporary, if not deserved. Above all, the church entrapped in the least progressive aspect of the *status quo* was unlikely to come forth with creative solutions. The evangelical revival issued in at best a social compassion that was essentially an attitude of charity toward those less fortunate.

However, just as the inadequacies of "reason" were to be challenged by the reaction of an idealistic Romanticism based upon feeling, so the time would come when the cracks in the wall of a system based upon automatic *laissez-faire* would become apparent, at least to those sensitive to the suffering of others such as an F. D. Maurice and even a Karl Marx!

PART III

THE NEW ORDER UNDER JUDGMENT

Chapter Seven

THE NEW AGE: ITS STRENGTHS AND WEAKNESSES

The failure of many studies to measure accurately the role of religion in the modernization of England has to a large degree resulted from too circumscribed a view of what was going on in English society over a sufficiently lengthy period. There is no magic in the turn of a century. The implications of what was occurring in the religious, political, economic and social life of England during the eighteenth century did not have its full affect for good or ill until at least the middle of the nineteenth century. Only then did a new political and economic order emerge, the barest outlines of which had been apparent in the eighteenth century. Only by then is it possible to see the consequences of that new order for religion and for society at large and to estimate what influence the so-called "evangelical revival" had in turn upon it. Only by then did the deficiencies in the new order itself become sufficiently clear for sensitive spirits to discern them in the interests of a deeper humanity. Here, then, we shall record in broadest outline the actual changes which took place and the movements associated with them from the early decades of the eighteenth century through the middle of the nineteenth as they worked themselves out in the social, political, economic and religious life of England.

I

Nothing illustrates more clearly the thesis that one

must take into consideration the whole spectrum of human life if one is to adequately account for social change than when we consider those changes which took place during the eighteenth century in England. Some have attributed them primarily to innovation in the economic and technical spheres, both of which were immensely important, but neither of which could have succeeded without new experimentation in education, to cite but one aspect of things, or without the acceptance of personal responsibility both on the part of those who were directing all kinds of new economic and social enterprises and that of a large mass of the labouring class. Others have attributed everything good which happened in this century to the influence of a great religious revival under Wesley and Whitefield. That revival accounts for everything from an increased sensitivity[1] to the sanctity of human life, exemplified in the movement to abolish the slave trade, to the creation of a sense of responsibility and dignity in a sufficient number of the poor to supply a labouring force for the new industry. A far more adequate assessment sees the causative factors for change in the whole complex interaction of human life from the specifically "religious" through the social to the political and economic.

Nor is this conclusion an abstraction born in the midst of the twentieth century. Rather, it was understood clearly by at least one insightful contemporary, Francis Place, who through his own empirical experience came to the conclusion that the vast changes he had known in his lifetime were to be attributed to varied causes. These range all the way from new habits of personal cleanliness, an improved system of law and order, to Sunday Schools and a new sense of personal dignity and worth on the part of the common people, partially made possible by the challenge to privilege of the French Revolution.[2]

From any adequate theological perspective one need not be less grateful for improvements in the human situation which take place in the "secular," as opposed to the traditional "sacred" realm, if those improvements as measured are *for* humankind. That the evangelical revival, made so largely effective by the profound personal concern for others and the organizing ability of John Wesley, was responsible for enabling vast numbers of poverty-stricken human beings, who prior to this time had hardly been considered persons at all, to become men and women with a sense of dignity and a new hope which gave them the capacity to be responsible, can hardly be doubted by any objective appraisal of the evidence. Yet the new developments in the economy gave outlet for the exercise of that responsibility and so reinforced it. With these forces working together, a vast change took place in the life of Britain and eventually of the whole western world, the effects of which have not yet been spent.

It is generally assumed that the eighteenth century was a period of improvement in English society. Yet that assessment can be made only after both sides of the ledger have been examined carefully. A rise in population is always a mixed blessing. That rise was both cause and result of change in the economic order. Surely the reason for the increase can be looked upon as a good, namely the fall in the mortality rate owing again to multiple factors such as improvement in foods, in personal hygiene, in medicine, in city planning and drainage, in the curbing of excessive indulgence in cheap gin and the final control of famine. These did not have their most notable effect until as late as the 1820's. In the early middle years of the eighteenth century infant mortality ranged overall from 74% to 99% of those on the poor rate in the city of London until as late as the 1820's.[3] The increase in longevity in turn gave a greater sense of personal security relative to life in this world and a deepened interest in it.

The fact if often cited that the Asiento Clauses in the Treaty of Utrecht of 1713 established Britain's right to a principal share in the slave trade. No one, it is claimed, objected to this use of human life. However, the greatest ethical merit of the Treaty of Paris, which brought peace to Europe in 1815, was its strong provisions against the trade. Contemporaries were convinced that this reflected a deepening sense of humanity which had occurred in the progress of the century.

The careful documentation of Francis Place, who had himself suffered many of the ravages of life in the century, testified that in his lifetime life had unquestionably improved for the great masses of people. He gives as evidence many of the factors we have named, above all the increased sense of dignity and freedom that was gradually being gained not only for the landed and well-to-do but for the artisan and the labourer. None of these could as easily be submitted to the press-gang or to false justice in the courts as had once been the case.

> The change in the attitude toward social questions,

says M. Dorothy George,

> which was the outcome of the new spirit of humanity, the new command of material resources and the new belief in environment rather than Providence as the cause of many human ills was at least parallelled by a progressive revolution in manners after about 1760.[4]

We could say much more, of course, about the vast increase of human knowledge which from Newton forward led men to a greater control over their environment if not over their abuses against each other. So much for the positive side of the ledger.

On the negative side, whatever may have been the case for the landed aristocracy and the growing middle class, vast numbers of the poor were the victims of famine. Every ten years throughout the century and every five years from the beginning of the nineteenth century through 1819 the country suffered bad harvests. The farmers, many of whom were themselves in a precarious and uncertain position economically, tended to hold out for high prices and to hoard their money against poorer times, contributing further to depression. Britain was at war more than at peace throughout the period, and when this was the case, prices rose, making it difficult for the poor. Whereas prices tended to be steady during the first half of the century, they fluctuated greatly during the vast changes which began to take place in the second half. Many, using the population problem as outlined by Malthus as excuse, wanted to keep the living standards of the poor down in order to decrease the population. Others, given hope by an expanding economy and the ideas of Adam Smith, thought the suffering would be taken care of "naturally." Both thus justified a lack of concern for others rather than expressed it.

While there were some industrialists who were deeply concerned about social conditions, the vast majority were too preoccupied with their business to do anything about it. Dorothy Marshall contends that the actual standard of living of the labouring classes went down during the last half of the century in the dislocations that were taking place and that overall there may have been a retrogression of living standards during the century which did not improve until the 1830's.[5]

The careful research of Robert Wearmouth has documented the thousands of riots which took place in which hundreds of thousands of the poor took part.⁶ The greatest number occurred over the high price of grain. There were others over wages, the introduction of tools and new machinery and over the Militia Act. Rarely did the government pass enabling acts to prevent the export of grain during famine periods. Here and there petitions were made to parliament, and not a few, including Wesley, sought to alleviate the condition of the poor. Yet the major response to the majority in most cases was to do nothing or to use the law repressively. While it is true that debtors prisons began to empty toward the close of the century, perhaps expressing a bias in favour of men of property who went bankrupt, one of the blackest years in English judicial history was that of 1785. That year over five hundred persons were sentenced to death and thousands transported overseas.

Throughout the century at least 50,000 persons who had committed felonies, some of them serious, the majority very minor, suffered this latter fate. As Wearmouth points out, the goal the poor sought was not to revolt against the state or even to revise the constitution but simply to provide for their basic necessities. The riots always coincided with distressing social conditions, yet there was little imagination used in the solution of their problems.

One could claim that this lack of sensibility was part of the order of the day except that there were men then, as there are now, who cried out against them. Among these were Jonas Hanway, John Howard and John Wesley. There are those at this very hour who seek to quell riots born of social injustice through the repressive exercise of the law. There were those then as now among the poor, especially among the Methodists, who were able to rise above their environment, aided by an expanding economy. *There were many more who were utterly defeated by it.* Then as now there were those ready to claim that the responsibility for poverty lay with the poor alone, but those such as Wesley, who knew the poor and cared about them, understood how viciously wrong that judgment was.

When the ledger is balanced, what is to be said? Was the eighteenth century one of improvement for the great bulk of the people? There can be little doubt that if our measure is simply "the greatest good for the greatest number in the long run," we must come down on the positive side. Though there was much that was unreformed in church and state that should have been changed long since and which compounded human suffering, changes that were taking place both in those structures and most especially in the economic augured for a greater well-being for mankind.

Yet, change itself is no guarantee that our last estate will be better than our first. The dislocation which took place in the lives of hundreds of thousands of people as a result of the new technology, and the fact that there was an absence both of planning and of structures for human service in society, meant that the benefits of the new ways of doing things did not accrue in any significant measure to the great bulk of the people until after the middle of the nineteenth century. Even then very much was left to be desired, so far as the labouring and poorer classes were concerned. Dorothy George is not altogether convincing when she insists that there was unquestionably a better way of life for everyone at the close of the eighteenth century than had ever been the case before. While there was an overall improvement in the standard of living which is clearly indicated in the fall of the mortality rate from one in fifteen at birth in the decade 1749-59 to one in 118 in 1799 to 1800, as T. S. Ashton records,[7] as we have noted above, it ranged from 74-99% among the poor through 1820!

The overall improvement must be attributed to several factors working in conjunction with one another. Among them were the improvement in diet brought about by the increased availability of fresh meats all year round and the other improvements in agriculture which made a more varied diet a possibility. New types of clothing made personal cleanliness an easier possibility as did the disappearance of the gin age after 1751. Moreover, the appearance of coffee houses created an attractive alternative, especially for the middle classes.

Brick was increasingly being used in housing and so simple a thing as whitewash cut down on dirt and rodents inside households. There was great improvement in drainage systems in the cities between 1780 and 1815, and, while at this later date a significant number of the Irish in particular were still living in cellars in the new industrial cities, these had been done away in London and for the most part in other cities.

Certain reforms in the administration of justice were also gradually being adopted, even though what we have said earlier of repressive measures lasting until after the Napoleonic Wars is true. The Fieldings strove to use their influence to take the city magistrates offices out of a system that made deals over justice profitable, and they were also instrumental in having a Metropolitan Police force established, though in its final form this did not take place until 1828. London life had become safer, especially for those who had anything to lose. While there were 60,000 in debtors prison in 1716, we are told by John Howard that there were only some 2,276 in 1779, though Colquhoun sets the number at 10,000 in 1802. Nevertheless, distinctions with regard to crime were being made and vast improvement was just around the corner, even though in the last two decades of the eighteenth century the law was especially repressive with regard to stealing and the like. This reflected the deep insecurity of the ruling classes because of the French Revolution which may also explain the difference in the figures for those in debtors prison.

The apprenticeship system based on the old type of manufacture, with its abuses, was beginning to crumble and was being replaced by that of a voluntary kind, even though parish apprenticeship lasted on until 1844.

Gradually the new economy was becoming more rationalized as the second generation of industrialists began to take over and the problems of the new factory system became more apparent. Indeed, Ashton excuses many of the abuses of this period by the optimistic yet true comment that scientific processes had outrun the adjustments that society had to make to them if they were to benefit more than a small proportion of the populace.

When all this has been said, we must never forget the great measure of human suffering undergone by the masses of the poor, men, women and children, as they were tossed to and fro, now in this direction, now in that, even as employment in the new factories opened up. Owing to great fluctuations in the market and the lack of advanced marketing techniques, employment was necessarily unpredictable. Inadequate poor relief could not begin to measure the need, and so there were numerous riots severely repressed, and countless women and children died while the mills and mines and factories ground on. In 1777 Wesley commented that the prisoners of Newgate were better off than his poor adherents in Bethnal Green, where poverty was the worst he had ever seen.

It is true that by the end of the century, due to the appearance of new machinery and the efforts of the reformers, both legislation and life were beginning to catch up with the very abuses of the new economy. This was beginning to affect beneficially the lives of women and also of the children of the poor. Dorothy George points to the fact that the Combination Acts had to be repealed as early as 1824, as evidence that the worker was even then coming into his own.[8] He was too necessary to the new system to have his rights ignored altogether. She also feels that the Chartist movement as well as other organized activity by the labouring class in the first half of the nineteenth century was evidence, not that the labourer's lot had in any sense declined, but that he had now experienced enough of the worthwhile in life to make him discontent.

While it is true that social conditions brought suffering to literally millions of persons, it is also true that the last half of the century saw a remarkable increase in legislation for social reform. The decisive action which brought the gin age to a close was not the passage of dry legislation inspired by a prohibition movement but rather the Act of 1751 when distillers were forbidden to sell by retail and when both spirit and license duties were again sharply raised. As Dorothy George points out, the measures to check excessive spirit drinking had been forced on the government in the teeth of vested interests through a protest led by the middle and trading classes, most of them Dissenters.[9] It had been the distillers, as well as the landed interests, who had surpluses of grain between 1720 and 1751, who had encouraged the abuse in the first place through making gin available at very low prices without benefit of health laws. As dispassionate an observer as T. S. Ashton not only recognized the abuse but regards the Act of 1751 as of great importance in the successful implementation of the new economy.[10]

Though the mania for gambling remained widespread and was the cause of ruin often to the financially solvent, and of pitiless suffering to countless of the labouring poor, it was at least curbed by an action of 1802 to cut down the number of days on which a lottery was drawn from forty to eight. This in turn helped to wipe out fraud and speculation connected with the lotteries.

Several licensing acts for public houses which lessened their number, as in 1752, and restricted their business to that of the licensing purpose also helped to raise the country from the stupor of the gin age and the abuses that went with it.

Also, an Act of 1787 brought about by the reforming activities of Wilberforce's Proclamation Society forbade the practice of paying wages in public houses which meant that more wage earners got home with their wages in their pockets.

We have already mentioned the reform of the municipal judiciary which took place largely through the efforts of the Fieldings and which took the profit as well as the burden out of the offices, granting the magistrates proper salaries and setting up a clerical service for conducting and recording the activities of the courts in an orderly fashion.

There were other very important acts for reform on the part of parliament such as those for prison reform in 1774, and at the turn of the century the Education Act of 1801 and the First Factory Act of 1802. However, effective acts against slavery as well as for real reform in the Factories had to wait for another forty years.

The great majority of parliamentary acts could not have been brought about without pressure from a concerned public aroused in turn by outstanding persons and the societies they formed. At the same time it is unlikely that lasting reformation could have taken place had those changes not been reflected in law and brought about gradually by effective enforcement agencies. Though there was resistance in parliament, frequently reflecting special interest, it is surprising that as much was achieved in an age when "the less government the best government" was a slogan which reflected the thinking of those who held both political and economic power.

The greatest agencies for reform during the period were those led by remarkable individuals and the societies they formed to promote particular issues. There were not only religious societies, such as the newly created missionary societies of the last decade of the century, but increased activity on the part of those such as the S. P. C. K. which had been in existence for a century. Every issue had its society. There was the society for the Reformation of Manners, for the Suppression of Vice, and a similar society, the Proclamation Society, which had both positive and negative influence in their dubious attempt to regulate other people's morals. There was the Society for the Relief of Persons Imprisoned for Small Debts and that for the Bettering of the Condition of the Poor. There was the Sunday School Society and there were among those who supported that society Wilberforce and Thornton and Zachary Macaulay and John Venn, who strongly supported and helped to bring about the State Education Act of 1801. There was the great Anti-Slavery Movement led by the members of the Clapham Sect who used both public petition and political influence to support their cause.

All of these causes were led by outstanding individuals. Most of them belonged to the upper middle classes or were among the "middling sort of men" who were to come into their greatest power after the Reform Bill of 1832. Their earlier efforts helped to make that Bill possible. The great majority of them were touched and motivated by "the evangelical revival" interpreted in its widest sense. The heroic story of those who began as early as 1772 to work toward the abolition of slavery, and did not finally succeed until 1833, is ably told in Ernest Marshall Howse's "Saints

in Politics."[11] It must not be repeated here except to say
that those who led this movement, such as the Venns,
Granville Sharp, the Thortons, Clarkson, Grant, and Shore,
Isaac Milner and Charles Simeon, were men of deep personal
piety, led in parliament by a man of the same stripe,
William Wilberforce. They had their limitations of insight
because they thought primarily in terms of doing things *for*
people, that is, in terms of personal charity. They also
had strength of will and a profound love of humanity
deepened by their evangelical faith in the love of God for
all men. It is true that they were committed to the sanctity of property and station and that they saw greater cause
for reform in the lower classes than in the upper. It is
even true that Wilberforce supported most of the repressive
action against the demonstrations of the poor at the beginning of the nineteenth century. Yet, at the same time, he
did support Peel's Factory Acts and every move for the
betterment of the poor through education and the like.
Later on in life, through his leadership and that of his
colleagues in the Clapham Sect, he was able to raise over
₤20,000,000 from the British people to indemnify those who
lost out when slaves were freed. And this was in an age
when men were accounted singularly opposed to "enthusiasm"
of any kind and when those who were striving for this
reform were fought by every force of economic interest
which claimed that a blow at slavery was a blow at "personal
property!" There were other factors, both political and
economic and humanitarian, that made for the abolition of
the slave trade, but without the leadership of the singular
individuals we have mentioned, as well as their readiness to
band together in common cause, success would not have been
won.

    It is not our intention at this juncture to assess the
relative importance of religious motivation in the varied

reform movements which sprang up in the latter half of the century, but we do want to draw further attention to the work of Wesley in this regard.

As early as 1744, and specifically in 1746, Wesley began a movement among the poor to help them help themselves through the Loan Societies. These were continued on a wider scale by others at the end of the century through voluntary Friendly Societies which, when at their best, were societies among the labouring class designed to help each other.

Wesley's efforts were singularly successful and through the Loan Societies a significant number of the labouring class were able to better themselves and eventually become not only responsible persons but sometimes wealthy in their own right. Indeed, this may well have been his most important social contribution to English life. If he failed to realize the importance of utilizing public agencies for reform because he was intent on individual repentance, he nevertheless recognized and spoke out against abuses, frequently before others had seen them. He encouraged those who were trying to bring about political measures to effect reform.

Long before John Howard awoke to the tragedy of the prison system Wesley and his followers were at work among prisoners. A follower who was in charge of the prison at Bristol had reformed it beyond recognition before the century was half through. Wesley encouraged John Howard in all his activities and regarded him as one of the finest Christian men alive. Moreover, Wesley recognized and condemned the judicial abuses that the Fieldings were seeking to reform.

In 1772 Wesley condemned the slave trade, then supported by others as economically profitable and therefore necessary to the good of the nation, as "that execrable sum of all villanies, commonly called the slave trade." In 1774 he wrote a pamphlet entitled "Thoughts upon Slavery" in which he commended the practice of the Quakers and roundly condemned the trade. The abolitionists regarded its circulation as one of the most important factors in their final success, even though Wesley, at the time he wrote it, could not conceive of any other method of reform than that of the personal abstinence of individuals from the possession of slaves. Finally, the Methodist movement did support the political agitation for abolition through the Arminian Magazine in 1788, while Wesley's last letter was a word of encouragement to Wilberforce in his efforts to free the slaves. On one petition against the trade of 352,404 nonconformist signatures 229,426 were Methodist.

As Methodism helped such men as Bundy of Bristol, Spence of York, and the Whitebread brothers of Rossendale, Oastler of Lancashire and the West Riding as well as the Ridgeways of Hanley to rise up from poverty and to join the ranks of the economically successful, so they in turn, through the Loan Societies and prison and factory reform, helped others. This does not mean that they were devoid of the relativity to their situation which plagues us all. Men such as Wedgwood were quick to join together with others to try to persuade the government to protect their special interests when they were challenged, yet they were also men who were ready to recognize that the deepest interests of humanity must always be one's major concern, if one has a serious commitment to the love of God as disclosed in Jesus Christ.

As we look over the entire century we would have to characterize it as one in which "men of property" had their way more often than not whether they owned land or belonged to the new "captains of industry." It was a period when local government and local privilege was strong. It was also one when men of privilege, as well as of financial and industrial power, were ready to use central government for their own interests. It was they who held back what might have been the earlier success of the movement for the abolition of slavery. There was great social distress beggaring the imagination among the poor which lasted well beyond the end of the century as adjustment was being made to the changes in agriculture and industry. Repression was frequently used and increased toward the end of the century as fear of the French Revolution dominated the horizon.

At the same time it was an age in which the rational application of men's minds to their environment made for real improvement in the standards of health and the length of life; when industry was slowly but surely, together with agriculture, lifting the overall standard of living. If "captains of industry" and the landed wealthy strove to further their interest at the expense of millions of the poor, it is also true that a few of them, though usually motivated by little more than charity, individually and together, dedicated themselves to the reform of abuses so obvious that they had to be made if in any sense humanity was to be recognized. It meant for some such men not simple acknowledgement of abuses but the giving of a whole lifetime to their cure.

II

At the beginning of the nineteenth century the industrial revolution empowered by the new capitalism had just begun to get underway. Merging as it has into the new technological revolution, its force has not yet been spent. The new industrial cities like Birmingham, Liverpool, Leeds and Manchester, to name only the most prominent, trebled and quadrupled their populations between 1800 and 1850. They

were again to go on to double and triple them and more by
1900. The uses and the abuses of the factory system were
yet to appear in their most virulent forms and the necessary
reforms set in motion. The political system remained unresponsive to the new economic order until the first Reform
Bill of 1832.

The necessary reforms in church-state relations did not
take place until 1828 and afterwards, while the Church of
England did not deal with its most pressing problems until
the 1830's.

The full-blown impact of individualistic *laissez-faire*
did not have its most forceful advocates in men like
Richard Cobden and John Bright until the agitation for the
repeal of the Corn Laws. While the opposition to, as well
as passage of, effective Factory Laws occurred only in the
1840's.

Yet, by the time our study closes at mid-century, the
whole new system has been called into question by a sensitive theologian, Frederick Denison Maurice, while its abuses
had been challenged all along by the equally sensitive
romanticist, Samuel Taylor Coleridge. At the very time
Maurice, the theologian, was subjecting the new order to the
full measure of Christian criticism, in the very same place,
namely the British Museum, another figure from a different
perspective was also subjecting it to criticism. That man
was Karl Marx. It is intriguing to speculate upon how influential the thoughts of the latter would now be if those
of the former had been given their due attention and had
been acted upon.

Vast economic changes continued to take place in the
life of England for the first three-quarters of the nineteenth century. It was still true in 1815, until the repeal
of the Corn Laws in 1846, that rural interests could triumph
over urban ones. There had been changes in the constitution

of the rural peoples during this period. Except for a few years between 1806 and 1832, the absolute numbers of small, independent farmers, the yeoman class, suffered a sharp decline. With the major part of the land enclosed within a decade after Waterloo, the large landholder, using the methods of the new scientific farming, put the little man to rout. The vast majority of land was either farmed by such men or let out to tenant farmers who could not continue to survive as small landholders against the efficiency of the larger farms.

William Cobbett inveighed uselessly against the new landed gentry who had made money abroad or in commerce and who then turned to the land to make money out of it. The Corn Laws represented the dominance of the landed class over the industrialists because they were thought to be in the interest essentially of the farmers and landowners, though this was not always in fact the case.

The repeal of the Corn Laws and of the Navigation Acts was evidence of the growing power of the Free Trade movement led by the new capitalists in whose interest it was to have access both to cheap, imported raw materials and to have foreign markets open to their manufactured goods. Inadvertently, their repeal also meant cheaper food for the poor and also worked in favour of lower wages, again benefiting the middle class industrialists. The victory of the Free Trade movement marks the economic ascendance of the new urban-based industrial leaders over the old landed aristocracy. This fact went alongside of, and itself made for, vast changes in political power in social and even religious relationships.

If the victory of the Free Trade movement by the mid-forties marked the ascendancy of the new middle class, many of whom were Dissenters or friendly to the Dissenting cause both religiously and politically, the Chartist movement marked at least the arrival of the competing claims of the labouring class. The labourer had nothing but the labour of his hands to sell and, at this time, in spite of agitation, frustration and untold suffering, failed to gain his full rights as a human being *because he had no share in political power*. The labourers were not men of property, either landed, or industrial, or commercial.

There were those among both the other classes such as Wilberforce and Shaftesbury, Bright and Cobden, who claimed to be agitating *for* the poor though they never envisioned a time when they would work *with*, and share *with*, the poor. It is interesting to note that Shaftesbury, whose wealth was primarily in land, worked for the Factory Laws and against Free Trade, while Bright and Cobden, who were middle class industrialists, opposed the Factory Laws on the basis that they interfered unduly with trade, while they claimed that Free Trade would bring cheaper food for the poor as well as benefit trade. So do the relativities of self-interest make themselves felt!

However, by the forties, skilled labourers, whose skills were necessary to the new economy, were beginning to discover that there was some power in their possession. They began to form Working Men's Associations among the miners and engineers and to band together jointly as associations for the protection of labour. They also provided mutual benefits of all kinds such as insurance and education. Their day, however, was a century off!

The significance of Chartism as a social movement must not be overlooked and will be dealt with in depth later on. It was essentially an effort on the part of the labouring class to right the wrongs against them *through political rather than economic means*. Labour was forced to change her tactics after the failure of Chartism, because it did not yet possess a base for political power either in sufferage or through property, which belonged to the other two classes. Labour had yet to learn that she was essential to the new economic system, and it was in order to secure her cooperation in this sphere that the other classes were gradually forced to share power with her. The Charter sought universal male suffrage, equal electoral districts, removal of property qualifications for members of parliament, secret ballot and annual general elections. Men of privilege were not yet ready to give it away in this measure, so that the movement petered out not only from apathy but from the consistent power of government arrayed against it which sapped its energies. Only the so-called "Christian Socialists" at mid-century saw clearly that man is always man-in-society, that his corporate nature and the mutual responsibility he shares for the welfare of others is religiously and therefore morally as fundamental as his individual rights. Karl Marx was making the same point on the basis of his dialectical materialism.

The really significant political change in the first half of the nineteenth century was the reflection of the actual change in economic power from the landed classes to the managers and owners of the new industrial economy. This could be stayed off through the influence of conservatives like Burke, Pitt and Wellington for a season using the bogie of the French Revolution. However, by 1830 the realities of foreign trade forced even a conservative like Canning to support the policies of the Whigs, Grey and Russell. Gradual liberalization was under way and made for the redistribution of political power both at the local and the national levels.

At the local level the justices of the peace had their power eroded as emerging problems became far too great for them to handle. Food riots, for example, became so frequent and massive after Waterloo that the old repressive penal methods would not work. Penal reform as well as the development of a more rational penal code plus the introduction of a proper police force all took power away from the justices of the peace. The whole system of poor relief was revised, which resulted in the Poor Law Amendment Act of 1834 which further reduced the role of parish vestries and the justices of the peace. It did not necessarily mean that the cause of the poor was better served because the rate had still to be raised locally and the efforts to separate the "deserving poor" from the "undeserving" were frequently arbitrary. They usually served the interests of the taxpayers. One of the inspirations for the Chartist movement was the hope of relieving the "deserving poor" from the nightmare of the "workhouse." The move away from the justices of the peace to the new forms of local government marks an essential social change from an agriculturally based society to a commercially and industrially based one.

The most important national political reform, of course, was the Reform Act of 1832, which, while it only added 217,000 persons to an electorate of 435,000, got rid of many of the rotten boroughs and gave the new towns something like adequate representation in the House of Commons for the first time. There was still a heavy property qualification so that once again it was not the labouring class who achieved the franchise but the merchants and industrialists. In 1867 a more radical reform bill was passed which doubled the electorate but still favoured the propertied classes over the labouring, though the more skilled labourer entered the electorate at this time.

From the standpoint of our interest the following pieces of legislation reflect not only the changes which took place in the distribution of power as between the landed and the industrial classes but also the significant if limited success of those movements for the humanizing of British society through 1850.

In the economic arena the battle for free trade was finally won with the final repeal of the Corn Laws in 1846 and of the Navigation Laws in 1849. Peel the Elder effected the First Factory Laws in 1802, but it took the long struggle led by Shaftesbury to put any teeth into them through the Laws of 1833 and 1847. With the help of Charles James Fox in parliament, slavery was abolished in England in 1807, but it took an indemnity to the owners raised by the Clapham Sect of ₤20,000,000 to abolish it in the Colonies by 1840. The harsh Combination Laws against labour were repealed in 1824, but new restrictive measures were passed in 1825 under the leadership of Peel. Repression was the response to outbreaks of violence occasioned by economic depression. It also reflected the fact that labour had as yet had no direct share in political power.

The Five Mile and Conventicle Acts were repealed in 1812 and the Test and Corporation Acts in 1828. A New Marriage Act of 1836 recognized marriages in other than parish churches and the University of London was permitted the right to grant degrees in 1836. However, Oxford and Cambridge were not opened to Dissenters until the 1870's, and the abolition of the church rate did not take place until 1868. Nevertheless, each of these reflected the growing power of the new industrialists and of the middle classes. On the other hand, the Established Church Act of 1836, the Pluralities Act of 1838 and the Dean and Chapters Act of 1840 represent the belated movement of parliament to finally deal with the worst abuses in the Church of England and were recognition that finally, like it or not, a new age had arrived.

The voluntary Societies of the eighteenth century became still more widespread in the nineteenth. The voluntary society was a middle class phenomenon while the associations of working men of the early nineteenth century took their model from the Methodist class meeting. The former was an effort at reform piecemeal in order to alleviate the worst abuses of the emerging order. Perhaps instinctively, though unintentionally, it blunted the edge of the radical movement among the labouring and poorer classes for a share in political power. The latter, though sometimes led by sympathetic men of goodwill who belonged themselves to the middle class, was a movement to better the condition of the working class through political action by the workers themselves. The gulf created by class distinction made it impossible for both groups to work together toward a more just society for all.

It is not too much to say that without the pressure from the voluntary societies none of the great reforms at this time in British society would have taken place. The Abolition Society collected millions of signatures over forty years in the struggle against slavery. Similar movements made the Factory Acts, the new penal codes and measures for the development of a modern educational system a possibility. While the movements for free trade represented primarily the economic interest of those who supported them, it can also be shown that in the wider suffrage movement, even in its earliest years, there were those of the middle classes who wanted to see the franchise extended to as many of the populace as possible.

While the movement for the new Factory Acts was led by a landed man like Shaftesbury who had little to lose economically, it was opposed by a man like Bright who advocated the repeal of the Corn Laws. Bright claimed it would make food cheaper for the poor while Shaftesbury, as a landed man, opposed it, thinking it would bring down the price of grain. The mixture of self-interest and altruism is then not easy to assess. That there was a close association between almost all of these movements and the religious convictions of those who took part in them we will show later.

The so-called Radical Movement as a political force must be considered here because it was a major political movement to achieve social justice in Britain at this time. In its effort to include all classes in the new social order it represented a genuine attempt to bring about a situation in which the benefits of the new economy would have been open to all. Its failure was a tragedy, the fullest implications of which the world is still suffering.

While there is little evidence that any of the landed classes were prepared to support the movement for universal suffrage and other movements, such as those for the repeal of the Poor Laws, from time to time it did represent a coalition of other interests that bridged the chasm between the middle and the lower classes. Due recognition should also be given to its pioneers in the seventeenth century, men like Paine, Godwin and Priestley. We must also include Jeremy Bentham who in 1817 had been one of the first to call for a radical reform against the aristocracy in land, church and government. He asked for a broad franchise, a secret ballot, and shorter parliaments, even though, unlike J. S. Mill two generations later, he could not see how a man could be a man without property. Nevertheless, the movement was primarily led either by skilled artisans like Cobbett, Lovett and Place, or by men frequently trained through the Methodist movement like J. R. Stephens who came from the ranks of the labourers themselves. Over three million persons, chiefly of the labouring classes, signed the Second Chartist petition.

The whole effort represented a struggle to improve the intolerable living conditions of the labouring classes

living in cities like Birmingham, Manchester, Leeds and
Newcastle, as well as to improve the lot of miners, men,
women and children who were living in conditions beggaring
the imagination. William Cobbett, Francis Place and Major
John Cartwright organized unions in the industrial areas
as early as 1815 in opposition to the Corn Laws of that
year.

It was the "massacre of Peterloo" which took place in
Manchester in 1819 which really precipitated serious
activity. On that occasion the military charged a crowd of
some 60,000 labourers gathered to hear the fiery orator
Hunt. Eleven people were killed and four hundred others
wounded, including some one hundred women. Popular indignation crossed class lines and made it possible for Place to
begin strong popular agitation against the Combination Laws.
With the help of Joseph Hume, a member of parliament, he
succeeded in 1824, but Peel was successful in countering
much of the progress made with repressive laws in 1825.
Though Place had a naïve faith that a free market would set
the labourer free to sell his labour at a fair price, he
soon saw, along with William Lovett, another artisan, that
no progress would be made unless the labourer had a share in
political power.

Continued fruitless strikes urged them on. Place and
Lovett drew up the first People's Charter in 1836 after
Lovett founded the London Working Men's Association. More
radical leaders like Attwood, O'Connor, Stephens and
Oastler in Birmingham, Leeds and Manchester presented a
second huge petition to parliament in 1839.

The final failure of the movement was due to at least
three factors. The first was the rise of the movements
leading to the revolutions of 1848 in Europe, which frightened middle class leadership; the second was the gradual
improvement in living standards among the labouring class

itself; and the third and the most important was the failure of those supporting the movement to agree over the way to achieve their goals. The wealthy Quaker philanthropist Sturge had even won John Bright to the cause until Fergus O'Connor and J. R. Stephens, as leaders of Physical-Force Chartism, declared that they were willing to use violence if necessary to achieve their goals. This made it easy for Russell and others in parliament to gather the forces of reaction in solid opposition to the goals of Chartism. He put down the great petition of 1839 easily. Moral Force Chartism took over, but the struggle over new Factory Acts and for repeal of the Corn Laws, as well as the forces mentioned above, sapped the strength of Chartism. Labour finally turned to the organization of industrial unions to achieve economically what it had failed to achieve politically.

III

When one turns to the religious situation in the first half of the nineteenth century, the empirical realities obtrude in an insistent way. The one inescapable fact was that the establishment, the Church of England, was not in fact the church of all the people, that a third of all those under the government in London were Roman Catholics, albeit Irishmen, and that half of all the people who had any *active* connection with the Christian faith in the census of 1851 were not Anglicans but Dissenters. *In effect, the situation was pluralistic not monolithic and no effective government could any longer ignore that fact.* Had the government of the eighteenth century not had so much power over the national church, the difficulties both for the church and the state might have been far less complex. The reality was otherwise. This meant that especially for the first half of the century there was not a major political issue that did not have its effect upon the established church, even upon its theology, and that the church and churchmen of all persuasions could do little that did not have political overtones.

During the conservative reaction to the French Revolution the Tories were able to pack the House of Lords with conservative bishops who resisted every attempt to bring about long overdue reforms in the church, to meet the religious needs of the hundreds of thousands moving into the cities or to deal fairly with either Dissent or the Roman Catholics. The Five Mile and Conventicle Acts were repealed in 1812, but the Test and Corporation Acts had to wait until Wellington was out of the picture in 1828. Russell was able to bring this about only when ironclad guarantees were given that the Dissenters would not use political power to disestablish the Church of England. The Catholic Emancipation Act of 1829 was passed only as a result of relentless pressure from the public and in order to deal with unrest in Ireland.

The struggle over the church rate beautifully illustrates the difficulties into which the government as well as the Church of England had gotten itself. By 1818 members of parliament finally began to recognize the tremendous shift of population that was taking place into the great urban centres. They had also witnessed the success of Methodism and the Dissenting churches in setting up chapels in these centres. They as well wanted to use the church and its influence to check unrest and later on to draw away support and interest from Chartism. Parish churches, especially for the poor, should therefore be established in the centres of unrest. This meant they had to be built from the church rate. That also led to the conclusion that funds either had to be taken from traditional sources of revenue, thus interfering with the old sacred system, or the church rate had to be increased. Since everyone had to pay the rate, Methodists and Dissenters were not prepared to meet the increase. Indeed, in 1868 they finally succeeded in having the rate done away with altogether. Since they could also attend parish meetings, they were able to vote down every attempt to alter things through increased church taxation. After all, they were already paying their tithe to build their own chapels and were not prepared to be double taxed. As a result, this belated attempt on the part of parliament to pay the price for having taken over authority that properly belonged to the church failed both the church and its own political purposes.

After it looked as though the bishops were going to vote against the Reform Bill of 1832, the hue and cry against church abuses rose to such a pitch that it could be ignored no longer. First Grey then Peel in 1835 set up a Commission to reform the church. Chadwick puts well what had to be reformed and we have returned to such abuses time and again from the beginning of this study:

> By English conservatism the church came through the Reformation altered in doctrine and liturgy, but still medieval in its legal framework. Parson's freehold, ecclesiastical courts, sinecures, parishes in commendam pluralities, wealthy livings with few parishioners, sale of advowsons, pocket boroughs of the church--it all smelt of the middle ages, an archaic order which encouraged the well placed and left the work to poor and ill-equipped curates at ₤80 a year.[12]

The composition of the Commission both of bishops, clergy and laymen was still conservative. The Archbishop of Canterbury chose the clergy and Peel himself chose the laymen. Peel also served on the Commission. After a period of time only the clergy continued to attend the meetings of the Commissioners regularly. So that, in effect, the clergy did have the freedom to make the necessary reforms.

As a result of its work, three main acts of parliament were passed: the Established Church Act of 1836, the Pluralities Act of 1838, and the Dean and Chapter Act of 1840. In the main, the first abolished livings held in commendam, distributed the bishops' stipends more equally and created two new sees while abolishing two others. It is significant that the two new sees were Ripon and Manchester. The Pluralities Act limited the number of benefices to be held by one person to two, which must be within ten miles of one another. Neither was to have a population of more than 3,000 and their joint value was not to be above ₤1,000. Both could be held only under the favour of the Archbishop of Canterbury. Also the bishop could require two full services each Sunday which were to include a sermon. The bishop was also given added powers to enforce residence in the parish. The Dean and Chapter Act of 1840 did away with the abuses that had grown up around cathedral appointments and made available, along with the results of the other reforms, a sum of ₤360,000 with which the Commissioners could begin to lift the salaries of the poorer clergy and to help the new parishes in the cities.

The extent to which the state had become involved in church affairs to everyone's embarrassment became clearly evident in the theological issues of the day. The famous Hampden and Gorham cases illustrate the predicament. Hampden was appointed Regius Professor of Divinity at Oxford by Lord Melbourne and finally made a bishop under Russell in 1848. In Gorham's case the courts of justice decided that, as an Anglican clergyman, his doctrine did not "contradict the formularies of the Church of England" over against the protests of Bishop Philpotts of Exeter. Hampden represented a position that was very close to the rationalism of Paley some years before, and Gorham, as an evangelical, claimed that baptism had no significance unless confirmed by the experience of regeneration in the heart of the adult believer. Both of these moves were strongly opposed by the Oxford Movement within the Church of England.

What the Oxford Movement saw in all this was a threat to the essential integrity of the Church of Jesus Christ. They represented the spirit of the Non-Jurors a century and a half before and the quality of the men they attracted to their movement was comparable. They were devout, ascetic, committed. They believed in the unity of the church on the basis of the early creeds and the teaching of the fathers. Rome was schismatical because it had separated itself but so were the Dissenters because they tried to find a unity on something other than the creeds and the Bible interpreted by the tradition and authority of the apostolic succession. The church, not the state, was the custodian of the truth, and one of the signs of the possession of the truth was the desire for unity within one church based on the ancient formularies. This was their reaction to the pluralism caused by the growing power of the Dissenting groups and the individualism, the authority of private judgment in matters religious, appealed to both by evangelicals and by Dissenters. Eventually their need for unity with authority was to lead Newman himself into the Roman Church along with many of his distinguished colleagues and followers. That move, however, was enough to vindicate the enemies of prelacy and popery like Russell and to make men like Philpotts draw back from secession in order to save the establishment. A fundamental disruption of the church as it occurred in Scotland, therefore, did not take place in England nor did the wishes of those Dissenters who wanted total disestablishment succeed.

All of these issues were reflected in the struggle of the Dissenting Deputies to get rid of the further disabilities under which Dissent still suffered. Under efforts of the Dissenting Deputies in 1833 and 1834 as many as 343,094 lay persons signed 1,094 petitions against their disabilities, while those opposed to them could only secure 230,000 signatures in favour of the establishment.[13] They were unsuccessful with regard to entrance into the universities, though by 1836 the University of London was granted the right to issue degrees. Disabilities continued because the Dissenter was still forced to pay the parish rate. Relief was granted if the vestry could not get a majority, but the irritation continued until 1868 when abolition of the rate took place. In 1836 the right for marriages, which, until then, had had to take place in the parish church, to take place in Dissenting chapels was passed. However, problems over the registration of children's births which had been previously through the church baptismal records alone continued throughout the century, as did problems over the use of burial grounds. Finally, disabilities at Cambridge and Oxford did not disappear until the early 1870's.[14]

Whenever the government acted to recognize the rights of Dissent, it could be accused of undermining the established church and of being indifferent to "objective truth in religion." This was the challenge on the right from the High Church party. When the government seemed to protect the established church, it could be accused of doing injustice to the consciences of millions of its subjects who did not adhere to that church. That the church establishment wobbled on as it did and was able to maintain itself at all was nothing short of a miraculous feat of compromise.

The long struggle over education was a further

reflection of the changing situation within the nation. We
have already mentioned the Dissenting Academies which developed in the eighteenth century as a response to the fact
that Dissenters were barred from the universities and to the
desire, especially on the part of the new industrialists, to
appropriate the new scientific learning for their purposes.
We recall, too, the efforts of persons like Wesley, as well
as many philanthropists, to set up schools for the children
of the poor. By 1811 a National Society for Promoting the
Education of the Poor in the Principles of the Established
Church was set up and from the outset regarded itself as
keeper of the truth and of the conscience of the nation. In
1814 the British and Foreign Schools Society began its
activities, using a knowledge of the Bible and of the new
sciences as the basis for its approach. It tried to take a
non-doctrinaire stance in matters religious. The financial
burden soon became so great that by 1833 the state had to
help and of course a dispute arose as to how the tax monies
were to be distributed. In 1839 Russell became alarmed at
the standards in some of the schools and set up a Committee
on Education under the privy council. He wanted the right
of school inspection, but this was finally won only if the
Archbishop of Canterbury and other religious officials were
granted a veto power over the decisions of inspectors. It
took until 1870 before a "conscience clause" could be in-
serted into provisions for grants whereby children of minority groups could be exempted from religious instruction.
Broad Churchmen, evangelicals and moderates broke away from
the National Society to set up one of their own, the Church
Education Society, in 1851.

    The High Church party and the members of the Oxford
Movement thought the church had, and ought to have, authority over all matters affecting faith and morals for the
people as a whole. For evangelicals and Broad Churchmen or

moderates religion was a matter that had to be appropriated by the individual inwardly and could not be coerced. It was not a matter of indifference, however. As a result, two incompatible systems arose reflecting the actual religious situation within the nation.

Education continued to be under the auspices of religious societies because the state did not have sufficient power over against the church to set up a secular system. Yet the establishment was not strong enough to insist even on principle that it was in fact the church of all the people. The power of Dissent was far too great for that. It might have been possible to deny Dissent its full rights during the eighteenth century, but by the middle of the nineteenth not only was Dissent more vigorous from a purely religious point of view but she was far more powerful because of the economic position which so many Dissenters, and those sympathetic with Dissent, held in the life of the nation. The education issue was a dispute between the landed and the industrial classes in which the labouring class itself had little say. The worker was to be made an orderly, Christian citizen through education for the extension of a burgeoning capitalist economy. In the final analysis the established church did receive more tax monies for educational purposes. This made it possible for her to regain some of her lost strength in the second half of the century and on into the present.

It is important to say a further clarifying word here about the composition of Dissent and about its relation to social reform. The reason we must use the term broadly is that there was a significant group of men who might have been low churchmen, or of the dissenting churches, or of the Wesleyan and other Methodist groups who were bound together by two things which they held in common and which were expressed in their political activity. *They were evangelicals in religion and they belonged to the middle classes, to the new industrial classes.* For example, on education even the Wesleyan Methodists were opposed to the National Society and the domination of education by the Church of England. On this issue they were with the Dissenters. After 1847, however, when the Dissenters were for complete disestablishment they would not go along.

The Methodist New Connexion, the Unitarian Methodists, the Protestant Methodists, and the Bible Christians, all offshoots of the Wesleyan movement, were with Dissent and were frequently even more radical because they were in general identified with the working classes. By the end of the nineteenth century Methodism was generally regarded as being part of Dissent.[15] In their reforming activities they were sometimes together and sometimes apart. If they were together, it was because their profound religious loyalties and moral sense of responsibility brought them together on issues. If they were apart, it was because the place from which they looked at the world around them, their standing in the society of that day, their relative stake in the old order that was passing away as opposed to the new one just coming upon the scene, was greater or less.

When we consider William Wilberforce and the majority of those who made up the "Clapham Sect," we find that they were in the main low churchmen who wished to further the interests of a truly reformed Church of England but who were ready to cooperate through the varied societies with other denominations because they shared a common evangelicalism with them. Thus Churchmen, Quakers and Methodists worked for the abolition of slavery, for penal reform, for temperance, for religious and civil liberties, and the like. At times the deep piety of a man like Wilberforce, while it did not overcome a deep sense of class distinction and fear of revolution, yet made it possible for him not only to struggle for the abolition of slavery but to rise above strictly class interest and to vote for parliamentary factory reforms.[16]

That Dissent was in the main middle class can be illustrated so clearly in the struggles both for religious reform and for political reform. The Wesleyan Methodists were for every reform which extended their right to propogate the faith as they understood it, but even though there were a few outstanding middle class leaders in the Chartist Movement, it was opposed by the Wesleyan Methodists and supported by the new Methodist sects which were of the labouring classes. While Chartism failed at the end largely because some of its leaders gave excuse to its enemies by advocating violence, it never enjoyed broad support among the middle classes. What is so impressive on the one hand was the number of outstanding leaders like Wilberforce and Shaftesbury, Joseph Fielden, Cobden, Bright and Sturge who, whether it was the slavery issue, the Factory Acts, Corn Law Repeal or Chartism, were prepared to act out of Christian charity on behalf of those less fortunate than themselves. However, their commitment to the *voluntary principle*, that is to the idea that if given opportunity each individual could, indeed, must save himself both in this world and the next, obscured the equally true fact that the way society is structured can either make for justice or injustice, can either assist men to be creative, free and responsible or encourage its opposite. Faith in the *voluntary principle* was encouraged by an equal faith in an expanding economy. It was as easy to believe in free trade as in free salvation. Those who questioned the efficacy of this combination were a tiny minority struggling against the stream of contemporary thought.

It is often forgotten that the nineteenth century was the great century of non-conformist expansion. The renewal that had begun with Whitefield and Wesley and the evangelicals of the established church lasted throughout the nineteenth century and had its greatest harvest in terms of numbers then. At the beginning of the nineteenth century there were 270 Presbyterian, 708 Baptists and 1,024 Congregational congregations with perhaps 400,000 members and adherents in all. [17] This means that much of what had been lost to Dissent in the middle years of the eighteenth century had been regained by them. If we add to these numbers the 109,000 Methodists recorded in 1800, plus the other four hundred thousand persons in the nation who were in some way touched by the Dissenting movement at the opening of the century, the phenomenal growth of the movement by the end of the nineteenth century can be seen by the fact that there were 2,125,275 Free church communicants as against 2,231,735 active Anglican communicants in 1910. Moreover, when one includes the number of adherents, it is likely that there was greater attendance at Free church services by 1900 than at Anglican, since the seating capacity of the Free churches was greater than that of the Anglican.

It is true that in the first few decades of the nineteenth century Methodism lost vitality because of the class divisions within it and the shortsightedness of the leadership. This was regained with the appearance of the Primitive Methodists among the working classes and the vigour of the United Methodist Free Churches from the middle of the nineteenth century. These figures indicate the extent to which toleration not comprehension had won out.[18]

We have also noted that the increase in the number of Dissenters took place precisely where the great increases in population due to changes in economic life were taking place. The religious division, therefore, was also an economic, political and social one. The fact that this was the case would seem to demonstrate that religious commitment was unable to overcome divisions owing to other human interests, and that these were frequently in control of the values at work in the social system more than those values that might have been expected from a commitment to the Christian faith, and which would have negated social differences. This was true insofar as the Church of England was still the captive of the old order, and to the extent that Dissent represented solely the growing political and economic interests of the middle classes.

The principal factor of change in the organization of the Dissenting churches in the years beyond the death of Wesley and the early years of the new century was the fragmentation of Methodism into the New Connexion in 1797 and the Primitive Methodists in 1812, the Bible Christians in 1815 and the Protestant Methodists in 1826 and the Wesleyan Central Association in 1837. The greatest break with the old connexion came in 1849 with the formation of the United Methodist Free Churches.

Sometimes the problems involved were ostensibly doctrinal or liturgical, but more deeply these divisions represented the ferment that was taking place in English society. Much of the Methodist rank and file wanted to move away from the conservatism and authoritarianism of the clergy and to have a greater share in the government of their churches at the local level in particular. Without the leadership of Wesley, a principle of authority was lacking at a time when authority itself was being challenged throughout English society. Because the laity played such a prominent role in local Methodist Societies it meant that leaders arose from among the common people who would not tolerate others dominating them. Methodism with its emphasis on the worth of the individual before God, its insistence that every man no matter how humble his birth should accept moral

responsibility for himself as well as share discipline over
his brethren, contributed not just to sectarianism but to
the capacity for leadership which gave the working class a
final voice in its own destiny.

IV

What was the role of Methodism in relation to political
and social reform during the first half of the nineteenth
century? The answer to that depends upon which group of
Methodists we are discussing. At the outset we must be
clear that at the beginning of the century the vast majority
of Methodist preachers and laity were of the working
classes. As W. J. Warner points out:
> Practically all of the regular preachers, there-
> fore, during this period of more than fifty years,
> were drawn from a single social stratum, located
> between 'unskilled labour' and the 'middle class.'[19]

The skilled artisans, the small tradesman, manufacturer
and farmer were on the whole about to share in the now expanding economy after severe periods of distress. These
were felt even more strongly by the miners and the unskilled
labourers who made up much of the rank and file of the growing Methodist movement. Generally speaking, those Methodist
sects that were closer to the tragic plight of the great
masses of labouring poor, such as the Primitive Methodists
and the Bible Christians, took a more active part in the
struggle against that plight than did the others. All
Methodists, however, were inhibited by a rigid interpretation of Wesley's "no politics rule." It was pervasive in
spite of the fact that Wesley himself, not only on the
slavery issue but on prison reform and on the American
Revolution, made his own biases quite clear. Part, of

course, of the passivity and submissiveness was due to the
oppressive nature of the conservative spirit during the
French Revolution as well as the Napoleonic Wars and their
aftermath. Objectively, the new religious movement had far
less legal standing than did Dissent in general, and so its
leaders, like Wesley before them, were grateful for what
protection they got from the authorities.

Before we go on to a discussion of the particular sectarian groups into which Methodism divided, we must assess
the numerical size and influence of the movement as a whole.
The approximately 90,000 Methodists in the population of
8 ½ million in 1795 had grown in the Wesleyan Methodist
Church in spite of all its difficulties to some 358,277 in
Great Britain alone by 1850, though the Wesleyans were to
lose some 100,000 as a result of the formation of the United
Free Methodists in 1857. Owing to poor strategy the latter
group only picked up some 40,000 of these persons, the
remainder being lost to other Methodist groups or to
Methodism altogether. In 1849 there were 17,556 persons who
belonged to the New Connexion, and in 1850 there were
104,762 Primitive Methodists. In 1852 there were 10,416
Bible Christians and some 19,411 who belonged to the
Wesleyan Methodist Association which was finally to lead
into the United Free Methodist Church a few years later. If
Methodist adherents are to be taken into consideration, we
must multiply these numbers by three arriving at some two
million persons influenced by Methodism in a population of
17,000,000 in the middle of the century. Thus 1 of 9
persons in the population was directly related to Methodism
and a great many more indirectly so. In the industrial
areas it was estimated that 1-6 was a Methodist or closely
related to Methodism while in Cornwall the numbers rose to
1-3 persons.[20] There was, therefore, a phenomenal growth
of Methodism in general in spite of all its internal

problems, reflecting the vitality of the evangelical revival which spread far beyond the bounds of Methodism itself and was in turn reflected in the first half of the century in the movement away from rationalism toward romanticism in intellectual and literary pursuits.

As Weber and Troeltsch have pointed out, the skilled artisan or small tradesman and manufacturer who also happened to be a Methodist exemplified all the attributes of the "Protestant ethic" which made it possible for him to take advantage of the new economic order. It is no accident that Wesleyan Methodism found it less and less possible, by mid-century, to be the preserve of the clergy as the laity became wealthier and gained in political power as well. It took until 1878 for Wesleyan Methodism to give equal rights to the laity and to learn the lessons that had led to the schisms of the first half of the century.

What this reflected more than anything else was that it was becoming not only theologically and ecclesiastically nearer to Dissent but that like them, economically and politically, it was also becoming a middle class movement. By the time that Hugh Price Hughes was chairman of the Free Church Union at the end of the century, this new class orientation was already apparent in the breakaway of William Booth's Salvation Army in protest against it. Few Methodists may have been among the wealthiest of the land, more were now more likely to be Liberal than Conservative in politics, but fewer still of Wesleyan Methodists were likely to give support to the labour movement as it rose to take its fair share in the common life.

Wesley had established a religious reform movement related to the Church of England. The next generation of Methodists faced a new situation. First, they had to face the problem of authority since Wesley, a benevolent despot, had kept power in his own hands. Secondly, they had to find a new relation to the Church of England, an issue that Wesley had refused to face since his intent had been to reform the Church of England not to start a new sect. However, his own action in ordaining men to the ministry in the United States as well as the fact that after his death his own people in England wanted to celebrate the sacraments and could not do so for lack of clergy led to the inevitable organization of a new sect.

The problem of establishing itself when it had no legal standing was not an easy one. It had to be organized and nurtured by one who knew what was at stake for the new enterprise. The one who did this did not appear at once on the scene. When he did so, he used the "Legal Hundred" as the heart of the new organization, and he sought to avoid every involvement of it that would threaten what he regarded as that organization's fundamental religious purpose. That man was Jabez Bunting. The "Legal Hundred" was a group of one hundred Methodist clergy who carried on the direction of the movement after the death of Wesley. Only the clergy could be elected to it. The "Legal Hundred" had every power belonging to the sect as a legal entity. Laymen could meet in a separate conference without powers at the same time as the official Conference of Preachers was meeting under the chairmanship of its president and secretary. The laity had no official authority.

Thus the organization of Wesleyan Methodism was essentially republican in character. In fact, it was dominated throughout his lifetime by Jabez Bunting who was by far the most powerful person in the conference year after year. He was a strong Tory. Though he cherished his Dissenting ministers license, he regarded Wesleyan Methodism as closer to the Church of England than to Dissent. At the same time, he had no use for the High Church sacramentalism of the Oxford Movement as Wesley might well have had. Under his guidance and that of the other Methodist sects Methodism became inevitably sectarian. Nevertheless, Wesleyan Methodism, choosing the path it did, could not help but move closer to Dissent and away from the High Church and the more traditionally catholic orientation of Wesley. When this was reinforced by the stress on individual freedom in the economic and political sphere, the direction was even more certain. *Any corporate understanding of the church was lost and individualism reinforced.*

Bunting was jealous for the right of the pastor to lead and to govern. He was profoundly concerned that "spiritual interest" not be swallowed up in this-worldly political considerations as he had contended had been the fate of the Dissenting radicals like Priestley during the eighteenth century. Wesleyan Methodism paid a heavy price for this course for it not only lost thousands to other groups in the first fifty years of the century because of autocratic rule by one man, and exclusive rule by clergy alone, but it led to the loss of 100,000 persons at the mid-century who could stand for this state of affairs no longer.

It may be that Wesleyan Methodism was saved as an institution among other religious institutions as a result of the path that was marked out for it so clearly by Bunting, but it did so at great cost in terms of a narrow understanding of the significance of religious faith for the whole of life and a lack of sensitivity to social justice. This made it possible to serve those whose economic and political interests were secure but cut it off from those whose needs were not met, namely the great masses of the lower working classes.

The political stance, then, of Wesleyan Methodism was politically passive, even submissive. It placed a great emphasis upon privileges received rather than rights expected from the body politic. This approach worked to its advantage during the period of social conservatism from the beginning of the French Revolution until the early 1820's. However, in 1819, at the time of the Peterloo massacre, it lost 5,000 members in one year because the labouring classes were so distressed by the outrage that the counsel to submissiveness was too much to bear. In 1816 and 1817 the Wesleyan Methodist Conferences openly opposed the working class societies and actively did so through its preachers.[21] Wearmouth suggests that it had to do so or it would have been wiped out as the radical movements were.[22] This seems hardly a valid argument, however, since the other Methodist groups did have many, if not a majority, of their membership involved in the radical movements and were not "wiped out." It is true that the radical movements suffered temporarily. To this extent it was not at that time in the interest of those seeking to build and to preserve an institution to be too close to them. Bunting and his followers were afraid of being identified as levelling "Jacobins," especially when the "secular" radical, political movements such as the Political Union and the Chartists began to use Methodist techniques which drew suspicion from the authorities upon all Methodists. Yet the separation between the "religious" and the "secular" here was most unfortunate. In the long run, it led to the diminution of the influence of institutional religion over the life of English society as a whole. In dingy towns the authorities were always consoled if the influence of the Wesleyan Methodists, rather than the "Ranters" and the Primitive Methodists, was strong because the former could be counted upon to keep their people quiet even in the midst of exploitation and indescribable poverty.

The Plan of Pacification, designed in 1795, provided that Methodists should have the sacraments from their clergy as long as they were not given at the same time as Anglican services. That plan made it clear that Methodism must become an organized denomination rather than a religious movement.

From that time forward there were those who did not like the autocratic way in which the denomination was organized. Nor did they like the "no politics" clause. In politics they were followers of Locke and Paine and were deeply sympathetic with the original ideals of the American and French Revolutions. They believed that the worth of the individual soul meant that all men were in fact equal before God and that that equality should be expressed in both political and economic freedoms. Their original leader was Alexander Kilham who died in 1798. They determined that their church should at least reflect their views in its organization if the state did not. Like their Dissenting brethren they were more concerned that the crown should be true to the English constitution than that they should be so careful about expressing loyalty to the crown. Thus they founded the Methodist New Connexion in 1797, determined that laity should have equal rights with clergy. *Whereas Wesley had appealed to the conscience of those in authority under God for social reform, they appealed to the rights of every man under God and claimed the New Testament as authority for their position.* They accepted "the sovereignty of the Bible" and the general evangelical scheme of salvation. They supported the Radicals in politics generally and eventually were made up of middle class intellectual entrepreneurs. They reflected the growing influence of the voluntary principle. Their position demanded too much sophistication to become widely popular among the lesser working class. It is not surprising, however, that their movement took hold in Leeds and the other industrial cities. While the Conference still had authority in their denomination as in the Methodist pattern, there was equal lay and clergy representation. To the Districts and Circuits they gave authority much like Presbyterian synods and presbyteries. From the outset Kilham, having taken out a Dissenting ministers license, regarded himself as part of Dissent and had little love for the Church of England. This was true of his followers as well. With them, too, Wesley's sacramental emphasis was lost. They were men of the new day, of individual initiative in religious faith as in economic and political life. Yet their sense of the "gathered church" was not absent. They were opposed to a national establishment of religion. In politics they were the forerunners of Mr. Gladstone's Liberalism. Their number remained relatively small and select in all amounting to less than 20,000 in 1851.

The Primitive Methodists were by far the most successful of the groups which split off from the parent body in the first half of the nineteenth century. It was a very strong lay movement and was most representative of the lower working classes. They were less concerned about formality and more concerned about spontaneity in the expression of religious enthusiasm. Hugh Bowne and William Clowes, skilled artisans and lay preachers, were among their founders. They broke away from Wesleyan Methodism when it refused to permit public tent meetings which had been introduced from America. Their leaders remembered the great outdoor meetings addressed by their original founder and felt this new movement was quite in order. Bunting and others were afraid that the meetings would get out of hand and bring disgrace to the Methodist cause for which they were seeking acceptability and respectability. Moreover, the authorities looked upon these meetings as potentially subversive.

At first the Primitive Methodists tended to be apolitical, but as the economic plight of their fellows became worse and worse, more and more of them found such a stance unacceptable. While the majority of their preachers cannot be said to have led in the movements for political reform and economic redress, during the first half of the century much of the leadership of those movements came from preachers who were, or had been, Primitive Methodists. They became leaders of the Friendly Societies and the Trade Unions.

At the outset the Primitive Methodists were opposed to domination by the preachers alone, so that by 1818 they had insisted in their conference that there should be two laymen for every full-time preacher. It was no wonder that their people, as they took a greater share of the leadership of the church at the center, as well as at the local level, learnt to speak in public and so were numbered among the natural leaders of the dispossessed workers. In this movement as among the Wesleyan Methodists, of course, there was a majority who felt that earthly economic and political concerns would take them away from the more important concerns of "religion." Yet the Primitive Methodists were never so hostile to the reform movements as were the Wesleyan Methodists.

Another movement away from the authoritarianism of the Wesleyan Methodists was that of the Bible Christians, sometimes known as "Quaker Methodists," led by William O'Bryan in Devonshire. They were strongly lay oriented but never became widespread. The significance of this movement was that it originated in a revolt against "The Legal Hundred," on the part of a local clergyman. The courts ruled that according to the Methodist system even local property was vested in the conference. Had the ruling gone otherwise, the future of Wesleyan Methodism as an ecclesiastical organization would have been very different. O'Bryan took the occasion to *"go local,"* to create an independent "gathered community."

# The New Age

The final significant division of Methodism took place in 1849 and 1850 when over 100,000 persons left the Wesleyan Methodist Connexion because of the refusal of Bunting and his followers to give up any of the powers belonging to the clergy. The leadership had refused to take note of what had been happening in English society since 1828, especially as that was reflected in their own membership. By virtue of the new freedoms given to the Dissenters as well as the new political reforms of 1832 the middle classes were gaining more and more power. The businessmen and industrialists, the new-type farmer and the wealthy mine owner were coming into their own. They did not mean to be submissive to church, crown and lords. They intended to be independent, to compete in the open marketplace and in society at large, to stand erect and not bow the head to their "betters." It was this breed of man, a cut above the ordinary labourer, sometimes wealthy in his own right, who felt he should have more and more say in the way the Methodist Chapel of which he was frequently a trustee, and for which he more often than not paid the bills, was run. That, according to Bunting, was just what he feared--a group of laymen would take over the church who had little thought for things "spiritual" and much for things "material." He remained adamant.

As early as 1839, therefore, an organization known as the Wesleyan Methodist Association, with 28,000 members and 600 chapels under its influence, came into being, led by Samuel Warren and Robert Eckett. Those who gave their support to the Association were *laissez-faire* liberals like Bright and Cobden and Place and Lovett, in matters political. They were not Owenite socialists and they were as unhappy about the anti-religious basis of "atheistic, Benthamite radicalism" as was Bunting, but they were nevertheless prepared to cooperate with any who would bring about

the middle class reforms they cherished. They had a growing
faith in "the people." Under the influence of Daniel
Isaac's "An Investigation of Ecclesiastical Claims," in
which he was strongly anti-clerical and in which he emphasized the priesthood of all believers, the Wesleyan
Methodist Reform Union was founded in 1849 to work for the
restructuring of the Wesleyan Methodist Church. It was led
by such leaders as Everett, Dunn and Griffith, all political
liberals. They tried to overcome the influence of Bunting
but were unsuccessful. Also, any desire to be associated
with the Church of England had disappeared from among them.
Indeed, they sensed a deep sympathy with those congregations
which had left the relationship with the state in the break
up of the Church of Scotland at this time. They possessed
a strong sense of their own destiny, affirming their right
to guide their own religious affairs. Thus, over 100,000
persons moved away from the Wesleyan Methodist Connexion
either to the other Methodist groups, to some of the Independent churches, like the Baptists and Congregationalists,
or finally moved into the United Methodist Free Churches
formed in 1857 on a strong congregational basis. As E. R.
Taylor says:

> Not only did Methodism lose its unity in this
> period; it moved away from its "Reactionary" posi-
> tion, and became simply the largest but most
> hierarchial of the Nonconformist Churches in
> England; it wasted Wesley's sacramental legacy;
> it forsook his belief in the Church as the Body of
> Christ, and substituted for it his High Churchman-
> ship and ideal of pastoral supremacy. Where he
> had been Catholic, it became authoritarian.[23]

We must emphasize again that while the majority of all
Methodists did not take an active part in the movements for
radical political reform, a very significant minority,

especially of the Primitive Methodists, did so. It is understandable that those who had a fear of non-respectability, who witnessed the use of force effectively against the political radicals at this time, should like Bunting himself have been badly frightened. It is still harder, however, when one listens to the government report of 1842 on conditions in the coal mines, as one example, to understand how the Methodist leaders could have continued to call for passivity and submissiveness in the fact of such brutality and degredation. The report revealed that the majority of those working in the mines were under thirteen years of age, that some had begun to do so at the age of four years, spending the daylight hours in the darkness and wet muck of the pits, that both sexes, naked and half-naked, worked together as children and adults, that babies were born in the pits and brought to the surface in the rag skirts of the women, some of the mothers who worked there still essentially children themselves. Meanwhile, in England's "dark Satanic Mills," the average life span of workers was from 15 in the industrial north and Midlands to 22 in London! Their lives were far shorter than those of paupers.[24] What tragedy it would have been had no churchmen spoken up! Leaders like Tommy Hepburn, a Primitive Methodist lay preacher, appeared among the miners to fight for their cause while the Tolpuddle martyrs were also Methodist leaders in the Agricultural Unions.

Wearmouth is able to show that there was a significant minority of such men who were or had been Methodist leaders.[25] During the Chartist movement some Methodist chapels were used. Yet the paucity of such numbers who were active Methodists is disquieting. The labouring movement as such had not been subjected to these experiences long enough to gain a sense of solidarity and a sense of direction for policy nor had society at large lived with the new problems of the industrial age for a sufficient length of time to know precisely what to do. Government regulations were passed as soon as the revelations of 1842 were made known, even though compliance was hard to secure. Moreover, the grip of *laissez-faire* doctrine, with its aversion to government regulation, was getting stronger, not weaker. Class was also a hindrance. Fear of levelling tendencies smelt "Jacobin" revolution whenever reform was mentioned. Moreover, among sectarian pietists there was the conviction that men would do out of pity, out of a spirit of Christian charity, what they would not do out of a sense of social justice reflected in laws that would recognize the rights of all men. If that was so, why had they not already done so? *It may be best for the legal institutions of religion to be quite separate from those of the state. Yet to believe that the religious life as such can be separated from the rest of life was the great error here. To call one part of life "sacred" and the other "secular" and to confine the activity of God to one is the tragic fallacy.* That, in fact, is what happened. Those who felt impelled to speak up against social injustice knew they would receive little sympathy from those who had authority in the very chapels they loved and which were symbolic of the God whom they felt they still served.

It was no accident, then, that those who did try to give leadership to working class reform movements in this period turned to the organizing techniques they knew from firsthand experience to be so effective for their chapels. The Class Meeting was the perfect answer after the authorities in the decade beyond 1810 refused to allow large political meetings. Radical class meetings were organized at this time and later on, after the Reform Bill of 1832, the Political Unions also used the class meeting technique. They even financed their reading materials by assessing

their members a penny a week as Wesley had done. The myriad
of societies which arose for every reform at the outset of
the century and beyond were themselves an imitation of the
Methodist Society. The Chartists not only used the class
meeting but the camp meeting as well. There were Chartist
Churches established after the failure of Physical-Force
Chartism, even though the moral appeal of men like Attwood
and Lovett as well as all other attempts of the working
class to achieve their economic objectives by the middle of
the century, through political agitation, had failed.

Again and again those who gave leadership in these
efforts were forced out of the religious community through
which they might have given leadership. While these movements erupted in violence from time to time, especially in
the great depression of 1837 to 1843, they were on the whole
non-violent. They sought, as through the charter, to use
the new techniques of petition to achieve their goals. The
labouring class had not yet discovered that they must seek
redress through economic means, since that was the base of
their power, rather than through the political where they
had little foothold. Unlike the rising middle class they
did not yet sense their economic power. They had no way
into political power as the various middle class reform
movements did who could rely on their own leaders in parliament, even before the Reform Bill of 1832. One wonders how
much sooner labour might have secured its just place in the
social order if the Methodist movement, recognizing the
sovereignty of God over the whole of life, had struggled for
the right of all to enter into the riches of the new order.
Instead, the "religious" was separated from "the secular."
This fateful division had tragic implications both for an
adequate understanding of the Christian faith and the
achievement of justice on a sound and secure basis in
Western society as a whole.

Methodism then moved more and more in the direction of middle class Dissent. It was inevitable that the sacramental High Church, and in this sense catholic, understanding of the church held by Wesley should have been lost. Wesley's soteriology, his Arminian conviction that salvation was for all but was dependent upon the response of those who chose so to respond, inevitably led to that view of the church which had come to be shared by Dissent, that is, of "a gathered community" of like-minded believers called out to serve God and God's world, yet called to what was more important--their own eternal salvation among the company of the elect in a life which encompassed far more than this life. An alternative to this view which was far more than the post-reformation view of the authority of the church as advocated by Rome and by the Oxford movement had yet to appear. When it did appear in the thinking of Frederick Denison Maurice, it found little acceptance because contrary factors in society at that time were far too strong for it.

Finally, those who did take part in the struggle of the working classes for radical political reform at this time, whether from religious conviction or out of simple humanity or out of the ideas of Jeremy Bentham, were but a minority, even of the working classes. They had not yet discovered that the source of their power lay in binding together to seek economic redress. They went down to defeat, overwhelmed by the power held by the landed and industrial classes. The majority even of them shared the view held by their "betters" that the new economy would bring, in its time, a better day in which all "deserving" individuals willing to work and strive would share.

## Chapter Eight

## A Fresh Vision: A Prophetic Alternative

A consideration of the ethical and social values held by the varying classes in Britain in the first half of the nineteenth century discloses the rise of a prevailing individualism over all other considerations. The organic ideal of medieval society like the landed economy on which it was based was cast aside. It had run aground on the shoals of exploitation and privilege, though the individualistic capitalism which took its place was to be no more noted for its sensitivity to justice and fair play.

There were those among the upper middle classes, like Wilberforce, Peel the Elder and Shaftesbury, whose deep religious conviction moved them through a sense of compassion to ameliorate the condition of the poor. They were evangelicals who had a profound sense of the worth of the individual soul, though they were unable to see how the structures of the new industrial order, as yet hardly discernible, themselves made for poverty. The new landlessness, for example, of men who had formerly been farmers, along with the complete political powerlessness of the already poor, hardly made it possible for either to cope with the new power of the industrialists. The complete lack of organization of the poor made it impossible for them to deal with their employers on economic terms. All of these issues were to be faced in the future, but they were not on the horizon of the thinking of men of goodwill at this time. Wilberforce and Robert Peel the Elder and Shaftesbury were prompted to bring in legislation for the new Factory Laws and the abolition of slavery on the basis of a concern for individuals. Their motivation was charitable and philanthropic, as was true for all of the "Clapham Sect." They were pietists who believed that men ought to be charitable to those classes beneath their own. *The idea of social equality did not occur to them.* Nevertheless, they were willing to use state intervention to bring about some measure of social justice for the dispossessed. Concern for individuals prompted by a spirit of charity was their basic motivation while they believed it was possible to leave social structures much as they were.

The middle class industrialists were for freedom in every respect--freedom in trade, freedom in government, freedom in religion. Earlier industrialists like Wedgwood, and later on men like Dale in New Lanark, felt a profound personal responsibility for the people who worked for them, men, women, and children. Even the Wesleyan Methodists, the most conservative among Methodist groups, worked for the abolition of slavery through acts of government. There were also Dissenters who supported the Factory Acts. Yet their main leadership in men like Cobden and Bright opposed them on the ground that if there was no interference by government in economic life, the welfare of all would be served. Thus there was to some extent a contrary tendency among the middle classes. Their sense of social justice and respect for the individual called for a certain amount, even if minimal, of government intervention. This tendency increased under the thinking of a person like J. S. Mill, who came to see that unless the interests of the whole group were taken into consideration the freedom and happiness of any great number could not be served. In his essay "On Liberty," therefore, he moved in the direction of democratic socialism, even though he had been reared in the extreme *laissez-faire* thinking of his father and of Jeremy Bentham.

Nonetheless, the great bulk of the new middle class had

# A Fresh Vision

a profound faith in the doctrines of Adam Smith--they firmly believed that the hand of providence would bring about the public good, when everyone was free to serve his own best interest. The main thrust of their political activity was aimed at getting rid of government restriction on religion and on trade and on encouraging the political activity of the individual. Both Bright and Cobden believed in voluntarism, in the man of goodwill rationally acting in such a way as to assert his own rights, but not at the expense of his neighbour. They were for social services on the part of government only where and when absolutely essential to individual welfare. Cobden, especially, worked and dreamed of forms of international government that would institute minimal regulations for the nations of men which would bring about peace through trade and rational behaviour in relation to one another so that war would no longer be in anyone's self-interest. It was an expansive and optimistic view of the human situation, prompted by the empirical situation in which Great Britain found herself at this particular time.

Skilled artisans like Attwood and Place, though they were for the Chartist movement, thought of labour as being best served through the sale of their labour on the market on equal terms with management. They sought an equal share in government for all classes, but they were convinced that when that occurred, the temptation to use government repressively would disappear. The role of government would, therefore, be more restricted. "The less government the best government" was a conviction they shared with others. They were certainly not opposed to the competitive market. Government would dispense justice in an even-handed manner to all rather than in the interest of the landed and industrial classes alone. They were thus within the orbit of the *laissez-faire* philosophy.

The real challenge to the new social philosophy itself,

representing for the first time a reassertion of social
solidarity which at least was an ideal of the middle ages,
came from those who felt that serious competition, as a
primary not a secondary factor in human relationships, led
not to the health and welfare of societies but to their
disintegration through the expression of self-interest.
There were at least three persons representing this challenge on different grounds who commanded a serious following. Robert Owen was the first. He had been placed in
charge of the model city of New Lanark by the great industrialist and philanthropist David Dale, a conscientious
Dissenter. At first Owen was motivated by a simple Christian charity for the interest of those under his charge as
he sought to improve greatly the living and educational
opportunities of the labourers. He came to believe that the
behaviour of many of the labourers which was brutish and
selfish was occasioned by the deprived environment in which
they had been raised. He also came eventually to believe
that the competitive system itself was a denial of one's
essential responsibility for his fellowman. Finally, he
tried to set up in America a New Lanark that would represent
a truly cooperative rather than competitive approach. He
had much to do with the origins of cooperatives as viable
economic units, even though his more ambitious schemes
failed. His analysis of the human condition was far too
unambiguous and optimistic.

A second challenge to the *laissez-faire*, competitive
approach was that of John Stuart Mill. We have already
mentioned the fact that he became sensitive to the great
sufferings of the people in mine and factory, to the vile
sanitary and slum conditions existing in the new cities. In
this he could see it was inhuman for one group of men to
claim the right to happiness or even to experience the possibility of it at the expense of others. He added to

utilitarianism the conviction that the greatest happiness itself ought to reflect a *qualitative* compassion for the whole society. This meant that he not only began to support a concept of government and of society that would supply services for persons but one that would also reflect a sense of corporate and mutual responsibility. Whether this was to lead to socialism or not he would leave for a further generation to decide.

A third challenge to the new system was a more basically religious one and was raised by the Christian Socialists under the leadership of Charles Kingsley, Thomas Hughes, J. M. Ludlow and the real leader of the movement, Frederick Denison Maurice. They were not socialists in the doctrinaire sense of the word, either of a democratic or Marxian kind. *They emphasized the fact that the Christian faith affirmed the solidarity of all mankind under the sovereignty of God.* Since every man was his brother's keeper according to Christian doctrine, it was sinful in the extreme to believe that the interest of mankind could best be served by every man serving his own interest. This they saw to be the exact contrary of the Christian ethic. Moreover, they attempted to symbolize their point of view by setting up Working Men's Associations in different trades, based on a profit-sharing principle, and they set out on a program of adult education aiming to bring the working class into full participation in British society. Objectively, their efforts finally petered out, but like all the other movements related to the working classes it had a cumulative effect which finally led to a deeper sense of corporate responsibility in British society. Maurice is highly significant because, apart from Marx, his thinking represents the first serious challenge to the inadequacies of a rampant individualism which obscured the corporate side of man's existence. He is religiously significant because his work, neglected because unacceptable at the time, illustrates the capacity of the religious dimension in human experience to produce creative alternatives.

I

By 1850 the tragic divisions in the religious community that had begun so promisingly as a result of the renewal of the Christian faith through the work of John Wesley had rendered Methodism incapable of providing that leadership which the dispossessed, labouring class needed so badly. For Wesleyan Methodism the question was, "How to preserve institutionally the witness to what they conceived to be the strictly religious concern of Wesley for the salvation of individual souls?" Methodism as such had no legal standing before the state and only gained it through identifying finally with Dissent. Bunting and the leadership in Wesleyan Methodism were interested in carrying their following into its inheritance in the new *laissez-faire* economy through the exercise of "the Protestant ethic." If men were regenerated spiritually, they would transform their own destinies economically and politically.

Indeed, more and more of the laity of the Wesleyan Methodist Connexion were in fact bettering themselves, and that in itself became a problem for the clergy-dominated sect which Bunting had organized. Thinking to escape the political and economic environment in which it lived, that environment, as it inevitably does, entered the fellowship to confound those leaders who had ignored the reality of such factors. Primitive Methodism had indeed been nearer the working man, but even here, because of the separation of the present world from that of one's eternal salvation, a clear understanding of social responsibility could not be grasped. At best it was only half-realized as Christians in their select "gathered" communities found it impossible to tolerate the physical sufferings of their fellow believers. The mundane search for social justice had to be taken up by the "secular" societies. As a result of the inadequacy of these movements, Marxian Socialism not only came into being but found a following.

The middle classes represented by Dissent and its friends stood for "liberty," so far as the franchise was concerned, if not for "equality" and "fraternity." Men like Cobden and Bright were confident that if individual men were free from the restricting bonds of autocratic or even aristocratic control, each would find a satisfying place which would enable him to make his contribution to society and reap from society rewards granted through competition with others. Such a system, one of open competition, would naturally work for the good of all classes. They were trapped in their total allegiance to *laissez-faire*, because the empirical expansive economic situation in which the British Empire found itself made it plausible enough, especially to those who benefited most by it—the middle classes. In the middle of the century we are still on the doorstep of this expansion. The difficulties of the new order had become apparent but its apparent strengths had not yet been fully realized. The landed aristocracy still had some capacity to resist, but the new "captains of industry" were not to be gainsaid. The ambivalence of Palmerston who "sensed uncertain winds" disappeared to be replaced by the confident leadership of a Gladstone and a Disraeli who reflect England at the height of her power and influence. It was not until the turn of the century that men like Hardy and Galsworthy would begin to really question the validity of a materialism which made property more important than people. "The Forsythes" as "men of property" reflected the pettiness of human life when reduced to the material.

At mid-century others began to inherit the benefits of the new order of England, but it was not for another generation that the general improvement in the economy made any substantial difference to a part of the working class. Toward the end of the century, as their common plight as well as common task gave them a growing sense of solidarity, the trade union developed among the working classes while the concept of a democratic socialism found its way into the thinking of the "Fabians," a middle class group of intellectuals like the Webbs and George Bernard Shaw.[1] These two sources were the springs from which the modern labour party developed. Poverty continued to exist for vast numbers of the unskilled poor who were always the victims of uncontrolled boom and bust. Labour did not secure a full share in the common life until the close of World War II.

In the meantime, Karl Marx, concerned for the plight of the labouring classes, influenced by Hegelian dialectic and the prophetic utopianism of Jewish eschatology, devised his "dialectical meterialism" through the impetus of which, reflected in the class struggle, the proletariat would finally usher in the classless society.

His, however, was not the only reaction to the suffering of the labouring classes. In the very years when Marx was at work on his theories in the British Museum, another equally dedicated man was at work there, but from a very different perspective. He was convinced that for too long the Christian church had been captive to the social order rather than a catalyst within it; that the Christian faith itself through a narrow evangelicalism, on the one hand, and an authoritarian ecclesiasticism, on the other, had been made impotent to perform its rightful life-giving, prophetic task in the life of human society. That man was Frederick

Denison Maurice (1805-1872). It was precisely Maurice's refusal to accept anything less than a whole view of the Christian life which makes his contribution so significant and makes him so different from the pietist Bunting, the individualistic or at best sectarian Dissenters, the charity-minded conservatives, the humanistic Benthamites, the simply service-minded reformers and the authoritarian sacramentalists like Pusey, Keble and Newman.

Though the gauntlet he threw down was taken up in heated controversy in his own day, he himself was an irenic spirit who felt that one better spent his time looking for the positive aspects in the arguments of those with whom he disagreed.[2] He could not escape controversy because, far more than he himself ever realized, his approach signalled the possibility for the renewal of faith on the part of those who continued to seek guidance from the Christian faith, while at the same time the implications of his view cut across the prevailing views of the time.

II

We shall begin with the practical work with which the name of Maurice is most often associated, though, except symbolically, it may be less significant than the contribution his theological insights have made. The phrase "Christian Socialism" Maurice used to indicate the practical outworking in the everyday life of human society of the Kingdom of God as he understood it. At that time the word socialism did not have the associations it has today when it is reduced either to the thought of Marx and of Lenin, on the one hand, or to the highly sophisticated democratic socialism which is the ideological underpinning of the British Labour Party and other democratic socialist movements. It meant simply the effort of the labouring classes to improve themselves in any way they could, to share in the growing prosperity of the technological revolution in its early stages. It was frightening to some because of the turn it had taken with the revolutionary violence of the French Revolution, but it had not hardened into any fixed creed. *Maurice meant it to mean the right of those who did not have a proper share in the common life to that share.*

Because of his faith in the Reality which makes all humanity one and which when experienced as concern for oneself, elicits both self-respect and the desire to contribute the talents one has to the common good, Maurice believed in the capacity of the working man to respond to opportunities to learn so that the labourer could become a responsible actor in society. As a result he helped found the first Working Men's College and later Queen's College for young women. He is regarded as a founder of the modern adult education movement.

On the basis of the same faith he helped establish various Working Men's Associations, for example, the Shoemaker's Association, the Working Tailor's Association, the Working Printer's, Builder's and Baker's Associations. These were producers' cooperatives. They were based on the principle that it was self-defeating for the labouring classes to allow their labour to be placed in competition with other men's labour. Rather, they should join together, and with the capital they could themselves supply, or which was supplied at low interest from friends, they would then produce their own goods and put them on the market. They would thus eliminate the middleman who would try to buy raw materials as cheaply as possible, then add the value of labour to them as inexpensively as possible, in order to make as large a profit for himself as he could.

Through the Associations the workers would themselves share in the profits. In textiles and shoes, for example, there was often quick profit made at the expense of labour.[3] The military would order large quantities of such goods through an entrepreneur, and he in turn, seeking to make a large profit, would hire labour as inexpensively as possible. The Associations, however, were a practical way for the labouring man to deliver himself out of this morass. Of course, the cooperative principle had already been attempted by Owen, and the men of Rochdale at this very time were beginning to institute consumers' cooperatives.

The Associations illustrated two principles that were dear to Maurice. First, the one of which we have spoken, that the labourer could help himself if given opportunity. Secondly, they illustrate the practical validity of cooperation over competition.

The Associations failed after a few years, largely for lack of capital resources. The enterprises were far too small, and there was no means of organizing a sufficient number of the labouring classes to successfully compete with the regular companies. However, both producers' and consumers' cooperatives exist and thrive today, albeit in competition with other types of economic enterprise. They were not, however, an answer to labour's practical plight at this time. Rather it became necessary for labour to band together to bargain with those who held capital for the sale of their labour on the threat of the withdrawal of their labour, in other words to strike, before labour was able to reach anything approaching an equal place with capital, first in the economy and then in the polity of the nation.

However, labour would not have been able to achieve the capacity to do that had it not been for two other factors.

The first of these was the rising prosperity of the nation as a whole which placed a great many more labouring families within reach of a humane life and which in turn made it possible for them to take an interest in bettering themselves in this life. The second was the inspiration to self-education that was provided through the pioneering work of organizations like the Working Men's College.

Maurice, J. M. Ludlow and Charles Kingsley, the principals in the "Christian Socialist" movement, would have been the last to have dared to believe that they had some panacea, some closed ideology, that had all the answers to man's dilemma. They did believe that it was possible for all men to live decently together and that they were meant by their Creator so to do. Maurice was not discouraged at the failure of these practical enterprises because he believed that there was a power for good at work on a larger scale who would see to the success of those human enterprises which were in themselves worthy of success.

Maurice, along with the political radicals, was fully aware that the Reform Bill of 1832 was at best the beginning of a reform on behalf of the middle classes. He was for full working man's suffrage. "Not owning a house but being a man should qualify one to vote," he wrote.[4] While it is true that certain of the Dissenters were for such reform, we have seen how the reform movements were cast out of the church and the sects and were regarded with at best suspicion and at worst hostility. In using the word "Christian" with "Socialist," therefore, Maurice was making a point both to those inside and outside the church. Labourers and radicals simply took it for granted that the church and therefore all Christians were opposed to them. A strong alienation of labour from the church dates from this very period. Maurice was pointing out to them that the church's stance at that time was not normative for Christianity, for he believed by its own nature those who professed one faith must be interested in the rights of all men. Maurice tells us in

his own words,
> It is by no means easy now to realize the aspect
> under which co-operation presented itself in 1849.
> It was completely identified in the minds of the
> workmen themselves with anti-Christian views. To
> the general public in England all proposals for
> co-operation came branded with the stigma of anti-
> Christian Revolutionary Communism.[5]

It was strange, therefore, for those all the way from the Owenites, who had given up on religion, to the Chartists, who had given up on the churches, to the Benthamite Radicals, who had tried to base their position on a purely rational utilitarianism, to be told that they were in fact working out the will of God on behalf of others, whether they recognized it or not. For churchmen to be told that brotherhood was a basic reality of the faith, the only basis upon which human life can be organized *here* and *now* because God would not have it otherwise, was to be told that their opposition to the right of the labouring man, or for that matter to the rights of any man, was fundamentally anti-Christian.[6] "Competition is put forth as the law of the universe," says Maurice. "That is a lie. The time is come for us to declare that it is a lie by word and deed."[7] "Human relations not property relations are basic."[8] M. B. Reckitt puts the situation in which Maurice recognized the church to be in that time with pristine clarity:
> Confronted by the rise of industrialism, the church
> failed to count because in relation to this sphere
> of human activity she had not begun to think. De-
> vout men entirely failed to realize what was going
> on, because the Divine Society to which they belonged
> had long ago surrendered so large a measure of ini-
> tiative to the world it was its mission to combat.[9]

The term "Christian Socialism" had a connotation at that

time given to it by Maurice and his followers alone. At the same time it was very apt and, for that reason, relevant.

After 1854 the Working Men's Associations went out of existence. The "Christian Socialist" movement declined for want of a deeper understanding of, and active support for, the interpretation which Maurice gave to the Christian faith and which he believed to be the most adequate interpretation of it. Had that support been forthcoming perhaps a sustained attack on the deprived position labour found itself in relative to capital would have been made.

Reckitt gets a firm hold upon the fundamental reason why the movement failed when he says:

> We shall never understand the violence of the antipathy with which the ideas of a Maurice and the projects of a Shaftesbury were met until we realize that *Accumulation*[10] was the unquestioned and almost exclusive purpose, for at least two full decades from 1851, of every class in England below that of landed gentry who had not need for it, and above the miserable hordes of slum dwellers who had no hope of it.[11]

The Working Men's College later merged with Queen's College for Women and is now Queen's College of the University of London, a continuing symbol of the practical relevance of Maurice's work and that of his fellow "Christian Socialists."

Yet the important thing for us to realize is, as Alec Vidler points out, that the work of Maurice must not be reduced for one moment to the work of the "Christian Socialists." It was not the collapse of the workers' associations which really mattered, but the continued apathy, worldliness and sectarianism of the nation's church.[12] The concrete views of Maurice were carried on to influence the development of the church and of the labour party in the last part

# A Fresh Vision

of the century by men like Stewart Headlam and Scott Holland. What is far more important is the fact that Maurice had a firm hold upon an interpretation of the Christian faith that was more adequate than he knew or that any of his contemporaries recognized. It has a tremendous relevance for us today who are able to hear it now, because through crisis after crisis we see the shortcomings of an essentially selfish social order through which men of an earlier and more prosperous era a century ago could not see, blinded as they were by that very prosperity.

Reflection does indeed suggest, says Reckitt,

> that the spectacular events of this century, which have ushered in what is in effect a new phase of western civilization, the post-Christian era, are in a large measure a logical consequence of the fact that these problems have gone for more than a hundred years unsolved.[13]

We turn to the theological convictions, then, and the values based upon them which were set out by Maurice a century ago. They witness to the self-renewing power of the Christian faith. On the one hand, they cut prophetically across the temper of his own time, challenging a view of the human that had been hidden since the middle ages and even then was at best very imperfectly seen. They are relevant for today because in catching up to them we may hope to emerge from the contemporary crisis in which the twentieth century finds itself.

## III

We will not go into a full exposition of Maurice's theology, but we will deal with those elements in it which help us to understand the genius of his particular insights into the crisis of his own day.

Maurice was brought up in a Unitarian clergyman's home, but eventually, to the heartbreak of the father, the whole family, including his mother and his sisters, as well as Maurice himself, moved away from Unitarianism. He found the Unitarian position unable to cope with the profound mystery and complexity of the human situation. Its rationalism was far too confining as an adequate ground for faith in life's meaningfulness as well as its ambiguity.

> They (the Unitarians) may build their theology upon certain deductions of the intellect, or upon certain individual consciousness, mine rest on the Eternal Love, which overlooks all distinctions, which embraces the universe.[14]

Rigg understood the difference between Maurice's view of the atonement and the forensic view, but he, along with some others, misses the mark when he claims that fundamentally Maurice was a Platonic Idealist or that his view of the logos, the Son of God, the Word, was one with the *nous* of the Neo-Platonists.[15] He himself admits that above all other things Maurice was convinced of the objective reality of a living God to whom man is related--such a God could not be reduced to any system or conceptualization, metaphysical or otherwise.[16]

That is why Maurice was so opposed to "systems" of any kind. That is why he does not begin, as does Thomas Aquinas, with philosophical theology and why, though he would appreciate the insights of natural law, he would not, like Hooker or even William Temple, regard them as a fit place to begin or upon which to frame a social order. Maurice, rather, begins with the logical priority of God's being to man's and with the objectivity of God's nature, of his love.[17] He begins with such a relation between God and man as defining fundamentally the nature of reality. His theology is basically *relational*, and if we are to speak of ontology at all, it is in terms of the fundamental relation between a living God who acts, who is first faithful and responsible and who elicits responsibility from man, who is himself the ground of all truly loving, responsible, faithful acts between men, whether they acknowledge that fact or not.[18]

It is in this sense that Maurice would interpret the prologue of the gospel of John, would interpret phrases like "it was not that we first loved him but that he first loved us" (I John 4:---), or Colossians 1:9...or Hebrews 1:1-3 or the cosmic views of Ist Corinthians 1 or of the early chapters of Ephesians and of the first eight chapters of Romans.[19] This interpretation is not reserved for the New Testament alone but is traced throughout the Old in his *Prophets and Kings of the Old Testament*.[20] The living God as Presence, as Sustainer-Creator, as Deliverer is objectively, dynamically working out his redemptive purpose in and through the whole of humanity.

The Redeemer God is the ground of man's being as well as the One who is related to nature. His redemptive purpose expressed as love in terms of the life and death of Jesus of Nazareth is prior to, and is related to, all men. "I am obliged," he says, "to believe in an abyss of love which is deeper than the abyss of death; I do not lose faith in that love. I sink into death, eternal death if I do. I must feel this love is compassing the universe."[21]

He was in the tradition of Anselm and of Pascal's God of "Abraham, Isaac, and Jacob." He began, like Wyclif, with God's sovereignty and not with his righteousness as did the followers of Calvin. But it was God's sovereign, righteous love.[22] Knox, he claims, as did Calvin, made God's righteousness, not his sovereignty, basic. *This was the ground of predestination, of the mistaken concept of an elect as distinct from God's universal purpose for all men.* "The will of God which makes for righteousness is what is sovereign," says Maurice.[23] Or again,

> The belief which a minister of God has in the eternity of the distinction between right and wrong should especially dispose him to recognize that distinction apart from mere circumstance and opinion. The confidence which we must have that the life of each man, and the life of this world is a drama, in which a perfectly Good and True Being is unveiling His own purposes, and carrying on a conflict with evil, which must issue in complete victory, should make him eager to discover in every portion of history, in every biography, a divine 'morality' and 'mystery'--a morality though it deals with no abstract personage--a mystery, though the subject of it be the doings of the most secular men.[24]

God is continually working out His purposes in terms of his Sustaining-Creating power, of His judgment which in turn is always for redemption.

The only judgment he knows, says Rigg,

> is a living self-manifesting power which operates perpetually and universally through the laws according to which God regulates all things. Probation according to him, is either done away, or it is protracted through eternity. Meantime he cherishes the trust that love will prevail eberywhere, and forever, over all evil.[25]

We cannot understand the unique contribution of Maurice unless we grasp his conception of the grace of God. Maurice was convinced that God was continually at work in the world

# A Fresh Vision

for the salvation of all creation. He was at work through all humanity and through all things. Nor was this just in some prevenient way as with Calvin and Wesley. No. Unless God were at work among us all at all times, we would long since have destroyed one another out of our selfishness. God was really at work in the efforts of labouring men to secure justice for themselves, through political Unions, through Chartism, through the Benthamite Radicals, when in this respect He was unable to be at work in the church because churchmen had frustrated His Purpose. "The unregenerate fight for righteousness and justice while we do not because we must wait upon mass regeneration."[26] The fact that working men are rising to loose their chains is a judgment on the church and those who say it is impossible.[27]

All must recognize the ground which alone makes brotherhood possible, but God does not have to await that full recognition, or even its self-conscious recognition, to effect certain of His purposes. God does seek such self-conscious recognition freely given by all mankind simply because God is the ground of all unity and of the truth upon which humanity is dependent. Without that recognition, self-righteousness threatens. Maurice expressed it forcefully and beautifully in the following reflection which he made on many sermons he had heard concerning the saving power of Christ:

> They might be a help for members in all states of mental darkness, of moral debasement, were it not for this frightful limitation, this huge practical contradiction. The grace of God is made not the ground of man's belief, but dependent upon it.[28]

Again Rigg is not mistaken when he interprets the Christology of F. D. Maurice in the following terms:

> Throughout they teach or imply that peculiar view of the preliminary justification and regeneration

of humanity, abstractly and universally, in Christ, which is now known as characteristic of the Maurice-Kingsley School.[29]

Again Maurice himself points out in *The Unity of the New Testament*, "Look upon Christ's death and resurrection as revelations of the Son of God, in whom all things had stood from the first, in whom God had looked upon his creature man from the first."[30] As to why God, who was in Christ and who was from the beginning the Regenerator of mankind, took flesh, he states, "The living Word took the flesh and blood of men that He might vindicate the order of Creation and overcome that which all men felt and knew to be its enemy."[31] He would add by implication that God from the first had been seeking all mankind as he sought him in Christ.

Moreover, Christ is that unity for which the world pleads as we experience a realized, and a being realized, eschatology in which the triumph of God in Christ is the one certain fact.[32] Christ is the truly human one. "There can be no Universal Humanity except there is a Universal One to whom, through whom all are related."[33] "I say it is the Christ whose name I was taught to pronounce in my childhood; the Righteous One, the Redeemer in whom Job and David and the prophets trusted, the ground of all that is true in you and me and every man; the Light that lighteneth every man who cometh into the world. Apart from Him, I feel there dwells in me no good thing, but I am sure that I am not apart from Him, nor you, nor any man."[34] Whenever any man anywhere does an act that is truly for his brother that man and that act are related to the living God in Christ in the following way:

> Admit Him to be the centre of them and they all fall into their places; each has had his separate protest to bear, his appointed work to do. Though

A Fresh Vision 267

>he may not have known in whose name he was minis-
tering, his ministry so far as it was one of help
and blessing to mankind, so far as it implied any
surrender of self-glory, may be referred to The
Man, may be hailed as proceeding from Him who took
upon Him the form of a servant.[35]

Christ, then, is the One who manifests to us, who discloses to us, the One who has been with us, and for us, from the beginning. The Incarnation *reaffirms* the continuing intent and purpose of God to redeem humanity. Against that purpose no evil does or will prevail.

As for the reality and the work of the Holy Spirit Maurice has this to say:

>I mean a reality; I mean that which has to do with
your innermost being. I mean something which does
not proceed from you or belong to you; but which
is there searching you and judging you. Nay! Stay
a moment. I mean that this light comes from a
Person--from the King and Lord of your heart and
spirit--from the Word--the Son of God. When I say
repent; I say turn and confess His presence. You
have always had it with you. You have been unmindful of it.[36]

The spirit of selfishness, of self-assertion, is the heart of the spirit of evil and the source of the power of evil, but as in Augustine, it has no standing except of a negative and self-defeating kind. The only fundamental reality is the goodness and the love of God. That is the source of man's true Life, but he is given it only as a true Father gives to his mature Son, in free response. The judgment of God is real, but it is always as the gateway to a renewed relationship with God and therefore with one's fellow human beings. Reckitt puts it succinctly:

>Maurice is here contending for a basic and too often

forgotten Christian truth, that God has acted before man is called upon to act, and that therefore His word is given to man first not in the imperative but in the indicative mood. The Kingdom of God, declared Maurice, is not to be thought of as an ultimate consequence of sanctified temporal effort it has been planted by the great acts of God, alike of Creation and of Redemption, in the very nature of things as constituted by the Father, and reconstituted by the Son, and maintained by the Holy Spirit.[37]

As for us humans we cannot understand ourselves from within our biological nature alone nor from our environment alone, for we are more than both. The self is one only when one understands oneself as in relation to One who sustains one, who grants one one's freedom. But in faithfulness to us humans God never lets our abuse of our freedom overcome His love for us. God seeks the same quality of love in all human relations. Christ as the elder brother of the race, as the second Adam who reaffirms the faithfulness of God, is seeking fellowship with us on the basis of His loving righteousness which is the source of all abundant life.

We apply the principle to the facts, when we say boldly to the man who declares that he has a righteousness which no one shall remove from him--'That is true. You have such a righteousness. It is deeper than all the iniquity that is in you. It lies at the very ground of your existence. And this righteousness dwells not merely in a law which is condemning you, it dwells in a person in whom you may trust. The righteous Lord of man is with you, not in some heaven to which you may ascend that you may bring Him down, in some hell to which you must

A Fresh Vision

dive that you may raise Him up, but nigh you, at your heart![38]

Pain is a sign and witness of disorder, the consequence of disorder. It is mockery to say otherwise. You describe it rightly; it is a bondage, the sign that a tyrant has in some way intruded himself into this earth of ours. But you are permitted to suffer the consequence of that intrusion, just that you may attain to the knowledge of another fact-- that there is a Redeemer, that He lives, that He is the stronger.[39]

Do we wish to know the difference it makes whether we are aware of, and consciously respond to, the love of God? Maurice clearly states his position:

Scripture sustains this conclusion. All it tells me of the Kingdom of Heaven shows me that man must anywhere be blessed, if he has the knowledge of God and is living as His willing subject, everywhere accursed, if he is ignorant of God and at war with Him.[40]

That everywhere to know God, and work for God, and with God, to help his creatures to cry and labour for the extirpation of evil, must be the good of spirit formed in God's image; that everywhere sympathy, fellowship, affection, must be the condition of right human existence; selfishness its plague and contradiction.[41]

Baptism is the acknowledgement of God's universal Reality, Light, Love for all men. It signifies to whom we all actually belong. It does not separate some men from others--in so far as we do not we

> are not. There is no separation on the basis of some who are chosen and others who are not. Any more than that some have done righteousness and others have not. We are justified by faith. In so far as we are faithful we embody the gift of God's righteousness as his gift and not our accomplishment.[42]

Again Maurice says:

> It seemed to me that except I could address all kinds of people as members of Christ and children of God, I could not address them at all. Their sin it seemed to me, must mean a departure from that state, it must be their true state that which Christ had claimed for them.[43]

If in the self-giving death of Christ we see the fulness of life, the love which God has for us and for all mankind, then we understand what it means to be alive, to be fully human, to have experienced the resurrection, to have entered into the new life.

In these thoughts we may see why Maurice believed that cooperation and mutual helpfulness was the only possibility upon which life could be lived while competition was its contradiction. Moreover, we may understand further an insight that is familiar to us as a result of the work of modern sociology but which should be evident also whenever we take the biblical record seriously. He looked upon man as one who understands himself only in society, in relation to others and in his dependence upon his brothers, all of whom like himself are related to a common father. "I cannot love another unless I do also love myself. Bring in the belief of the One Head and Brother of each man, the Centre of Society, and that great moral contradiction is felt to be the great moral necessity; one which we can welcome and rejoice in, and act upon.[44] The point is, I am

# A Fresh Vision 271

called to be a self-conscious centre of responsibility, as
one who is loved infinitely but by that token my humanity
means that I must if I am to be human show that same concern
for every person, for all those upon whom I am as dependent
for life as they are upon me. I may resist my responsibility, but I cannot sustain that resistance without utter
frustration. No more can my brother or sister. At the same
time I can through that resistance make it sometimes impossible, at other times almost impossible, for others to
believe in the sustaining grace of God in relation to them.
I can so surround another's life with evil circumstances, as
was true for tens of thousands of men and women and children
in the slums of Maurice's England, that they cannot discover
their own true nature. Seldom has the pressure of environment been better described than by Maurice in the following
words:

> The sottishness which accompanies despondency,
> which is sometimes the consolation of solitide,
> sometimes the effect of a craving for society and
> which may always be looked for where any causes
> have destroyed domestic life, helps to degrade the
> man still farther, to make his body as unhealthy
> and as feeble as his spirit. Here are the influences
> which are at work to drag the English labouring man
> into a very deep pit.[45]

He goes on to illustrate how the human spirit then
longs for escape and finds it either by projecting a utopia
beyond this life, as sectarian religious groups have always
done, or by a utopian view of the possibilities of this life
when transformed. Just how insightful the passage below is
becomes apparent when we remember that the name of Karl Marx
was at this time unknown for he was writing precisely in
these years. While Maurice could not approve of any abso-
lutization of such a utopian vision as this, of any

finalization of it in history, he regards the fact that
human beings can respond to such a vision at all in the
midst of degrading circumstances as evidence of the presence
and the grace of a living God. That is why he regarded
certain aspects of the working class movements in such a
positive light. He goes on to say of the working man
trapped in the circumstances of which we have spoken:

> But he has hopes of escaping from it, dreams of a
> world quite different from the one in which he is
> living, a 'new moral world' that may be created for
> him, a world where there shall be order and not
> anarchy, fellowship not rivalship, where intellec-
> tual improvement shall be possible, where the physi-
> cal powers shall have their proper development.
> He has a dream of this kind which he believes
> that certain new arrangements of society would enable
> him to realize....The dream at all events would make
> him a more energetic man, ashamed of acts which
> turn him into a beast, inclined to feel more for
> his fellows and with them.[46]

And Maurice concludes in words which remain a judgment
over the Christian Church for the past century. "These
visions," claims Maurice, "should lead the church to ponder
its task for their 'atheistic vision' is a challenge to a
better one. We ought to see that we have not been advocating Christ as the ground of human society."[47] Christ as
the elder brother of the race is that force which is at work
fighting selfishness in self and others.

On this deeper ground rests "Christian Socialism,"
while at the same time it challenges the pride and self-
glorification of those who claim to be Christian but whose
works betray them. Far, then, from it not being important
that man should acknowledge self-consciously the God who has
disclosed himself in Christ, the one who does so has a

confidence and a joy and a sustaining power that is not his
own. He is like a man about to drown whose striving is
necessary to keep him alive but who has discovered that
there is a buoyancy in the water upon which he can depend
for his very life.

The views of F. D. Maurice, while a radical departure
from thinking about the church by others in his day, were
not iconoclastic, even institutionally, and they had their
roots deep in traditional English views of the church. However, Maurice saw that the church is called to symbolize the
Kingdom of God, the reign of God on earth--a reign that
alone is supreme here and now and against which all that
evil men can do cannot prevail. He thought of the Church of
England as an attempt to express the dominion which God
claims over the whole of life, a dominion to which all men,
ruler and ruled, alike are responsible. He traces this
state of affairs, as Hooker did, back to the anointing of
Saul by Samuel as a symbol of the stewardship of rule under
God for, and on behalf of, the people. Maurice regarded the
monarchy in England to be under the law since law is given,
as it was to Israel, for the sake of the community as a
whole. The English constitution reflects that fact.
Charles I was therefore no true king, nor in a sense was
James II, because they tried to place themselves above God
and the constitution.

Of course, no one church, not even the Church of
England, established, reflected in fact God's intention for
it, though everyone in so far as they were faithful to the
rule of the living God in Christ had a unity with others as
a result of the reality of that fact. For this reason
Maurice could support the establishment while at the same
time he could regard the Dissenting churches in an entirely
positive light. The churches are always instrumental to the
underlying purpose of God which is to bring all men under

the loving and righteous rule of his kingdom. In the measure which the churches are true to this purpose, they are the church as God normatively expects it to be. In so far as they are not true to that purpose by that measure they are not the church and are under the judgment of God. The church normatively is co-extensive with God's reign so that wherever that reign is acknowledged in and through the quality of human relationships which exist, the church is in that measure there. In this sense there is no salvation outside the church, that is, there is no salvation of man in the deepest sense that can be apart from, and other than, an expression of the grace of the living God.

These views are strewn throughout his works from his earliest, like the *Kingdom of Christ*, to the *Workman and the Franchise* of 1866.[48] Baptism is the symbol of "the true state of men in Christ, from which every sin was a cowardly departure; because of which every righteous endeavour had the hope of eventual success." The Lord's supper is a celebration of our utter dependence upon the grace of God expressed in and through the whole of life. It is the reality of that grace through which all men are bound to one another. It is impossible, therefore, for the church to be truly the church without being ecumenical. It is equally impossible for the church to be the church of a part of the people, of a class of people, and not of all the people, since all are in truth children of God.

Moreover, since all men are bound together as brothers under the Fatherhood of God, we are only truly human when throughout the whole of life we express that brotherhood. Insofar as we deny it, we are inhuman. That is why ruthless competition is a lie, as Maurice understood it, and why cooperative action based upon a recognition of our mutual dependence under God is alone a reflection of an humane way of life. In the *Theological Essays* Maurice has this to say:

> The Church is, therefore, human society in its
> normal state; the world, that same society irregular
> and abnormal. The world is the Church without God;
> the Church is the world restored to its relation
> with God, taken back by Him into the state for
> which he created it.[49]
>
> God is the heart of all: The head of the whole
> family. There is only salvation in this society--
> in this church and nowhere else.[50]

Here, of course, he is speaking of what to him is the objective spiritual truth. By the "church" he means that community which is in fact, not fancy, under the rule of God. The resurrection took place for the whole of humanity as Jesus Christ in his self-giving death triumphed by that act over every evil force, over the very power of selfishness, which separates us from God and from one another. That act therefore reunited the whole of human society.[51]

In his doctrine of the church, in its breadth and its profundity, he cut across the narrowness of groups like the Evangelical Alliance, who were a reflection of the individualistic doctrine of salvation which is still with us, and the views of the Oxford Movement which sought to reassert the authority of the church in terms of some institutional sign such as the apostolic succession. All such narrow definitions pale into insignificance compared with this deeper understanding of the church which Maurice restored. At the same time he understood a basic emphasis of Wesley which had been all but forgotten by his disciples but which was the basis of Wesley's doctrine of assurance. In speaking of the eighteenth century collier, Maurice says, "The saved 18th century collier spoke of an infinite Sin, yes-- but he also spoke of an infinite Love."[52]

The soteriology, or doctrine of salvation, which

Maurice held in distinction to so many in his own day ought to be apparent by now. It is important because what men believe at this point radically affects the value judgments they make relative to the nature of their responsibility in society. It eventually affects the whole social structure. In 1857 Maurice wrote an essay entitled *The Worship of the Church--a witness for the Redemption of the World.*[53] In it he stated:

> I agree with you that it is impossible for any man whatsoever to have a conception of Eternity. I agree with you that every man whatsoever stands in the closest relation with Eternity, and ought to know what his relation to it means.--You say that God's life is the true life, the fountain of life. So I think St. John calls *that* life the Eternal life.[54]

> His atonement has been made once for all; that our business is to announce it as *complete*; that to speak of anything but the sacrifice of Christ as completing it, is to introduce endless efforts of men to what they cannot do, efforts which must result in superstition, in distrust of God, in despair.[55]

> Surely there is no respect of persons with God. He hates evil, not because it is in this man or that, but because it is in his own image, that which he sees perfectly in His son.[56]

> I say that Righteousness has only begun to work here, which I believe it will finish by methods the same in kind as those which it is using here. I utterly deny that this is a new doctrine.[57]

Judgment to come, we should be setting before all
people as that which must be; as that which must
be good because it is the change of darkness for
light; as that which must be terrible to all who
love darkness rather than light.[58]

In his theological essay *On Regeneration* Maurice contends that "we are the partakers of it now, not to be partakers of it in some future ideal state."[59] It is the restoration that has already occurred in Jesus Christ which makes this restoration possible. In *A Letter to the Right Honourable and the Right Reverend the Bishop of London* he points out the seriousness rather than the lack of it with which he regards human sin. Indeed, he equates it with selfishness when he insists that it be taken seriously now, rather than in relation to the fear of punishment later. When we concentrate on the consequences of our sin for some later eternal punishment we may indeed sometimes do the right thing, but it will be for the wrong reason. It will be out of a selfish preoccupation with the self, and we will fail to see the serious, practical consequence of our inhumanity now. "What I complain of," he says, "is that our rhetorical preachers do not recognize this fact; that they strive to awaken the conscience by images of that which may happen to it hereafter when it wants a message of emancipation from that which is oppressing it now."[60]

It is not hard to see how deeply Maurice's views differed with the view of the pietist. The latter had been so deeply influenced by the evangelical revival that he thought of his salvation as an individual response to a price paid for one's sins, for which an angry God required a price. The believer could only be assured of a place in the eternity to come as a result of a probationary period here during which he would prove by his good works his right to his place in the life to come. Such a view might encourage one to do some good works, along with others of his kind, called out by God into his special company. It might stimulate him to disciplined hard work, rather than the indulgence of the flesh, but it could not permit him to believe that God was at work in his whole world calling all men to that life here and now, in all its aspects, a response which God craved for all. Maurice's view *sacralized* the *secular* in the sense that since God is the Lord of the whole of life, all of life is unified in Him, has its special dignity in relation to Him. Every calling, every pursuit of truth has its special dignity in its own right because of its relation to God. There was no special "religious" sphere which could be separated from the "secular," with walls dividing them. We see at once how Maurice's views are just now finding some acceptance and how they cut across accepted views, with all their implications for the social order characteristic of his own day.

Maurice had no particular skills or practical insights as to what was specifically to be done in his own day, but far more important than that his conception of the nature of humanity and of human society contained an understanding which, if acted upon, could have produced those values which would have transformed British society in that day, as it could in this. His view is a universal one. His conception of social solidarity, of the whole nature of political man derived as it is from his relational theology, has only recently come to the fore among some theologians. Maurice sounds precisely like the contemporary Paul Lehmann when the former says:

> It is marvelous how he (Aristotle) is free from the temptations of the mere schoolman: How little he trusts in mere formulas: *how every virtue of which he speaks is only a virtue as it becomes formed in man.*[61] (italics mine)

# A Fresh Vision

He prefers Aristotle's *oecumene*, his household, and his *polis* built upon it to the Universal Communism of Plato's *Republic* which instead of exalting relationships which are reflected in the family bases relationships upon an ideal, an ideology.

According to Maurice, family relationships are the starting point for all other relationships.[62] Thus human relationships precede human law. All law is meant to further such relationships. All property in turn must serve persons and not the reverse, and all human relationships, normatively, are to reflect our mutual dependence. Cooperation, then, not competition, is the *condition* of life. Its opposite spells death and that is why mid-nineteenth century England was in such danger. Indeed, those who keep society from falling apart because of its inhumanity, its sin, are those who struggle against the forces of competition, of self-assertion:

> If the desire of possession and rule is stronger in any man than the sense of brotherhood, he may be a tyrant and a slave; or both in one. He in whom the sense of brotherhood is uppermost may be a sufferer and a victim, but he will help to preserve society from destruction.[63]

The basis of every true society as of every family which finds it possible to live together rather than to fall apart is trust.

> So there will be discovered beneath all the politics of the earth, sustaining the order of each country, upholding the charity of each household, a City which has foundations, whose builder and maker is God. It must be for all kindred and races; therefore with the sectarianism which rends Humanity asunder, with the Imperialism which would substitute for universal fellowship, a Universal Death, must it wage

implacable war. Against these we pray as often as we ask that God's will may be done in Earth as it is in Heaven.[64]

In *The Workmen and the Franchise* Maurice made it very clear that he understood precisely where the social order of which he was a part stood in the year 1848. He pointed out that the middle class had indeed inherited its own but that the benefits of new opportunity were being denied to the working classes of men and that that was what the revolution of 1848 in Europe was all about. He claims that such revolutions are inevitable unless and until a fully integrated society is developed in which all classes of men will have their rightful share. He is convinced that society must be viewed as an organism dependent on a common Source of Life to which all men are related and as a result of which they are related to one another. We may and do resist that fact, but our resistance causes suffering and frustration and is self-defeating. Maurice states so well the relationship of the Christian faith to the social order in his interpretation of the sheep and goats in Matthew 25 that we must let him speak again here:

> To whom are the structures of God's judgment directed?--they are addressed to those who turn from outcasts--'ye have not known the Father nor me,'--The Shepherd is seeking His sheep; you do not enter into his mind. Your minds are altogether alien from His; those whom He loves you hate; therefore your house will be left to you desolate. You shall be cast out of the stewardship which you have refused to fulfill. You count yourselves unworthy of the Eternal Life, the life of the Everlasting God; therefore He will cut you off.... I would seriously consider how our Lord speaks of His gathering all nations before Him; what he says

> would constitute the faith of those on the right
> hand, the infidelity of those on the left--that
> one saw Him, that the other did not see Him in the
> least of His brethren whose nature he had taken....
> The threatenings then are still against those who
> will not believe in a God who delivers men out of
> moral and spiritual bondage, who will not confess a
> Son of Man in whom He has justified and glorified
> humanity....And that converting Spirit still goes
> forth as in the case of Saul of Tarsus (who always
> speaks of himself as a specimen of the grace which
> can overcome the most obstinate pride) to bring
> men out of their unbelief in a God absolutely good
> into a humble acknowledgement of His goodness; by
> degrees into a perception of the eternal purpose
> which he proposed in Himself before the world was,
> to gather up all things in Christ, both things in
> heaven and things in earth.[65]

This, then, is the nature of man's social responsibility. This is the only way for man not in the dim and distant future, not in some world where the willing response of man to its demands will no longer be required, but here and now in the midst of this world and this order.

The catholicity of Maurice's view is all encompassing because God encompasses all, is related to all. The unity of the church is in its Lord who is the ground of its unity. That same Lord hallows every human calling and every human state. Through them the Divine enters into the human making sense of the latter, granting it meaning and fulfillment. Maurice expresses this beautifully in a letter to his fiancée:

> No, I do trust and believe that God has enabled me
> by your means, to feel now as I always ought to have
> felt, not to joy in a human blessing when I could

not joy in a divine one, *but to feel the truth of
the divine through the human.*⁶⁶ (italics mine)
Every "middle wall of partition is broken down" in and
through the all-inclusive Lord.

Maurice's understanding of the gospel then cut clear
across "the Protestant ethic" which had developed in later
British evangelicalism and which regarded life in this world
with its responsibilities as a test by God through which man
might prove his special, individual election for the world
to come. That this ethic did contribute to the development
of high capitalism is hard to dispute. Reinforced by the
*laissez-faire* doctrine of Adam Smith and even by the disciples of Bentham, Spencer and, to a lesser extent, Mill
in their concern for freedom and for rights if not for
brotherhood, the ethos which governed, and still to a very
great extent still governs, the modern western world, was
born. In its failure to include social responsibility,
concern for one's fellowman within its system of values, it
produced at best charity and services for those unable to
manage while it severed the Christian faith from social
justice and from anything save confirmation of the *status
quo* as such. It relegated religious faith to the inner
private life of the individual and to the "gathered community" of a select church.

Again Rigg, in his criticism of Maurice and his followers, identified exactly what Maurice was saying:

> Maurice is never and nowhere the preacher of a
> Gospel of Salvation to a guilty and fallen race
> through faith in the atoning merits of Christ's
> blood. Never does he preach to a sinful world of
> a future judgment, or exhort men 'to flee the
> wrath to come.' Whatever else he may preach he
> does not preach Christ's gospel!⁶⁷

And Reckitt states exactly the challenge Maurice represented to that period and still represents to a similar point of view today:

> Indeed the religion most characteristic of mid-Victorian England is an only too Marxian reflection of its economic values. Its aim was primarily to make good, in this world and the next, and to do good principally with an eye upon that. Its spiritual life its industrial discipline was one of rewards and punishments. Here again we have a clue to the hostility which the challenge of Maurice inspired among the pious, to whom Eternal life was much more like a post dated cheque than an ever-present reality.[68]

The point is, had Maurice been heard in that day by those who called themselves disciples of Christ, the appeal of Marxist analysis and of contemporary Communism might have fallen on deaf ears, for social justice would in fact be a far greater reality among men everywhere than it is today.

Because men were ready to accept something less than the whole gospel, they invited a result which is at very best a mixed blessing and at worst a false ideology which has trapped over one-third of the human race in a false totalitarian ideology which can further enslave men rather than free them for one another. The way ahead is the way Maurice sensed, a way that promises a world in which freedom and justice and mutual concern spring up to complement one another, to challenge selfishness in individuals and in social structures. Such a way continually beckons us to a fuller life in every sense in spite of our temptation to settle for less. *The Life* concludes in a tribute to Maurice which is in no sense an exaggeration of his contribution to posterity,

> Whenever rich and poor are brought closer together, whenever men learn to think more worthily of God

in Christ, the great work that he had laboured at
for nearly fifty years shall be spoken of as a
memorial to him.[69]

We have gone into the life and work of Frederick
Denison Maurice at such great length because his work illustrates the capacity of the Christian faith in this context to respond to the deepest needs of men and the fullest
understanding of human life. Because he would not be
satisfied with a faith that was a reflection of the world as
fallen beings would have it, rather than as it was intended
to be for a sustained and redeemed humanity, he provided
that prophetic criticism of life which, in so far as it has
been followed, has mitigated the shortcomings of an economic
and a political system that has fallen prey to the privilege
of a few more frequently than it has been open to justice
for all.

However, the sense of justice has not been entirely
lacking. It is not lacking, Maurice would have said,
because in some measure we have begun to understand what
kind of human life it is to which as human beings, in the
Maurician sense, we are called. In a world that is half-starved, half-overfed, in an affluent society in which millions still lack the basic necessities of life, facing an
international order marked by anarchy and threat of nuclear
disaster, our hope, he would claim, still remains in the
capacity for self-criticism both individually and socially,
which the Christian faith may evoke when we are open fully
to its claims. Only along such a pathway may fuller life be
a possibility, one in which the kingdoms of this world are
continually being transformed into the Kingdom of our God
and of His Christ, understood not in some narrow sense but
one which embraces truth wherever it is found.

It only remains that one deal with recent assessments

of the significance of Maurice that at points differ from my own.

In his *Church and Society in England 1770-1970* the British historian E. R. Norman devotes seven pages to the life and work of F. D. Maurice and to the influence of the Christian Socialists.[70] The treatment is at best patronizing, at worst misleading.

Norman suggests that Maurice's book *The Kingdom of Christ*

> ...was, indeed, the old Confessional State, dressed up in the style of German Idealism. Maurice was, in plain language, a Tory paternalist with the unusual desire to theorize his acceptance of the traditional obligation to help the poor. Gladstone moved on from the hopeless and un-English attempt to express traditional relationships in philosophical language: he abandoned his Coleridgian inheritance. But Maurice never did; he always remained in intellectual detachment from the realities of practical political experience.[71]

In another place Norman goes on to say,

> He believed that his Kingdom of Christ was already in physical existence. It was the English State in his own day.[72]

Nevertheless, he is forced to add of Maurice's view,

> If men would reconcile their differences by recognizing the purposes of God in the State as it was, they would find the State truly ethical.[73]

The qualifying "if" Norman is forced to add makes a very great difference. No one who has studied the matter closely would deny that Maurice's efforts to relate his underlying theological insights to the practical issues of his own day were at times ambiguous and inconsistent. As F. M. McClain says, "Maurice never really solved the problem of the difference between what he saw in the world around him and what he believed to be the underlying state of things."[74] He was a Victorian Englishmen who never traveled beyond the confines of the British Isles. He did think that British institutions of Church, State, Nation and Family as they had evolved could provide, *if properly used*, the best of all possible worlds. He obviously feared social disorder and violence. He believed in the right to a national identity because in his organic view of reality he thought the parts essential to the whole. Thus he approved Germany's emergence as a nation, but he was deathly opposed to imperialism.[75] At the same time he approved of his son Frederick's vocation as a soldier, though he wrote of warfare as though it were a matter of a London "bobby" putting down a disturbance. It is instructive that his second son, Edmund, to whom Maurice was very close, eventually became a pacifist.[76]

The clue, however, to understanding Maurice's attitude to all practical political action lies in his "realized eschatology." McClain attributes this, I think rightly, not to any "German Idealism" and Platonism that he may have inherited from Coleridge's influence but to the influence of the clergyman Joseph Adam Stephenson.[77] Maurice believed that the Kingdom of Christ is already present beneath all imperfect manifestations of it. When we awake to discover what it means to be a citizen of that Kingdom, we are transformed and become transformers of all human relations and all human structures. Maurice believed, rightly or wrongly, that nothing was more important than the discovery of that Reality and thus all other action, political and economic, was superseded for him by this concern. Only the transformation of all less adequate interpretations of the human predicament could set them free to be truly helpful, as they were meant to be helpful. Whatever the work of other men,

# A Fresh Vision

Maurice regarded his own work as that of enabling himself, and others, to discover through one's relation to Christ, who one really was.

Norman derides the political and economic relevance of Maurice's approach, preferring that of Gladstone and the British empiricists. Unless the Cambridge Platonists are to be described as "un-British," however, Norman can hardly deprive Maurice so handily of his citizenship.

Norman is also scornful of Maurice's concern for education, but the former does not clarify what the latter meant by education. We shall discuss below what Maurice owed to the Bible, to Platonism and to "German Idealism" via Coleridge and Hare. What Maurice did believe was that there is "a light which lighteth every man who comes into the world." Education consists not simply in the impartation of intellectual knowledge of the world but also, and of even greater importance, the discovery of our relation to the Eternal who discloses to us what it means to be our true selves and what it means to be in true relations with others and the natural world. Education, properly ordered, discloses the wisdom essential to personal and social life. It makes it possible for us to use the world in a way that establishes trust and human solidarity rather than its opposite.

What Maurice further believed was that the scriptual admonition, "he that loseth his life, will find it," is to be taken as the very essence of truth about the nature of Reality here and now. Love expressed through mutual self-giving is the only kind of action that makes us truly human. That is what the Godhead is as expressed eternally in the Trinity and historically in Jesus Christ.

We know this truth through the conscience. Whether the latter is enlightened or not does not depend upon one's station in life but upon the degree to which one understands the wisdom of this truth. Maurice frequently insisted that a lowly labourer might better understand such wisdom than an Oxford don. The test of it was in the quality of one's life expressed in one's relations.

Maurice believed that the British Constitution, as it then was, made it possible for all classes of men to struggle peacefully for justice and freedom. In this sense he may be looked upon now as a conservative. After all, according to him, family relations based upon mutual trust were to be the model and inspiration for the State. Whether in the conflict between good and evil, about which he wrote so much, evil can be as restrained as he contended it could be is a question over which the human race still agonizes and to which it seeks practical solutions. If the answer is in the negative, the future for the human race in the nuclear age looks tragic indeed.

Whether the faith Maurice had in the power of education as he understood it was misplaced or not depends upon one's deepest convictions. Norman obviously believes it does not, but their difference is one of fundamental conviction. It is not over the role of education as education is usually understood today.

It is hardly necessary to repeat that what is most significant about Maurice was not whether he was a Socialist in any contemporary use of that word. It is that he grasped the theological inadequacy of other alternative solutions to the predicament in which mid-nineteenth century England found itself. He understood the inadequacy of a false individualism and of a competitive approach to human relations that denied our profound interdependence. That he also be asked to have understood fully the implications of his insights is to ask too much of any man.

The second assessment of F. D. Maurice and his work to which we turn, and the much more important one, is contained

# A Fresh Vision

in Torben Christensen's book entitled *The Divine Order*. This is an exhaustive study of the theological works of Maurice. It can hardly be too highly praised. It is only at one point that one might take slight issue and then it is to develop an interpretation further rather than to differ.

Throughout his work Christensen attempts to assess Maurice's indebtedness not only to the Bible and the Christian tradition but to Plato and Platonism. At one point in the final chapter Christensen comments,

> Unfortunately he (Maurice) never directly indicated what Plato had actually taught him--the explanation for this is undoubtedly that he was convinced that the essentials of Plato's thought were to be found in the Bible.[78]

He goes on to say,

> Maurice's view of God as the personal will of love, acting in and through Christ, is so dominant in his exposition of the Divine Order that the Platonic ontology is often difficult to detect. Nevertheless it forms the basic structure of his thinking. This is most evident in his concept of reality and his theory of knowledge but is also to be discerned in his interpretation of God's history of revelation as contained in the scriptures. Maurice's continual insistance that man must take his starting-point in the eternal God in order to arrive at true knowledge presupposed the Platonic idea of reality.[79]

Undoubtedly, Christensen finds it hard to give up the conviction even against the evidence he himself has uncovered that Maurice was somehow imposing on the Biblical record Platonic views rather than taking it for granted, as Maurice apparently did, that Plato was to be interpreted through the Biblical record.

This view is strengthened when one takes into

consideration the "realized eschatology" to which Maurice
adhered as discussed above. Christensen seems unaware of
Maurice's indebtedness to Stephenson's approach to Biblical
history as discussed by McClain.[80] He also makes little of
Maurice's references to the epistles of Paul as well as
those of John. Maurice was as much indebted to Paul for
his view on the spiritual faculty in man as to John. One
also could say the same of his organic view of reality and
his convictions on renewed and transformed life.

Christensen insists that a phrase Maurice uses in an
essay on Plato in the *Encyclopaedia Metropolitana* is the
basic key to an understanding of Maurice.[81] The phrase is
"that which is." The true order, for Maurice, is the real
order underlying all appearances in the empirical world.
However, Christensen appears to be convinced that for
Maurice there was really no dynamic connection in history
between the acts of Divine revelation and the ongoing course
of history.[82]

This may be true if we read the Bible through Plato
but not the reverse. In his disputes with Ludlow, in his
insistence on the relational character at the heart of our
self-understanding grounded in all our dealings with a
living God, in the life, death, and living presence of the
Christ, in his disavowal of Plato's impersonal universalism,
in all of these we have evidence that Maurice did not subscribe to some static, abstract otherworldliness. He believed, rather, that the Eternal was continually breaking
into the temporal to create, to judge, and to transform.

Where Christensen helps us most in our understanding
of Maurice is in terms of his epistemology which is in turn
important for our understanding of what Maurice meant by
education.

It is true that Maurice was influenced by Coleridge,
and thus indirectly by Schleiermacher, in his own criticism

of Kant. Maurice did not accept Kant's categories of pure reason which make it possible for us to interpret the phenomenal world as the only faculty at our disposal through which we can gain understanding. Nor did he accept the view that the practical reason, the moral sense, was of another order which required the invocation of another world to justify it. Maurice believed that there is a third factor, a spiritual nature, which unites Kant's practical and pure reason and gives us intuitive insight as to their proper use. As well, our spiritual nature also relates us to the Divine. All of this is dealt with with great clarity in the first chapter of *The Divine Order*.

All that we have to add is that while there is indebtedness to Coleridge here and affinity with Schleiermacher, it is also clear that there is indebtedness to the Cambridge Platonists, to Clement of Alexandria and surely to the epistles of Paul and of John. Maurice really did believe that a true Comprehension really did exist and that it was continuously at work seeking the uncoerced acknowledgement of those prepared to open themselves to its life-giving power.

CHAPTER NINE

## CONCLUSION

It may be dangerous to generalize from any particular historic event or period. Yet generalize we must if we are to learn anything from historic analysis at all. It is as great an error to assume that every event is absolutely unique as it is to assume its opposite. If it were otherwise, cultural barriers could not be crossed at all, and that is patently false to human empirical experience. There *is* a common human residuum of understanding based upon common human needs. The test of any model for social analysis is whether it is able through its generalized concepts to bring about both an understanding of similarity and difference in human situations or whether it is not. If it is able to do so, we can then use such insights as at least one helpful factor in making contemporary value judgments. That has been the sole purpose in undertaking this book.

Among the generalizations which this study would seem to support are the following:

(1) Late twentieth century humans, notwithstanding a whole generation of theology dating from the 1920's to the contrary, still persist in the effort to claim that "religion," properly speaking, is that area of life which relates the individual to the ultimate. They would insist that, quite apart from the legitimacy of speaking of religious structures as among the specific interests of men for purposes of social analysis, they may take that separation as theologically and existentially normative. Religious thought, institutions and concerns are at best only

secondarily related to other human pursuits and should therefore be kept in their proper place.

This is a fateful failure both theologically and sociologically. Theologically the failure is to see the intimate relationship which exists between whatever faith of an ultimate kind we hold and the penultimate, human, social situation in which we are continually immersed as actors and in which we are constantly making value judgments. Sociologically Max Weber was the first to show in his varied works that we are never in isolation from each other but that we are always persons-in-society. We have certain basic "interests" which are universals for mankind and upon them are built the structures of any and every social order. We must eat so that wherever we are we build an economy, simple or complex, in which every member of the group participates and from which we learn certain ways of doing things. The same is to be said for politics for we must have some way of ordering our common life and of establishing a share for each. So it is with the family, with the arts and religion as well as with the associations of various kinds which we create for all manner of voluntary recreational interests.

The role of religion in this construct does not contradict our normative theological statement above because *sociologically* religion here refers not to a whole configuration of a society, to a whole "way of life," but to *the specific function* of religion which is to develop, preserve and promote such a configuration. That has been the role of institutional religion in traditional societies. Even today in pluralistic societies the only real difference is that there are competing claims for our ultimate allegiance. The point we would stress at the moment is that every individual learns to participate in these structures and he, or she, in turn contributes a share through them to the commonwealth.

In contrast to this organic view of life *the strength*

# Conclusion 295

*of the individualism that had its seeds in the subjectivism of the dissenting groups in the late seventeenth century and which gradually took hold also through the doctrines of "possessive individualism" and of "laissez-faire" in the eighteenth and nineteenth centuries in England is still a powerful force in the minds of late twentieth century North Americans.* It is reinforced by the contemporary conviction that religion itself is optional, one of the many voluntary special "interests" which, as individuals, we may or may not have. Yet, in spite of that fact, every person has some integrative scheme of priorities, conscious or unconscious, by which one orders one's life. Such a scheme enters into the common life affecting its values and goals just as the values and goals of society affect and influence the individual. Such values and goals are the basis of *the actual working faith* of those who make up the membership of a society at any given time, even though differing formal claims as to what one's religious faith is may be made. In this sense every one is "religious" and every society has its "religious" developments.

While it may be difficult for many to appreciate the interrelatedness and mutual dependence characteristic of all human life, the evidence for the reality of this position speaks from almost every page of our study. For example, church, crown and land were inextricably interwoven through those persons related to each who followed Hooker, while Presbyterians were also lawyers, or country gentry, who followed Cartwright. Dissenters were city merchants or new tradesmen or new industrialists, or themselves landed gentry into the bargain. In each instance the economic interest and the political and religious interest mutually supported one another. The bondage of the established church to the land was a fateful relationship in a society which was in the process of social change to a different economic base.

We remember how well Paley reflected the *status quo* at the end of the eighteenth century and how, earlier, Laud hitched his wagon to a falling star. Both had a theological rationale for their positions and much of it went when the new forces took over. It is not possible to understand adequately what is occurring in the realm of religious faith and religious institutions at any given point in the historic process without at the same time taking into consideration a comprehensive analysis of a whole society. On the one hand, one must discern how religious life and institutions function as independent variables influencing the rest of society and, on the other, how they are acted upon as dependent variables by the other structures of a social order.

(2) A corollary of our first generalization is that whenever men claim to be able to practice religious "apartheid," to separate their "religion" from the rest of life, what they in fact do is practice an alternate faith alongside of the formal faith which they and the larger society profess. It may not be recognized as their existential faith, yet it is, because they make their most vital value judgments upon the basis of it. They are practical henotheists. For example, the eighteenth and nineteenth century Dissenter did to a certain extent express neighbourly love through charity and through concern for special causes as a witness to his formal religious faith. His alternate faith was in the laws of the marketplace which, as John Bright believed, automatically worked for community good through each attending to his own economic self-interest.

As Tawney has pointed out long since, these two points of view held by the same person are hardly compatible. One must accept the final authority of the one or the other. It has never been possible in this way to serve both God and Mammon. The expanding marketplace of eighteenth and

# Conclusion

nineteenth century England, together with the novelty of the new social problems arising from the industrial revolution, confused the issue and made this difficult for many to understand.

(3) The close relationship between the nature of the evangelical revival and the empirical situation which obtained in the other structures of English society discloses another important insight from the side of religious faith itself. The doctrine of "possessive individualism" arising from the middle of the seventeenth century coupled with the freedom for individual enterprise reflected in *laissez-faire* matched the emphasis of the revival on individual salvation. *The redemptive relationship of God to the world as a whole, characteristic of the Bible, not simply to the church of the elect, was a conception totally absent from the thought of the revival.*

The redemptive purpose of God was related essentially to the elect and not to the whole of his creation, save in a negative sense. Those who led the revival had no conception of a universal corporate salvation as did F. D. Maurice. Great reforms of particular abuses were undertaken largely under the influence of those won by the revival into a deepened commitment to the welfare of their fellowmen as individuals capable of becoming children of God. But there was no sense of the reality of the structures of society which must also change if the men who participate in them are in fact to change the whole basis of their behaviour and thus reflect what it means to be a child of God. The significance of the "new economics" for the predicament of the labouring class as a whole was understood neither by Baxter, nor by Wesley, nor by the great majority of the Wesleyan Methodists of the early nineteenth century. Even the primitive Methodists whose members suffered most from the current abuses were confused because their own leaders

had an understanding of religion incapable of giving them
adequate insight into their problems. It awaited the
response of F. D. Maurice within the community of faith, and
of Marx outside of it, before a more creative advance could
be made.

The basic problem lies in one's theological understanding of the relationship of God to the world and of one's understanding of the nature and the purpose of the church which arises from it. If God's purpose is to bring *all humanity* into the fullest possible relationship with God and if God is sovereign over the terms upon which life may be had in this world, then the total life of *humanity*, consciously or unconsciously, is in fact related to God and to God's purposes. The purpose of the church, then, becomes to try to discern what that relationship means for *human beings* and to be faithful to that vision in its own life.

Furthermore, if God is truly sovereign and related to us all and if, apart from our worthiness, God seeks our good, then our good is dependent upon God's sovereignty and God's will for what constitutes the good. God does not will our good only *after* one has made a response. Calvin, according to Maurice, made the error of believing God's good will toward us depended on our response to God's righteousness and therein lies the basis for the fateful, and fatal, separation of the elect from the non-elect, the saved out of the world from God's saving purpose for the whole of creation.

The practical upshot of the Calvinist view, which was not changed by the Arminian modification of it, was that the revivalists felt a compassion out of charity for those suffering from social abuses, but they did not feel they had a religious mandate to challenge the social basis from which the abuses themselves arose. The "gathered community," the "church of the elect," substituted for the sovereign

demands of the universal kingdom of God. The result was
that while many of the poor as members of the "gathered
community" were given a new sense of self-respect and thus
became productive individuals, their solidarity with, and
responsibility for, the plight of the poor as a whole was
abandoned. The issue of justice for the poor began to be
fought *extra ecclesia*, which goes far to explain the modern
divorce of such problems from any formal religious base.

(4) A further conclusion to which our study leads
strengthens the view that if religious thought and action
incorporated within religious institutions does not guide
the other structures of a social order, those institutions
will be guided by the other structures.

While it is never possible for the institutions of
religion to be detached from the contemporary structures of
the society which supports them, the almost complete cultural captivity of the Church of England from the Restoration on is an ominous warning to those who have responsibility for maintaining religious institutions. The Church of
England was so immersed in the old feudal order that she
could not be free to serve the new day. Unresponsive to
general social change, she was victim of, rather than guide
to, the emerging society.

The obverse criticism could be made of Dissent. Institutionally she was forced into a ghetto situation relative
to the social order as a whole. Her concept of the "elect"
allowed her to conform to her empirical social situation.
Had she held a more inclusive, universal view, *even though
this can never be achieved in more than a relative sense,*
she might have been both more creative and critical in her
response to the new order. If the institutions of religion
try to discern what must be retained of the passing order
and what must be welcomed in the new, the resultant tension
may prove creative enough to make them a constant source of

renewal. They will then help to provide the values and the criticisms necessary to maintain at least a degree of health in corporate society.

(5) Another conclusion which arises from our study and which continues to face us has to do with the inescapable relationship between religious faith and its institutions and the exercise of power and authority as such in society. How should the ultimacy of the authority of religious faith be recognized by those delegated to wield political authority? How should religious institutions properly seek to wield influence? These are sticky questions. They seem to defy any static answer. Two things at least seem to be clear from the above. On the one hand, clerics have rarely been more sensitive in their use of power than have the laity and under duress may be quite as open to the abuse of it. On the other hand, the laity has had direct access to political power in Great Britain and then in North America since the Restoration. In the uses of the church for purposes of political patronage as well as in the effort to confine religious faith to individual moral responsibility alone, to take but two examples, the laity has been hardly more responsible than the clergy. During its access to unchallenged power, alternate idolatrous faiths such as extreme nationalism have wreaked havoc upon mankind. It is not only a question of *who* holds the power and influence of a critical kind in relation to a particular society. It is rather a question of *how* and *to what end* power and influence are used.

In matters of ultimate religious faith our study would confirm the wider experience of mankind that no one ought to be coerced. This means that churches *as institutions* ought not to have coercive power of an absolute kind relative even to their members, if that power involves external, civil disabilities. This does not make it impossible for

# Conclusion                                                                301

religious associations as such to exclude from their group
if they choose to do so. Since England is a peculiar case
arising out of the past, the present relationship of the
establishment to government may be tenable enough and may
issue in general good for society, as well as for other
religious associations, as William Temple claimed. In the
United States of America the experience of keeping the institutions of religion and government separate has been
highly salutary. This does *not* mean that the churches,
laity and clergy alike, ought not to exert whatever influence they can muster in order to achieve social justice, so
long as they do not do so as holding *direct* political power.
One could argue from the content of these chapters that when
they fail in this duty, truth is ill-served and justice
subverted.

(6) The final major conclusion to which our study
leads us is that even though the Christian churches of the
West have had a way of becoming moribund, of succumbing to
culture, of both embracing it and rejecting it, they have
also demonstrated a remarkable ability to renew and reconstruct themselves from within. Moreover, especially through
creative individuals, they have continued to influence the
wider society. Even in the sterile periods of the late
seventeenth and early eighteenth centuries there were those
who rose above their environment. intellectually and spiritually, and gave gifts to mankind. A Tillotson may inadvertently succumb, but a Law will stand strong even against
the stream. A Hoadly may settle for a lifeless conformity
and then will be challenged by a Gibson, a Berkeley and a
Butler. If there are fanatics, there are also profound and
stable men, such as Baxter. A Wesley appears and what has
been dead comes to life. A tradition which seems to have
lost its power and significance is renewed by the response
of a particular individual who utilizes its resources to

make the most helpful and trenchant criticisms. That is the significance of Frederick Denison Maurice. He sensed the need for a comprehensive view of life, since for him the living God was related to all men and to all things both creatively and critically. Thus he was able to discern the cracks and the crevices, the inadequacies and the injustices in the England of his own day, even though he had his own blind spots.

Maurice's comprehensive view led him to a deep awareness of the corporate nature of human life, to a profound sense of our mutual dependence. His criticism marks the beginning of the end of that period which began with the general breakdown of the feudal orders of the late sixteenth and early seventeenth centuries, to be replaced by "men of property," to be in turn displaced by "captains of industry" who were confident that individual initiative and a free marketplace were enough to serve the needs of all men but who turned a deaf ear to those who toiled in mine and factory and to those who were among the utterly destitute. Maurice would have us embrace a sense of responsibility for the whole of society because of his conviction that God's love in Jesus Christ was not for some but for all now. He regarded God as at work in all that was going on for good in every age and throughout the world. God was not confined to the church. In the fullest sense, Maurice anticipated the contemporary emphasis upon the dynamic "God-world-church" formula rather than the "God-church-world" view of so much traditional church history.

As we move towards the final decade of the twentieth century, western society (which in terms of the revolution in technology is becoming increasingly a world order) faces two particular crises in self-understanding that are

# Conclusion

inherited directly from the inadequate values and goals held by British and American society from the middle of the seventeenth century.

One of those critically inadequate value judgments was that property was more important than people. This judgment, which dies hard, is being challenged wherever men are striving for social justice, whether in the ghettoes of the great American cities or in the struggle of "the third world" for a greater share in the affluent, if not always good, society. We are discovering that people are more important than what they own and that when this is not taken into account inevitable chaos is the result. Law and order are then used to restrain those whose needs are unmet. "Systemic Violence" is built into the structures of society and violent upheaval is the natural result until some greater measure of justice is achieved. Such justice, it would seem, must be planned for in an open society which places men before things because reality dictates that it cannot be otherwise if we are to survive as a race. That is the relevance of the doctrine of the love of God for all men as Maurice understood it.

Another unexamined premise that has been increasingly accepted, especially from the eighteenth century until the present, is that it is possible for individuals and for societies to proceed into increasing specialization while at the same time the need for the integration of human experience is simply overlooked. Fragmentation of both the individual and society results.

Both in the external world of politics, where an international order must be achieved, and within each man, the need now is overwhelming for some method of integration, of unity which leaves room for difference, for novelty, for the parts as well as the whole. Should this need be answered, it would mark the end of a period which began with the

Renaissance and Reformation and the breakdown of the old medieval synthesis with all its inadequacies to be replaced by the new values of individualism, of industry and technology, all of which contributed much to mankind but now threaten to become his master rather than servant. They do not have within them the capacity to create the conditions for a truly whole and humane society. Should we recognize our need for wholeness, we may well respond to the challenge in such a way as to open up vast new possibilities prepared for us by the One through whom "all things hold together."

# NOTES

## INTRODUCTION

1. Of course, many worthy studies have been done of eighteenth century England, but the objection still holds that few have attempted to see the relationship between religious thought and action and *the total human context* in that period. Two major studies familiar to almost everyone and inspirations for this work are Max Weber's *The Protestant Ethic* and *The Spirit of Capitalism* and R. H. Tawney's *Religion and the Rise of Capitalism*. My purpose here is to build on them through moving out from the largely economic relationships traced by them to the wider human context. Another older and very worthy study from which I have drawn is W. J. Warner's *The Wesleyan Movement in the Industrial Revolution*.
One of the areas upon which this study touches only tangentially is the aesthetic. The interrelationships between literature and society are frequently dealt with by scholars, but the visual arts would doubtless render insights and relationships that have remained hidden here.

2. See J. Milton Yinger, *The Scientific Study of Religion* (London: Collier-Macmillan, 1970), esp. Chps. 5 and 6. Strictly speaking, our study accepts a phenomemological approach to the study of Religion.

3. Mihaljo Mesarovic and Edvard Pestel, *Mankind at the Turning Point* (New York: E. P. Dutton, 1974).
One of the most recent theological studies to adopt such an approach is Delwin Brown's *To Set at Liberty* (New York: Maryknoll, 1981). One of its great strengths is that it shows how such an approach can account for both incremental and radical change depending upon the historical circumstance. It is as dynamic as Marxian dialectic and, at the same time, more inclusive.

## CHAPTER ONE

1. Any attempt to give a detailed account of events prior to the eighteenth century is beyond the scope of this study. Several excellent accounts of the periods involved may be found in the select, annotated bibliography.

2. I am using the term "presbyterian" throughout this

study, sometimes in combination with puritan, rather than "puritan," the term by which this party has usually been known. The term "puritan" is so ambiguous in modern use that it cannot correctly identify the positions held by either of the two parties. Both parties were concerned for the "purification" of the life of the church.

3. H. Richard Niebuhr, *Christ and Culture* (New York: Harper and Brothers, 1951). According to H. Richard Niebuhr's classification, Hooker would fall into the "Christ above Culture" type.

4. Ernest Troeltsch, *The Social Teachings of the Christian Churches* (London: George Allen and Unwin, 1956), 2 vols. Vol. II, Chap. III, 3. See esp. pp. 580,581 and 607. Also François Wendel, *Calvin* (New York: Harper, 1963), p. 79. Calvin and his Geneva are relevant here because they were determinative for the Elizabethan presbyterians even as they were less so for the English dissenting movement of the late 17th and 18th centuries. See also Andre Bieler, *The Social Humanism of Calvin* (Richmond: John Knox Press, 1964), p. 24.

5. V. L. K. Brook, *Whitgift and the English Church* (New York, Macmillan, n.d.), pp. 149-153.

6. R. G. Usher, *The Presbyterian Movement in the Reign of Queen Elizabeth as Illustrated by the Minute Book of the Dedham Classis, 1582-1589* (London: Royal Historical Society, 1905), p. xxv.

7. Christopher Hill, *Economic Problems of the Church* (Oxford: Oxford University Press, 1956), p. 14 ff.

8. Christopher Hill, *Puritanism and Revolution* (London: Secker and Warburg, 1958), Chap. 14.

9. Usher, op. cit., Vol. I, p. xxiv.

10. Hill, *Puritanism and Revolution,* p. 217.

11. Leonard Bacon, *Select Practical Writings of Richard Baxter* (New Haven, Durrle and Peele, 1844), Vol. I, p. 19.

12. William Perkins, *Works* (London: John Legett, 1635).

13. I. Morgan, *Prince Charles Protestant Chaplain* (London: George Allen and Unwin, 1957), Vol. I, p. 438; Vol. II, pp. 19-24; Vol. III, pp. 493-520.

14. Ibid., passim.

15. Charles H. George and Katherine George, *The Protestant Mind of the English Reformation* (Princeton, N. J.: Princeton University Press, 1961), p. 443.

16. Rosalie L. Colie, *Light and Enlightenment* (Cambridge: Cambridge University Press, 1957), p. 15.

17. J. H. Overton and F. Relton, *The English Church* (London: Macmillan, 1906), V. 5, p. 321. See also, John R. H. Moorman, *A History of the Church of England* (New York: Morehouse-Barlow Company, 1959).

18. In further illustration, the "Feoffees for Impropriations" was an interesting effort to try to achieve "presbyterian-puritan" purposes through buying back former church lands. They succeeded during the ascendancy of John Preston at court when he was in favour with Buckingham and Buckingham in turn was dominant in the councils of the king. There were twelve original "feoffees" in the city of London, four ministers, four lawyers and four merchants. The idea was to support ministers and lectureships, not on the old church properties themselves, but in London, where new interest and activity lay. The lay initiative taken here encouraged the idea of the voluntary society later on when Dissent had to fend for itself. This whole movement was suppressed by the Exchequer court at the insistence of Laud, and the moneys involved were put to the king's use. This brought still greater opposition from city and parliament to king and church.

19. R. H. Tawney, "The Rise of the Gentry 1558-1640," *Economic History Review*, Vol. XI, 1941.

20. Ibid., pp. 5-9.

21. Perkins, op. cit., Vol. I, pp. 62-63.

22. R. H. Tawney, *Religion and the Rise of Capitalism* (New York: The New American Library, 1961), passim.

23. C. and K. George, "Protestantism and Capitalism in Pre-Revolutionary England," *Church History*, December 1958, p. 165.

24. Christopher Hill, *The Century of Revolution* (Edinburgh: Nelson and Sons, 1961), p. 340, and *Economic Problems of the Church*, op. cit., passim.

## CHAPTER TWO

1. R. H. Tawney, *Religion and the Rise of Capitalism* (New York: Harcourt Brace, 1926. Mentor edition, 1947), p. 219.

2. *Ibid.*, pp. 212-215.

3. J. L. Thomas, ed., "Autobiography of Richard Baxter," *Reliquiae Baxterianae* (London: J. M. Dent, 1931), pp. 154, 177-185.

4. Gerald R. Cragg, *Puritanism in the Period of the Great Persecution* (Cambridge: Cambridge University Press, 1957), passim.

5. Hill, *Century of Revolution*, p. 207.

6. Aharon Lichtenstein, *Henry More* (Massachusetts: Harvard University Press, 1962), passim.

7. Leonard Bacon, *Baxter's Select Works*, Vol. I, "A Sermon of Repentance before the House of Commons, April 1660," p. 351 ff; "A Life of Faith: A sermon Preached before His Majesty," pp. 386-454.
  _____, *Select Practical Writings of Richard Baxter* (New Haven: Durrle and Peck, 1844), Vol. I, Vol. II.

8. Bacon, *Baxter's Select Works*, p. 459; Thomas, "Autobiography of Richard Baxter," p. 35.

9. C. B. MacPherson, *The Political Theory of Possessive Individualism* (Oxford: Clarendon Press, 1962), passim.

10. Tawney, (Harcourt Brace/Mentor), pp. 126 ff, 160. Also Schlatter, *Social Ideas of Religious Leaders* (Oxford: Oxford University Press, 1940), p. 168.

11. Hill, *Century of Revolution*, p.294;also *Puritanism and Revolution*, p. 281 ff, 296, 382.

12. Bacon, *op. cit.*, Vol. II, p. 539 ff.

13. Troeltsch, *op. cit.*, Vol. II, p. 617 ff.

14. Bacon, *op. cit.*, p. 539.

15. Cragg, *op. cit.*, passim.

16. *Ibid.*, p. 193.

17. J. Hastings, *Encyclopedia of Religion and Ethics*. See article on Convocation.

18. Norman Sykes, *From Sheldon to Secker* (London: Cambridge University Press, 1959), p. 211 ff.

19. J. Milton Yinger, *Religion in the Struggle for Power* (New York, Russell and Russell Inc., 1961), pp. 22, 24; also Tawney, (Harcourt Brace/Mentor), passim.

20. G. M. Trevelyan, *History of England* (London: Longmans, Green and Co., 1926), p. 465.

21. Tawney, (Harcourt Brace/Mentor), p. 14.

22. *Ibid.*, p. 35.

23. Does theory follow practice or anticipate it? The answer would seem to be that there is a perpetual interconnection between them so that practice affects theory and theory in turn perpetuates, modifies and introduces new practice. Some of the process is therefore reflective and thus rational, but much of it is also accidental. Something is accounted useful and effective and thus accounted a good. A place is then found for it in a dynamic and changing theory.

24. Hill, *Century of Revolution*, p. 236.

25. *Ibid.*, p. 275.

26. *Ibid.*, p. 265.

27. *Ibid.*, p. 208.

28. M. Dorothy George, *England in Transition* (Middlesex: Penguin Books Ltd., 1931, 1953, 1962), Appendix pp. 150-151.

29. S. Paul Schlatter, *The Social Ideas of Religious Leaders* (Oxford: Oxford University Press, 1940), p. 122.

30. *Ibid.*

31. Tawney, (Harcourt Brace/Mentor), pp. 222, 223.

32. Hill, *Century of Revolution*, p. 206.

33. *Ibid.*

34. *Ibid.*, p. 268.

35. Tawney, (Harcourt Brace/Mentor), quoting Dafoe and Young, p. 223 ff.

36. Schlatter, op. cit., pp. 9-93.

*CHAPTER THREE*

1. As a result of the resolution of matters at the Glorious Revolution of 1688, the dissenting movement within the church lost out. The effort at Comprehension within one ecumenical, institutional church body had failed. Though sectarian movements had existed at least from the time of the Interregnum, it was now possible to openly belong to a sectarian congregation, even though certain disabilities existed.
To mark this legal, institutional distinction, Dissent in the text is now capitalized.
The same reasoning applies to Tory and Whig as these groupings took on formal identity in the political arena during the eighteenth century.

2. J. H. Plumb, *England in the Eighteenth Century* (Great Britain: Hunt, Bernard, Penguin Series, 1959) p.34.

3. Dorothy Marshall, *English People in the Eighteenth Century* (London and Toronto: Longmans, Green, 1956), passim.

4. Dorothy Marshall, *Eighteenth Century England* (London: Longmans, 1962), p. 231.

5. Ibid., p. 244.

6. Plumb, op. cit., Chapter 8, part II.

7. Marshall, *Eighteenth Century England*, p. 520.

8. Ibid., p. 21. "Only by the compelling force of hunger could the poor be forced to work." It was such attitudes that accounted for the fact that the population as a whole was unconcerned for the low standard of living of vast numbers of people. These ideas had been taken for granted as necessary for so long that they did not easily change. If anything, Adam Smith thought he had found the secret to their change on behalf of all.

9. Paul Mantoux, *The Industrial Revolution in the Eighteenth Century* (New York and Evanston: Harper and Row Publishers, 1962), passim.

Notes 311

10. Ibid., p. 36.

11. Ibid., pp. 69, 90.

12. Ibid., p. 83.

13. Marshall, *Eighteenth Century England*, pp. 40-49; also Mantoux, op. cit., p. 135, Chapter 3.

14. Mantoux, op. cit., pp. 141-142.

15. Ibid., pp. 134-135.

16. Ibid., p. 216.

17. Ibid., p. 377.

18. Ibid., p. 25.

19. Ibid., p. 348.

20. Ibid., p. 367.

21. Ibid., pp. 370-373.

22. Ibid., p. 388.

23. Ibid., p. 395.

24. T. S. Ashton, *An Economic History of England: The 18th Century* (London: Methuen, 1955), p. 22.

## CHAPTER FOUR

1. Norman Sykes, *Church and State in England in the XVIIIth Century* (Cambridge: University Press, 1934).

2. Sykes, *From Sheldon to Secker*, pp. 61, 409.

3. Ibid., p. 147.

4. Ibid.

5. G. F. A. Best, *Temporal Pillars* (Cambridge: Cambridge University Press, 1964), p. 71.

6. Ibid., p. 73.

7. Sykes, *Sheldon to Secker*, p. 270.

8. Ibid., p. 296 ff. (Chapter VII contains an excellant explanation of the positions taken by the various defenders of the doctrine of the church in the eighteenth century.)

9. Ibid., p. 326.

10. Ibid., p. 188.

11. Ibid., p. 330.

12. Best, op. cit., pp. 47, 70; Sykes, Ibid., p. 406.

13. Best, op. cit., pp. 71, 139-140.

*CHAPTER FIVE*

1. Gerald R. Cragg, *From Puritanism to the Age of Reason* (Cambridge: Cambridge University Press, 1950), p. 230.

2. Horton Davies, *The English Free Churches* (Oxford: Oxford University Press, 1952), p. 141.

3. Mantoux, op. cit., pp. 350-353; also, R. F. Wearmouth, *Methodism and the Common People of the Eighteenth Century* (London: Epworth, 1945), p. 182.

4. Gerald R. Cragg, *The Church and the Age of Reason* (Middlesex: Penguin Books, 1960), p. 60.

5. Davies, op. cit., p. 119.

6. Bernard Lord Manning, *The Protestant Dissenting Deputies*, Omerod Greenwood, ed. (Cambridge: Cambridge University Press, 1952), pp. 497, 16.

7. Ibid., p. 21.

8. Henry W. Clark, *History of English Non-Conformity*, 2 Vols. (New York: Russell and Russell, 1965), Vol. 2, p. 78.

9. Wearmouth, op. cit., p. 182 ff.

10. Ibid., p. 168.

11. L. E. Elliott-Binns, *The Early Evangelicals:*

*A Religious and Social Study* (London: Lutterworth, 1953), p. 420.

12. Wearmouth, op. cit., p. 105.

## CHAPTER SIX

1. Excellent sketches of the intellectual life of the eighteenth century are available in, for example, the works of Gerald Cragg and Ronald Stromberg. Gerald Cragg, *The Church and the Age of Reason* (Pelican), and *Reason and Authority in the Eighteenth Century* (Oxford: Oxford University Press, 1954). Ronald Stromberg, *Religious Liberalism in 18th Century England* (Oxford: Oxford University Press, 1954).

2. Sykes, *Church and State*, p. 327.

3. Stromberg, op. cit., p. 49 ff.

4. Cragg, *Reason and Authority*, p. 177.

5. Albert C. Outler, *John Wesley* (New York: Oxford University Press, 1964), p. 119.

6. Quoted in Outler from Wesley's *An Earnest Appeal to Men of Reason and Religion*, p. 389.

## CHAPTER SEVEN

1. J. Wesley Bready, *England before and after Wesley* (London: Hodder and Stoughton, 1939), p. 463.

2. M. Dorothy George, *London Life in the Eighteenth Century* (New York: Harper and Row, New Edition, Harper Torchbook 1964-65), p. 321.

3. Thomas S. Ashton, *The Industrial Revolution* (London: Oxford University Press, 1948), p. 158. Claims that when an overview is taken the material standard of living for the people as a whole rose through the century. He points out the fact that though the estimated cost of living between 1790 and 1831 rose 11%, wages had gone up 43% and a greater proportion of the people were sharing in the gross national product.

4. M. Dorothy George, *London Life*, p. 321.

5. Marshall, *Eighteenth Century England*, p. 170.

6. Wearmouth, op. cit., Section I, p. 276.

7. Ashton, *The Industrial Revolution*, p. 4.

8. M. Dorothy George, *London Life*, passim.

9. Ibid.

10. Ashton, *An Economic History of England*, pp. 6-7, 57.

11. Ernest M. Howse, *Saints in Politics* (Toronto: University of Toronto Press, 1952), passim.

12. Owen Chadwick, *The Victorian Church* (New York: Oxford University Press, 1966), p. 35.

13. Ibid., p. 81.

14. See Manning, *The Protestant Dissenting Deputies* for a thorough discussion.

15. Raymond G. Cowherd, *The Politics of English Dissent* (New York: New York University Press, 1956), p. 17.

16. Howse, op. cit., p. 127 ff.

17. Horton Davies, *Worship and Theology in England 1690-1850* (Princeton, New Jersey: Princeton University Press, 1961), p. 175.

18. See U. Henriques, *Religious Toleration in England 1787-1833* (Toronto: University of Toronto Press, 1961), 224 pp. for a full account of this particular issue.

19. W. J. Warner, *The Wesleyan Movement in the Industrial Revolution* (London: Longmans, Green, 1930), p. 250.

20. R. F. Wearmouth, *Methodism and the Working Class Movements of England, 1800-1850* (London: Epworth, 1937, reprint 1947), Introduction.

21. Ibid., p. 145 ff.

22. Ibid., p. 155.

23. E. R. Taylor, *Methodism and Politics, 1791-1851* (Cambridge: Cambridge University Press, 1935), p. 197.

24. Wearmouth, *Working Class Movements*, pp. 182-202.

25. *Ibid.*, Part III, passim.

### CHAPTER EIGHT

1. Maurice B. Reckitt, *Maurice to Temple* (London: Faber and Faber, 1942), p. 100.

2. See Sir John F. Maurice, *Life of Frederick Denison Maurice* (1884), Vol. I, p. 127.

3. F. D. Maurice, *Tracts on Christian Socialism* No. 2 (London, 1850-1), p. 12 ff.

4. *Ibid.*, No. 1 (London, 1850-1).

5. Sir John F. Maurice, op. cit., Vol. II, p. 6.

6. F. D. Maurice, *Tracts*, No. 3, p. 6 ff.

7. Sir John F. Maurice, op. cit., Vol II, p. 32.

8. *Ibid.*, Vol. II, p. 114.

9. Reckitt, op. cit., p. 25.

10. Italics mine.

11. Reckitt, op. cit., p. 99.

12. *Ibid.*, p. 92.

13. *Ibid.*, p. 64.

14. Frederick Denison Maurice, *Theological Essays* (Cambridge: Macmillan, 1853), p. 150.

15. J. H. Rigg, *Modern Anglican Theology* (London, 1857), pp. 124, 134. See especially, T. Christensen, *The Divine Order: A Study in F. D. Maurice's Theology* (Leiden: E. J. Brill, 1973), p. 73.

16. Rigg, op. cit., p. 113.

17. Bradley H. Alford in his *Frederick Denison Maurice: Founder of the Working Men's College* (London: Glaisher, 1906) properly interprets Maurice in the following: "The spirit of his clerical life comes out in one of his written answers to a question put before him at ordination:
   Q.: What are the strange and erroneous doctrines you promise to banish and put away?

A.: The doctrine that men are more anxious to attain the knowledge of God than He is anxious to bring them to that knowledge."
See Wm. J. Wolf and J. F. Porter, eds. *Toward the Recovery of Unity* (New York: Seabury, 1964), p. 63 for reference.

18. F. D. Maurice, *Theological Essays*, p. 11: "Bible and church speak of Charity. My consciousness responds to that speech and so I imagine does yours. I hold this charity to be the ground and the centre of the universe. I believe God himself to be charity. I start from that maxim. It is what has explained to me the different points or articles of the creed which I receive and confess."

19. Frederick Denison Maurice, *The Unity of the New Testament* (London: Macmillan, 2nd ed., 1884), 2 Vols., especially commentary on the passages noted.

20. Frederick Denison Maurice, *Prophets and Kings of the Old Testament* (Cambridge: Macmillan, 1853), see especially Sermons III and IV.

21. F. D. Maurice, *Theological Essays*, pp. 476, 118.

22. Frederick Denison Maurice, *The Workman and the Franchise* (London: Strachan, 1866), p. 115.

23. Frederick Denison Maurice, *The Conflict of Good and Evil in our Day* (London: Smith Elder, 1865), pp. 60-61.

24. Preface to Charles Kingsley's, *The Saint's Tragedy* (London, 1848), p. vi ff.

25. Rigg, op. cit., p. 108.

26. F. D. Maurice, *Tracts*, No. 7, p. 9.

27. Ibid., No. 8.

28. F. D. Maurice, *Conflict of Good and Evil*, p. 66.

29. Rigg, op. cit., p. 111.

30. F. D. Maurice, *Theological Essays*, Ist ed., p. 367.

31. F. D. Maurice, *Conflict of Good and Evil*, p. 102.

32. Ibid., p. 206 ff.

33. Frederick Denison Maurice, *Social Morality* (London, 1869), p. 428.

Notes

34. Ibid., p. 76.

35. Ibid., p. 109.

36. F. D. Maurice, *Theological Essays*, p. 118.

37. Reckitt, op. cit., p. 84.

38. F. D. Maurice, *Theological Essays*, p. 67.

39. Ibid., p. 76.

40. Ibid., p. 183.

41. Ibid.

42. My interpretation of Essay No. 9. in *Theological Essays*.

43. Sir John F. Maurice, *Life*, Vol. I, p. 236.

44. F. D. Maurice, *Theological Essays*, p. 238.

45. F. D. Maurice, *Tracts*, No. 8, p. 11.

46. Ibid., p. 11 ff.

47. Ibid.

48. Frederick Denison Maurice, *Kingdom of Christ* (London: J. Clarke, ist ed. 1838, 2nd ed. 1842), 2 Vols.

49. Ibid., p. 396.

50. Ibid., p. 397.

51. F. D. Maurice, *Theological Essays*, p. 496.

52. Ibid., p. 27.

53. Frederick Denison Maurice, *The Worship of the Church* (London: Macmillan, 1857), 46 pp.

54. Ibid., p. 10.

55. Ibid., p. 11.

56. Ibid., p. 16.

57. Ibid., p. 17.

58. *Ibid.*, p. 23.

59. F. D. Maurice, *Theological Essays*, p. 225 ff.

60. *A Letter to the Right Honorable and the Right Reverend, the Bishop of London*, pp. 21, 31.

61. F. D. Maurice, *Social Morality*, p. 21 ff.

62. *Ibid.*, p. 3.

63. *Ibid.*, p. 83.

64. *Ibid.*, p. 482.

65. *A Letter*, op. cit., p. 41 ff.

66. Sir John F. Maurice, *Life*, p. 231.

67. Rigg, op. cit., p. 113.

68. Reckitt, op. cit., p. 101.

69. Sir John F. Maurice, *Life*, p. 643.

70. E. R. Norman, *Church and Society in England 1770-1970* (Oxford: Clarendon Press, 1976), 507 pp.

71. *Ibid.*, p. 172.

72. *Ibid.*

73. *Ibid.*

74. F. M. McClain, *Maurice: Man and Moralist* (London: S. P. C. K., 1972), p. 150.

75. F. D. Maurice, *Social Morality*, p. 481.

76. McClain, op. cit., pp. 133-134.

77. *Ibid.*, pp. 54-62.

78. Christensen, op. cit., p. 295.

79. *Ibid.*, p. 297.

80. McClain, op. cit., Chapter 3, esp. pp. 54-62.

81. *Ibid.*, p. 71.

Notes

82. Christensen, op. cit., p. 297.

## Select Bibliography

Addison William. *The English Country Parson.* London: J. H. Dent, 1947.

Alford, Bradley H. *Frederick Denison Maurice: Founder of the Working Men's College.* London: Glaisher, 1906.

Allen, Arthur B. *Eighteenth Century England.* London: Rockliff, 1955.

Ashton, T. S. *Economic Fluctuations in England 1700-1800.* Oxford: Oxford University Press, 1959.

_____. *An Economic History of England: The 18th Century.* London: Methuen, 1955.

_____. *The Industrial Revolution.* Oxford: Oxford University Press, 1948.

Bacon, Leonard. *Baxter's Select Works,* Vol. I, "A Sermon of Repentance before the House of Commons, April 1660."

_____. *Select Practical Writings of Richard Baxter.* New Haven: Durrle and Peele, 1844, Vols. I and II.

Baxter, Richard. *A Call to the Unconverted to Turn and Live.* Glasgow: Porteous and Hislop, 1863.

_____. *Autobiography.* London: J. M. Dent, 1931 ed.

Beach, Waldo and H. Richard Niebuhr. *Christian Ethics.* New York: Ronald Press, 1955.

Bebb, E. D. *Non-Conformity and Social Life.* London: 1935.

Best, G. F. A. *Temporal Pillars.* Cambridge: Cambridge University Press, 1964.

Bennett, G. V. *Essays in Modern English Church History.* J. D. Walsh, ed. New York: Oxford University Press, 1966.

Bieler, Andre. *The Social Humanism of Calvin.* Richmond: John Knox Press, 1964.

Bready, J. W. *England Before and After Wesley.* London:

Hodder and Stoughton, 1939.

Brook, V. L. K. *Whitgift and the English Church*. New York: Macmillan, n.d.

Brown, D. *To Set at Liberty*. New York: Mary Knoll, 1981.

Carpenter, S. C. *18th Century Church and People*. London: Murray, 1959.

Chadwick, Owen. *The Victorian Church*. New York: Oxford University Press, 1966.

Christensen, Torben. *Origin and History of Christian Socialism, 1848-54*. Aarkus: Universitetforlaget, 1962.

_____. *The Divine Order: A Study in F. D. Maurice's Theology*. Leiden: E. J. Brill, 1973.

Clark, Henry W. *History of English Non-Conformity*. New York: Russell and Russell, 1965 ed., 2 Vols.

Clark, S. D. *The Developing Canadian Community*. Toronto: University of Toronto Press, 1962.

Colie, Rosalie L. *Light and Enlightenment*. Cambridge, 1957.

Collins, Wm. Edward. *Typical English Churchmen: Parker to Maurice*. Oxford: S. P. C. K., 1902.

Courtney, Janet E. *Freethinkers of the Nineteenth Century*. New York: E. P. Dutton, 1920.

Cowherd, Raymond G. *The Politics of English Dissent*. New York: New York University Press, 1956.

Cragg, Gerald R. *The Cambridge Platonists*. N.Y.: Oxford, 1968.

_____. *The Church and the Age of Reason*. Middlesex: Penguin Books, 1960.

_____. *From Puritanism to the Age of Reason*. Cambridge: Cambridge University Press, 1950.

_____. *Puritanism in the Period of the Great Persecution*. Cambridge: Cambridge University Press, 1957.

_____. *Reason and Authority in the 18th Century*. Oxford: Oxford University Press, 1954.

Select Bibliography

Davies, Horton. *The English Free Churches*. Oxford: Oxford University Press, 1952.

_____. *Worship and Theology in England 1690-1850*. Princeton, New Jersey: Princeton University Press, 1961.

Defoe, Daniel. *A Tour Through the Whole Island of Great Britain*. Revised by S. Richardson. London: 1742, 4 Vols.

Demant, V. A. *Religion and the Decline of Capitalism*. London: Faber and Faber, 1952.

Derry, T. K. and T. L. Jarman. *The Making of Modern Britain*. New York: New York University Press, 1956.

Edwards. Maldwyn. *John Wesley and the Eighteenth Century*. London: George Allen and Unwin, 1933.

Elliott-Binns, L. E. *Religion in the Victorian Era*. London: Lutterworth, 1964.

_____. *The Early Evangelicals: A Religious and Social Study*. London: Lutterworth, 1953.

Eyck, Erich. *Pitt versus Fox. Father and Son*. London: G. Bell, 1950.

Flynn, John Stephen. *The Influence of Puritanism (on the Political and Religious Thought of the English)*. New York: E. P. Dutton, 1920.

Frazer, N. L. *English History Illustrated from Original Sources*. London: Adam and Charles Black, 1914.

Frere, W. H. *History of the English Church*. London: Macmillan, 1904.

Gardiner, S. R. *The Constitutional Documents of the Puritan Revolution*. Oxford, Clarendon Press, 1906.

Gee, Henry and W. J. Hardy. *Documents Illustrative of English Church History*. London: Macmillan, 1896.

George, Charles H. and Katherine. *The Protestant Mind of the English Reformation*. New Jersey: Princeton University Press, 1961.

_____. "Protestantism and Capitalism in Pre-Revolutionary England," *Church History*, Dec. 1958.

George, M. Dorothy. *England in Transition*. Middlesex: Penguin Books, 1931.

_____. *London Life in the 18th Century*. New York: Harper Torchbook, 1964.

Gonner, E. D. K. "The Population of England in the 18th Century," *Journal of the Royal Statistical Society,* LXXVI, 1913.

Green, J. Brazier. *John Wesley and William Law*. London: Epworth, 1945.

Green, Vivian H. H. *The Young Mr. Wesley*. New York: St. Martin's, 1961.

_____. *Religion at Oxford and Cambridge*. London: S. C. M., 1964.

Halevy, E. *History of the English People*. 6 Vols., 1947.

Haller, William. *Liberty and Reformation in the Puritan Revolution*. New York: Columbia University Press, 1955.

_____. *The Rise of Puritanism*. New York: Columbia University Press, 1938.

Hammond, J. L. and Barbara. *The Rise of Modern Industry*. New York: Harcourt, Brace, 1926.

Hastings, J. *Encyclopedia of Religion and Ethics.* 1921.

Hearnshaw, F. J. C. *The Social and Political Ideas of Some English Thinkers of the Augustan Age*. New York: Barnes and Noble, 1923.

Henriques, U. *Religious Toleration in England 1787-1833*. Toronto: University of Toronto Press, 1961.

Hetherington, W. M. *History of the Westminster Assembly*. New York: Robert Carter, 1875.

Hill, Christopher. *Economic Problems of the Church*. Oxford: Clarendon, 1963.

_____. *Puritanism and Revolution*. London: Secker and Warburg, 1958.

_____. *The Century of Revolution*. Edinburgh: Nelson and Sons, 1961.

Select Bibliography                                              325


_____. *The English Revolution*. London: Wishart and
    Lawrence, 1949.

Hooker, R. R. W. Church, ed. *Book I of the Laws of Ecclesiastical Polity*. Oxford: Clarendon Press, 1876.

Houk, R. A. *Hooker's Ecclesiastical Polity Book VIII*. New
    York: Columbia University Press, 1931.

Howse, Ernest M. *Saints in Politics*. London: George Allen
    and Unwin, 1953. Toronto: University of Toronto
    Press, 1952.

Jenkins, Claude. *Frederick Denison Maurice and the New
    Reformation*. 1938.

Kingsley, Charles. *The Saint's Tragedy*. London, 1848.

Knappen, M. M. *Tudor Puritanism*. Chicago: University of
    Chicago Press, 1939.

*A Letter to the Right Honorable and the Right Reverend, the
Bishop of London.*

Lichtenstein, Aharon. *Henry More*. Boston: Harvard
    University Press, 1962.

MacCoby, S. *The English Radical Tradition*. London:
    Nicholas Kaye, 1952.

MacPherson, C. B. *The Political Theory of Possessive
    Individualism*. Oxford: Clarendon Press, 1962.

Manning, Lord Bernard. *The Protestant Dissenting Deputies*.
    Cambridge: Cambridge University Press, 1952.

Mantoux, Paul. *The Industrial Revolution in the Eighteenth
    Century*. New York and Evanston: Harper and Row, 1962.

Marlowe, John. *The Puritan Tradition in English Life*.
    London: The Cressit Press, 1956.

Marshall, Dorothy. *English People in the Eighteenth
    Century*. London and Toronto: Longmans, Green, 1956.

_____. *Eighteenth Century England*. London: Longmans,
    1962.

Maurice, Sir John F. *Life of Frederick Denison Maurice*.
    1884, 2 Vols.

Maurice, F. D. *Christian Socialism*. Oxford: 1849.

———. *Christian Socialists--Tracts on Christian Socialism*. Nos. 1, 2, 3, 4, 6, 7, 8. London: 1851.

———. *Christmas Day (and other Sermons)*. London: 1843.

———. *The Church and the Family*. London: 1850.

———. *The Conflict of Good and Evil in our Day*. London: Smith Elder, 1865.

———. *Kingdom of Christ*. London: J. Clarke, reprint 1959, 2 Vols.

———. *On the Reformation of Society*. 1851.

———. *The Prayer Book*. London: Clarke, 3 ed., 1966.

———. *Prophets and Kings of the Old Testament*. Cambridge: Macmillan, 1853.

———. *Social Morality*. London and Cambridge: 1869.

———. *Socialism* (a Dialogue). London: 1898.

———. *Theological Essays*. Cambridge: 1853.

———. *On Theology*. London: 1849.

———. *The Unity of the New Testament*. London: Macmillan, 1853.

———. *The Word Eternal and the Punishment of the Wicked*. 1853.

———. *The Workman and the Franchise*. London: Strachan, 1865.

———. *The Worship of the Church*. London: Macmillan, 1857.

McClain, Frank M. *Maurice: Man and Moralist*. London: S. P. C. K., 1972.

Mesarovic, M. and E. Pestel. *Mankind at the Turning Point*. New York: E. P. Dutton, 1974.

Moorman, John R. H. *A History of the Church of England*. New York: Morehouse-Barlow Company, 1959.

Select Bibliography 327

Morgan, Ironwyn. *Prince Charles's Puritan Chaplain*.
London: George Allen and Unwin, 1957.

Morris, William Dale. *The Christian Origins of Social Revolt*. London: George Allen and Unwin, 1949.

Nelson, Benjamin N. *The Idea of Usury*. Princeton: Princeton University Press, 1949.

Niebuhr, H. Richard. *Christ and Culture*. New York: Harper and Brothers, 1951.

Norman, E. R. *Church and Society in England, 1770-1970*. Oxford: Clarendon Press, 1976.

Outler, Albert C. *John Wesley*. New York: Oxford University Press, 1964.

Overton, J. H. and Frederic Relton. *The English Church*. London: Macmillan, 1906.

Overton, J. H. *The Evangelical Revival in the Eighteenth Century*. London: Longmans, Greed, 1907.

Payne, E. H. *The Free Church Tradition in the Life of England*. London: S. C. M. Press, 1944.

Perkins, William. *Perkins' Works*. London: John Legatt, 1635.

Plumb, J. H. *England in the Eighteenth Century*. Great Britain: Hunt, Bernard, 1959.

Reckitt, Maurice B. *Maurice to Temple*. London: Faber and Faber, 1942.

Reynolds, J. S. *The Evangelicals at Oxford 1785-1871*. Oxford: Blackwell, 1953.

Rigg, J. H. *Modern Anglican Theology*. London, 1857.

Robertson, H. M. *Aspects of the Rise of Economic Individualism*. Cambridge: Cambridge University Press, 1933.

Routley, Erik. *English Religious Dissent*. Cambridge: Cambridge University Press, 1960.

Saunders, H. W. *The Official Papers of Sir Nathaniel Bacon*. London: Offices of the Society, 1915.

Schilling, S. Paul. *Methodism and Society in Theological*

*Perspective*. Nashville: Abingdon, 1960.

Schlatter, Richard B. *Richard Baxter and Puritan Politics*. New Jersey: Rutgers University Press, 1957.

_____. *The Social Ideas of Religious Leaders*. Oxford: Oxford University Press, 1940.

Smith, Adam. *An Inquiry into the Nature and Causes of the Wealth of Nations*. Chicago: Encyclopedia Britannica, 1952.

Spinka, Mathew. *Christian Thought from Erasmus to Berdyaev*. Englewood Cliffs, New Jersey: Prentice Hall, 1962.

Stromberg, R. N. *Religious Liberalism in 19th Century England*. Oxford: Oxford University Press, 1954.

Sydney, William Conner. *Social Life in England (1660-1690)*. New York: Macmillan, 1892.

Sykes, Norman. *Church and State in England in the $XVIII^{th}$ Century*. London: Cambridge University Press, 1934.

_____. *The English Religious Tradition*. London: S. C. M. Press, 1953.

_____. *From Sheldon to Secker*. London: Cambridge University Press, 1959.

Tatham, G. B. *The Puritans in Power*. Cambridge: Cambridge University Press, 1913.

Tawney, R. H. *Business and Politics under James I*. Cambridge: Cambridge University Press, 1958.

_____. *Religion and the Rise of Capitalism*. New York: The New American Library, 1961.

_____. "The Rise of the Gentry, (1558-1640)," *Economic History Review*. Vol. XI, 1941.

Taylor, E. R. *Methodism and Politics, 1791-1851*. Cambridge: Cambridge University Press, 1935.

Thomas, J. L., ed. "Autobiography of Richard Baxter," *Religuiae Baxterianae*. London: J. M. Dent, 1931.

Thomson, David. *England in the 19th Century (1815-1914)*. Pelican Series, 1963.

Select Bibliography 329

Trevelyan, G. M. *History of England*. London: Longmans, Green and Col, 1926.

_____. *English Social History*. New York: Longmans, Green and Co., 1942.

Troeltsch, Ernst. *The Social Teaching of the Christian Churches*. London: George Allen and Unwin, 1956, 2 Vols.

Usher, Roland G. *The Presbyterian Movement in the Reign of Queen Elizabeth*. London: Spottiswoode, 1905.

Vidler, Alec R. *F. D. Maurice and Company*. London: S. C. M. Press, 1966.

_____. *The Theology of F. D. Maurice*. London: S. C. M. Press, 1948.

_____. *Witness to the Light*. New York: Scribner, 1948.

Warner, W. J. *The Wesleyan Movement in the Industrial Revolution*. London: Longmans, Green, 1930.

Wearmouth, R. F. *Methodism and the Common People of the Eighteenth Century*. London: Epworth, 1945.

_____. *Methodism and the Working Class Movements of England 1800-1850*. London: Epworth, 1937.

Weaver, Franklin J. *English History Illustrated from Original Sources*. London: A. and C. Black, 1918.

Weber, Max. *The Protestant Ethic and the Spirit of Capitalism*. New York: Charles Scribner, 1958.

_____. *The Sociology of Religion*. Boston: Beacon Press, 1963.

Wendel, François. *Calvin*. New York: Harper, 1963.

Wesley, John. *Sermons on Several Occasions*. New York: Nelson and Phillips, 1855, Vols. I and II. Vol. I published by Carlton and Phillips.

_____. *Works*. Grand Rapids: Zondervan, 14 Vols., 1958.

Whiteley, J. H. *Wesley's England*. London: Epworth, 4th ed., 1959.

Wolf, Wm. J. and J. F. Porter, eds. *Toward the Recovery of Unity*. New York: Seabury, 1964.

Yinger, J. Milton. *Religion in the Struggle for Power*. New York: Russell and Russell, 1961.

_____. *The Scientific Study of Religion*. London: Collier-MacMillan, 1970.

# INDEX

*SUBJECTS*

Abolition Society,217 (see also slave trade)
Act of Indulgence,60
Act of Settlement,65,72
Act of Submission,63
Act of Toleration,58,59,60, 72,138,148,153
Act of Uniformity,47,49,58
Agreement of the People, the,41,46
Arianism,167,168
Arminianism,16,17,20-21, 168,183,184,298 (see also Dort,Synod of)
Association for the Reformation of Morals,91
Association Movement,96
Bangorian controversy,171 (see also Hoadly, Benjamin)
Baptists,149,155
Benthamism,182,191,241,255, 259,265
Bill and Book,8
Bill of Rights,66
Broad Church Party,226-227
Calvinism,150,154,155,158
Cambridge Platonists,47-51, 165,167,177,186,287,291
Catholic Emancipation Act, 221
Catholic Relief Bill,96
Chartism,204,212-214,215, 218,219,220,221,229,237, 243,245,249,259,265
child labour,105,116,117, 118,243
Christian Socialism,214, 251,254-261,272
church and state, separation of,8,19,43,301
Clapham Sect,161-162,185, 206,207,216,228,247

Clarendon Code,49,58
Clerical Disabilities Act, 43
coercion in religion,77, 300-301
Combination Acts,96,204, 216,219
common law,29,46,58,66
Congregationalism,149,155, 158,159
Conventicles Acts,49,58,59, 216,220
Convocation,49,62,63,86, 122,123-124,132,135
Corn Laws,211,212,216,219, 220
cultural heritage,9
Dean and Chapter Act,223
Declaration of Indulgence, 59
Deism,56,62,167,168,182,183
differentiated organic model,xiii
Dissenting Deputies,225
Dort, Synod of,17 (see also Arminianism)
Education Act,205
enclosures,45,70,102,103
Established Church Act,223
Evangelical revival, Evangelicals,116,119,140, 158,161,164,173,179,182, 183,184,195,197,206
Fabian socialists,254
Factory Acts,101,109,116, 117,119,162,205,211,213, 216,217,220,247
Feathers Tavern Petition, 124,136,139,168
Five Mile Act,216,221
Free Trade movement,212, 213,216,217
French Revolution,93,96
General Chamber of Manufacturers,109

gentry, rise of,11
Gilbert's Act,118
Gordon Riots,96,118,161
Hampton Court Conference, 19,21
High Church Party,225
Humble Petition and Advice, 41,43
Indemnity Acts,156
individual salvation,52,297
individualism,109,190,247, 251,275
Instrument of Government,46
Latitudinarianism,61
lay patronage,23,24
Loan Societies,208,209
market,marketplace, the,27, 28,30,35,44,70,76,77
Marriage Act,216
Methodism,115,116,142,147-148,157,159,160,161,184, 191,200,209,217,221,222, 227-246,248,252,297-298 (see also Wesley, John)
Militia Act,200
Mortmain Act,131
Navigation Acts,212,216
Non-jurors,62,173-175,224
nuclear family,74
numbers, the importance of, 145
Occasional Conformity Act, 85,91,143,152,155
organic social order,36,290
Oxford Movement,224,226, 235,275
passive obedience,174
Petition of Rights,25
Plan of Pacification,237
Pluralities Act,223
Poor Law Amendment Act, 215
Poor Laws,33,45,70,72,79, 105
Poor Tax,215
political parties, rise of, 65,84(see also Whigs, Tories)
possessive individualism, 46,53,76,77,297
Presbyterian movement, party,7,8,9,10,13,15,23, 33,36,40,48,49,149,150, 155,159,168,295
Proclamation Society,205, 206
property, rights of,24,32, 36,39,44,46,54,55,66,68, 78,91,218,253,303
Protestant Dissenting Deputies,155
public petitionary meetings,95
Queen Anne's Bounty,129, 131,135
Radicalism,218,238
Reform Bill of 1832,66,96, 109,113,206,211,215,222, 258
religion, separate from life,36,293-297
representation in Parliament,90
Rockingham Whigs,95
Romanticism,181,182,191
Salter's Hall Convention, 154-155
Savoy Conference,15,48,49, 58,150
Schism Act,85,152-153,155
secularization,44,66
Septennial Bill,90
Seven Years' War,93,94
slave trade,198,205,206,247
Society for the Propagation of Christian Knowledge, 153,206
Society for the Propagation of the Gospel,153
Society for the Propagation of Manners,153,206
Society of Friends (Quakers),150,158,177
Socinianism,167,168
Statute of Monopolies,25,29
suffrage,217
Sunday Schools,140,196,206
taxation, power of,65
Test and Corporation Acts, 58,137,143,151,155,216, 221
Tolpuddle martyrs,243
Tories,84-85,129,155,174,

189,221,235
Trade Unions,240
Treason and Sedition Acts, 96
Treaty of Paris,198
Treaty of Utrecht,65,198
Unitarianism,150,155,158
usury,30,36
voluntary religious community,25
Wesleyan revival,116,119, 140,227,228,229,233,237 (see also Methodism)
Westminster Assembly,40
Whigs,85,129,155,181,214
women,116,219,251,254,256-257
Working Men's Associations, 213,219,251,254,256-257
Working Men's College,256, 260
York House Conference,17

*NAMES*

Abbott,George,17
Addison,Joseph,126,146
Alinsky,Saul,187
Ames,William,15,30,31
Andrewes,Lancelot,16
Anne(Queen),49,63,66,85, 102,129,139,148,152,154, 156
Anselm,165,186,263
Aquinas,5,262
Aristotle,278,279
Arkwright,Richard,106,107, 108
Arminius,21
Ashton,T.S., x, 116,201,203, 204
Atterbury,Francis,124
Attwood,Thomas,219,245,249
Augustine(of Hippo),184,267
Bancroft,Richard,4,12,16, 18,19,21,22,24,34
Barclay,Robert,150
Baxter,Richard,15,16,18,19, 30,31,35,43,47-49,51-52, 57,58,61,64,71,162,183, 297,301

Bentham,Jeremy,95,97,169, 218,246,248,282
Berkeley,George,88,147,177-178,301
Best,G.F.A.,129,131
Booth,William,234
Boulton,Matthew,106,107, 112,114,119
Bowne,Hugh,239
Bready,J.W.,x
Bright,John,211,213,217, 220,229,241,248,249,253, 296
Buckingham,Duke of,17,18
Bunting,Jabez,616,235-236, 237,239,241,243,252,255
Burgh,James,96
Burke,Edmund,95,96,136,140, 147,161,168,175,179,180, 181-182,214
Butler,Joseph,88,121,123, 130,147,155,173,178,301
Calvin,John,5,6,7,9,19,30, 50,52,57,76,171,184,186, 263,265,298
Canning,John,214
Cartwright,John,96,219
Cartwright,Thomas,4,5,7,9, 10,13,18,295
Chadwick,Owen,222
Charles I,6,7,18,20,21,25, 26,56,63,135,273
Charles II,14,39,46,59,60, 69,135
Christensen,Torben,289-291
Clarke,Samuel,167
Clement of Alexandria,291
Clement of Rome,48
Clowes,William,239
Cobbett,William,212,218,219
Cobden,Richard,211,213,229, 241,248,249,253
Coleridge,S.T.,181,182,211, 285,286,287,290,291
Collins,Anthony,168,213
Cosin,John,16,
Cragg,Gerald,49,58,146,166, 180
Cromwell,Oliver,23,32,42, 43,45,46,67
Cudworth,Ralph,50

Cunningham,W.,149
Dale,David,119,248,250
Danby,Thomas,66
Davies,Horton,140,148,159
Descartes,Rene,53,55,165,
    177,186
Disraeli,Benjamin,253
Doddridge,Philip,147,152,
    153,155,157
Donne,John,17
Dryden,John,167
Eckett,Robert,241
Edward VI,47
Elizabeth I,3,10,11,12,32
Elliott-Binns,L.E.,158
Engels,F.,xii
Fielden,Joseph,229
Fielding,Henry and John,
    202,205,208
Figgis,J.N.,66
Fox, Charles James,95-96,98,
    181,216
Fox, George,69,150
Franklin,Benjamin,112
Fry,Elizabeth,162
Galsworthy,John,253
Gay,John,169
George,M. Dorothy,198,201,
    203,204
George II,92
George III,64,93,94,124,154
George IV,102
Gibson,Edmund,122,123,127,
    133,136,137,154,157,173,
    301
Gilbert,T.,118
Gladstone,W.E.,239,253,285,
    287
Godwin,Wm.,168,175,181,218
Gorham,G.C.,223-224
Green,J.R.,148
Gregory of Nyssa,189
Grey,Lord,214,222
Hampden,R.D.,223-224
Hanway,Jonas,200
Hardwicke,Lord,123,133
Hardy,Thomas,253
Hare,Julius,287
Hargreaves,James,106
Harrington,James,54,55
Harvis,Howell,153

Headlam,Stewart,261
Henry VIII,10,18,26,63,121
Hepburn,Thomas,243
Herne,Nathaniel,69
Hill,Christopher,15,39,75
Hoadly,Benjamin,133,136,
    137,171,301
Hobbes,Thomas,53,54,55,164,
    174,178
Holland,H. Scott,261
Hooker,Richard,4,5,6,7,8,9,
    10,13,16,18,21,48,50,172,
    262,273,295
Howard,John,162,200,202,208
Howes,E.M.,206-207
Hughes,Hugh Price,234
Hughes,Thomas,251
Hume,David,146,164,178-179,
    182
Hume,Joseph,219
Hunt,Henry,219
Huntingdon,Countess of,147,
    148
Hutcheson,Francis,169
Ireton,Henry,32,45
Isaac,Daniel,242
James I,6,8,11,18,19,20,21,
    24,25,34,63
James II,60,69,273
Kant,Immanuel,164,166,179,
    291
Kay,John,106
Keble,John,255
Kierkegaard,S.,180
Kilham,Alexander,238,239
King,Gregory,33,70,72,105,
    149
King,Martin Luther,187
Kingsley,Charles,251,158,
    266
Knox,John,263
Laud,William,7,15,16,17,18,
    19,20-23,24,26,27,29,33,
    34,36,40,42,45,56,63,64,
    67,122,123,131,135,173,
    296
Law,William,88,121,123,133,
    137,147,155,173-174,177,
    180,301
Lehmann,Paul,278
Leland,John,170

Index                                                                    335

Lenin,V.I.,255
Lichtenstein,A.,51
Locke,John,51,53,54,55,68,
   78,139,164,165-166,167,
   168,173,174,175,176,177-
   178,179,181,183,238
Lovett,William,218,219,241,
   245
Ludlow,J.M.,251,258,290
Macauley,Zachary,206
MacPherson,C.B.,46,53,54,66
Malthus,Thomas,199
Manning,Bernard,151
Mantoux,Paul,100,102,107,
   111,112
Marshall,Dorothy,90,92,98,
   199
Marx,Karl,xi,xii,191,211,
   214,251,254,255,271,283,
   298
Maurice,Edmund,286
Maurice,Frederick,286
Maurice,F.D., xi , 191,211,
   246;*his Christian Social-
   ism*,251-261;*his theology*,
   262-291;297,298,302,303
McClain,F.M.,285-286,290
Melbourne,Lord,223
Mill,J.S.,218,248,250-251,
   282
Milner,Isaac,207
Montagu,Richard,16,17,20
More,Henry,47,50,51
Naylor,James,40
Newcastle,Duke of,87,89,133
Newman,J.H.,224,255
Newton,Isaac,53,54,77,198
Norman,E.R.,285-288
North,Lord,94
Oastler,Richard,209,219
O'Bryan,William,240
O'Connor,Fergus,219,220
Outler,Albert,185,188
Owen,John,62
Owen,Robert,250,257
Paine,Thomas,164,174,175,
   218,238
Paley,William,130,138,140,
   170,172,173,181,224,296
Palmerston,Lord,253
Parsons,Talcott,xii,xiii

Pascal,Blaise,177,180,186,
   263
Peel,the Elder,Sir Robert,
   112,113,119,120,207,216,
   247
Peel,the Younger,66,112,
   216,219,222,223
Pelham,Henry,84,88,92 (see
   also Duke of Newcastle)
Perkins,William,15,16,17,
   18,30,51
Philpotts,Henry,224
Pierce,James,167
Pitt,the Elder,William,
   Earl of Chatham,69,84,92-
   93,97
Pitt,the Younger,66,69,84,
   95,97,98,214
Place Francis,196,198,218,
   219,241,249
Plato,3,279,289,290
Plumb,J.H.,89,95
Preston,John,15,16,17,18,
   19,58
Price,Richard,95,181
Priestley,Joseph,95,97,152,
   158,161,168,175,181,185,
   191,218,236
Pusey,E.B.,255
Reckitt,M.B.,259,260,261,
   267,282
Richardson,Samuel,75
Rigg,J.H.,262,264,265,282
Rousseau,Jean-Jacques,178
Russell,Lord John,214,220,
   221,223,224,226
Sancroft,Silliam,174
Schlatter,Richard B.,71
Schleiermacher,F.D.E.,181,
   290,291
Shaftesbury,First Earl of,
   60,66
Shaftesbury,Seventh Earl
   of,116,120,169,213,216,
   217,229,247,260
Sharp,Granville,207
Shelburne,Earl of,95
Sheldon,Gilbert,63,135
Simeon,Charles,185,207
Smith,Adam,55,67,68,97,98,
   109,163,164,169,170,184,

191,199,248,249,282
Smith,John,50
Spencer,Herbert,282
Stephens,J.R.,218,219,220
Stephenson,Joseph Adam,286, 290
Stromberg,R.N.,166
Stuart,James "the old Pretender,"154
Sturge,Joseph,220,229
Sykes,Norman,121,126
Tawney,R.H.,30,32,41,54,55, 64,66,67,72,170,296
Taylor,E.R.,242
Taylor,John,184
Temple,William,262,301
Thomas a Kempis,188
Thornton,Henry,185,206,207
Tillotson,John,51,53,56,57, 71,76,78,153,170,301
Tindal,Matthew,168,177
Toland,John,168
Travers,Walter,4,5,7,9,10, 13,18
Trevelyan,G.M.,66
Troeltsch,E.,234
Tull,Jethro,102
Usher,R.G.,31
Venn,Henry and John,185, 206,207
Vidler,Alec,260
Wake,William,140
Walpole,Robert,84,85,86,87, 88,89,97,133,143,151,154, 155,156,157,171,173,181
Warburton,William,133,137, 157,171-172
Warner,W.J.,188,232
Warren,Samuel,241

Waterland,Daniel,167
Watson,Richard,86,122,127, 128,138-139,155,172-173
Watts,Isaac,147,153,155, 157,167
Wearmouth,Richard,157,158, 160,199,200,237,243
Webb,George and Beatrice, 254
Weber,Max,xii, 234,294
Wedgwood,Josiah,104,106, 107,112,114,119,209,248
Wellington,Duke of,214,221
Wesley,John,27,44,86,105, 121,125,142,147,148,157, 158,159,160,161,164,173-175,179-180,182,184,185-191,196,197,200,201,203, 207,208-209,226,227,230-232,234-236,238,239,242-246,252,265,275,297,301
Wesley,Samuel,153
Whichcote,Benjamin,50
Whitefield,George,121,147, 148,157,158,184,196,230
Whitgift,John,4,5,12,13,18, 21
Wilberforce,William,97,116, 119,180,185,205,206,207, 209,213,228,229,247
Wilkes,John,94,95,161
William III(and Mary),60, 153
Woodforde,James,125,134
Wordsworth,William,181
Wycliffe,John,67,263
Wyvill,Christopher,96
Yinger,J. Milton,64

TEXTS AND STUDIES IN RELIGION
   I. Elizabeth A. Clark, **Clement's Use of Aristotle: The Aristotelian Contribution to Clement of Alexandria's Refutation to Gnosticism**
  II. Richard DeMaria, **Communal Love at Oneida: A Perfectionist Vision of Authority, Property and Sexual Order**
 III. David F. Kelly, **The Emergence of Roman Catholic Medical Ethics in North America: An Historical-Methodological-Bibliographical Study**
 IV. David Rausch, **Zionism within Early American Fundamentalism: 1878-1918**
  V. Janine Marie Idziak, **Divine Command Morality: Historical and Contemporary Readings**
 VI. Marcus Braybrooke, **Inter-Faith Organizations, 1893-1979: An Historical Directory**
VII. Louis William Countryman, **The Rich Christian in the Church of the Early Empire: Contradictions and Accommodations**
VIII. Irving Hexham, **The Irony of Apartheid: The Struggle for National Independence of Afrikaner Calvinism Against British Imperialism**
 IX. Michael D. Ryan, ed., **Human Responses to the Holocaust: Perpetrators and Victims, Bystanders and Resisters**
  X. G. Stanley Kane, **Anselm's Doctrine of Freedom and the Will**
 XI. Bruce Bubacz, **St. Augustine's Theory of Knowledge: A Contemporary Analysis**
XII. Anne Barstow, **Married Priests and the Reforming Papacy: The 11th Century Debates**
XIII. Denis Janz, ed., **Three Reformation Catechisms: Catholic, Anabaptist, Lutheran**
XIV. David Rausch, **Messianic Judaism: Its History, Theology, and Polity**
 XV. Ernest E. Best, **Religion and Society in Transition: The Church and Social Change in England, 1560-1850**

Ernest Best is professor of religious studies at Victoria College, University of Toronto and has published another book **Christian Faith and Cultural Crisis.**